CONVERSATIONS IN COLOMBIA

CONVERSATIONS IN COLOMBIA

The domestic economy in life and text

STEPHEN GUDEMAN

ALBERTO RIVERA

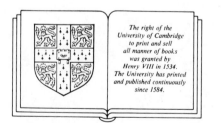

The right of the
University of Cambridge
to print and sell
all manner of books
was granted by
Henry VIII in 1534.
The University has printed
and published continuously
since 1584.

CAMBRIDGE UNIVERSITY PRESS

Cambridge
New York   Port Chester
Melbourne   Sydney

Published by the Press Syndicate of the University of Cambridge
The Pitt Building, Trumpington Street, Cambridge CB2 1RP
40 West 20th Street, New York, NY 10011, USA
10 Stamford Road, Oakleigh, Melbourne 3166, Australia

First published 1990

Printed in Great Britain at the University Press, Cambridge

British Library cataloguing in publication data
Gudeman, Stephen
Conversations in Colombia: the domestic economy in life and text
1. Colombia. Economic conditions
I. Title II. Rivera, Alberto
330.9861
ISBN 0 521 38322 6

Library of Congress cataloguing in publication data
Gudeman, Stephen.
Conversations in Colombia: the domestic economy in life and text
Stephen Gudeman, Alberto Rivera.
    p.   cm.
ISBN 0 521 38322 6. – ISBN 0 521 38745 0 (pbk.)
1. Indians of South America – Colombia – Economic conditions. 2. Indians of
South America – Colombia – Land tenure. 3. Economic anthropology –
Colombia. 4. Subsistence economy – Colombia. 5. Colombia – Economic
conditions – 1970– 6. Peasantry – Colombia.
I. Rivera. Alberto.   II. Title.
F2270. 1.E3G83   1990
330.9861'0632'08998 – dc20   89-23945 CIP

ISBN 0 521 38322 6 hard covers
ISBN 0 521 38745 0 paperback

SE

For Annabella and Amelia
Roxane, Rebecca
Elise, and Keren

CONTENTS

FIGURES

Figures 1–6 reproduced from Planning Bureau, Gobernación, Nariño.

TABLES

ACKNOWLEDGMENTS

Grants from the Graduate School and the McMillan Fund of the University of Minnesota plus a Scholar of the College award to the first author generously supported part of the field research. A Bush Sabbatical Fellowship, also from Minnesota, provided timely assistance for the period of writing. We thank Keith Hart, Adam Kuper, and Enrique Mayer for their suggestions and comments. Portions of chapters 1 and 2 were first published in *Current Anthropology*, vol.30, no.3, © 1989 by the Wenner-Gren Foundation for Anthropological Research.

Chapter 1
CONVERSATIONS

Good conversations have no ending, and often no beginning. They have participants and listeners but belong to no one, nor to history. Inscriptions of them broaden the community of conversationalists but close the discussion to those without access to the written word. The conversations about which we write began in the mid-1980s and in 1976, and earlier than that. They took place in the Andes of Colombia and other parts of the Americas. But the full discussion – which has shifted continuously between voice and text, practice and inscription – began 2,000 years ago in Europe. Neither we and the reader nor we and the Colombian folk make up a bounded community of conversationalists, for all of us hear voices "in the air"; and many of us, including theoreticians, are inscribers of discussions "on the ground," even when we suppose otherwise. Our text is about all these conversations, but it centers upon the voices and practices of the rural Colombians who talked about and showed us their model of a house economy.

In recent years there has been much talk about "rational" peasants and "moral" peasants, "decisive" peasants and "fetishized" peasants, "exploited" peasants and "rebellious" peasants, as if some writers were using ethnographic data to verify processes of human history and a face of human experience that they felt were already known to them.[1] Our project is different. In the marginal areas of Colombia and much of Latin America, the house is the principal grouping for carrying out the practices of livelihood. We think that an examination of the domestic economy as a model – how it works, where it came from, the ways its practices have been inscribed by theorists of the center – has important implications for understanding the processes of the periphery as well as theory at the core.

We also think that we have made unusual discoveries about the house model.[2] The ethnography comes from the eastern Andes of Colombia, an area stretching from the Department of Nariño in the south through Cundinamarca and Boyacá to the southern end of Santander in the north. Locally, this area is known as Andean Culture.

1

Judging from our experiences elsewhere, we surmise that similar models are found from the Yucatan Peninsula of Mexico right through Central America and the Isthmus to many parts of South America. We propose that this model of the domestic economy dates to late medieval and early modern Europe and that it was brought to the Americas at the Iberian conquest. Because it has mostly disappeared from its place of origin, a brief summary of the Colombian example may be useful.

The rural folk or *campesinos* claim that the earth – and only the earth – provides the "strength" for life. This strength, given by the "might" of God, is contained in crops and transmitted in food to humans, who "use it up" in "work" to "gather" more. All material practices are organized through the house, and the lexicon for them comes from the vocabulary for the physical dwelling: the house as shelter is a metaphor for the house as economy. Within the house, returns from the crops and animals are used up in an ordered sequence of named expenditures. Good management ensures that after these expenditures there will be leftovers for other uses. The relation between expenditure and leftover is expressed by the repeated admonition to "be thrifty" or to "make savings." This model of domestic management differs in important ways from the profit-and-loss calculations of a business. As the rural folk say, the house is not designed to "make money" like a business. Of course, they also "trade" on the market for "necessities" which the earth does not give, but they complain about "unjust prices" and the power of traders who possess large holdings. In the rural folk's view, the monetary power of outsiders explains why they are "poor." But the market and exchange also mark the boundary of the house model, for here it reaches the limits of its power to make a world. In the larger arena, the house comes into contact with the profit-seeking corporation. The corporation – a different model, a different means of grouping – is hegemonic in all markets and through its financial control persistently consigns the house to the margin of profit making. To understand the domestic economy, therefore, we shall also consider the articulation of the house and corporate models "at the margin," and argue that this connection has much to do with persistent underdevelopment in rural areas as well as with the historical development of theory in the center. These latter topics – the contrapuntal relation of house and corporation, the impact of the margin on both, and the connection of practice and text within a long conversation – are leitmotifs of the book.

CONVERSATIONS: HERE AND THERE, NOW AND THEN

The realization that our own research was embedded within a long and complex conversation grew slowly. Only toward the end did we see more clearly that our way of conducting field investigations, our mode of analysis, and the shape of this text itself were closely connected. But the emphasis we give to both practice and inscription as parts of longer conversations is at variance with some contemporary views in anthropology. Much attention has recently been given to the rhetorical forms that anthropologists use, for – according to one argument – ethnographers, by drawing upon their own culture's forms of persuasion and canons of expository style, significantly control the way one culture "reads" another.[3] According to this thesis, the texts that anthropologists write do not provide a window upon the "facts" of social life nor even a clear view of the theory that shapes those "facts" which ethnographers collect and report. The anthropological text is a controlled communication that the author uses to persuade or critique, invent, justify, or reaffirm a theoretical position. Considerable attention, therefore, is given to analysis of anthropological writing itself, its figures and metaphors, the historical position of the ethnographer and its impact upon the text produced, and the shifting, reflexive relation between observer and observed.

The critique is useful, but one consequence of this attempt at an epistemological shift of the discipline is to minimize and to undermine the importance of anthropological practice or fieldwork itself. To be certain, one must by very wary of adopting the view that the "facts" are "there" to be collected. But according to the recent "textualists," the claim to have had the "experience" of "being there" is itself a rhetorical figure, a culturally and historically dated ideology used to justify the authority of the text in which it appears (Clifford 1983, 1988). Anthropologists do go "there" and bring back evidence of this experience – in photographs, recordings, journals, "verbatim reports," and artifacts – but apparently only to legitimate, in a discipline-specific way, the texts that they write. It follows, of course, that if fieldwork is deflated as a way of human learning, text production is the more exalted as the singular moment of anthropology.

We take issue with this view that would pass over the special anthropological practice of listening to other voices and evade consideration of the many skills anthropologists have developed and learned, used and refined, in their research. Curiously, the "postmodernist" argument would deny that anthropology itself has a history of learning and change, for it seems to consign the imaginative and hard work of learning about others' lives to a passing moment on the way to text production, and it disregards the complex, evolving relation between practice and inscription. We think that field skills, so varying in scope, so demanding of the faculties, profoundly differentiate the texts that anthropologists produce. And perhaps we have become the more aware of these skills as our own collaboration has revealed the gains to be made by joint work and the shortcomings any single person experiences on being surrounded by the total demands of field research. Despite the obsessive grip that the Malinowskian myth still has upon our imaginations (Hayes and Hayes 1970), the anthropological project has never been the feat of a singular hero. Fieldwork itself is a perpetual discussion, and we propose the model of conversation as the practice of anthropology and as the activity of other cultures – which, incidentally, are surely not "texts." Texts are frozen, they are conversation-stoppers that deny the continuous remaking of social life. Through our fieldwork methods we have tried to make our dependence on broader communities more explicit, to shift the conception of the anthropological project from singular to communal venture, and to expand the scope of the conversation. The anthropologist produces a text, as we do here, but only as one part of several larger conversations; and the anthropologist must certainly have a "good ear" as well as a facile pen.

Our own conversations about these and connected issues began some time ago. In 1977 we undertook an initial survey of the *llanos* or low plains to the east of Bogotá and of regions in the Department of Nariño. Further work had to wait several years, but from the outset we were aware of the torrid relation between power and knowledge in anthropology. During the 1970s, Colombia and other Latin American nations were concerned about the activities of foreign researchers who would enter the country, undertake investigations directed to questions and theories current in their First World nations, and then leave with their results. Anthropological research seemed to be a metaphor for "dependency" relations, especially the exploitation of natural resources by transnational corporations who were aiming for short-term profits to be dispersed or reinvested in the home country. In Colombia, one response to this critical awareness was the passage of a law requiring a foreign researcher to make over a part of his or her grant to the disciplinary community. But it seemed to us then, as it does now, that the issue of anthropological responsibility should be focused more on power in relation to the very production and dissemination of knowledge. This issue was central to us, for we had to come to terms with our own differing backgrounds – one from Colombia, one from the United States – and with what was then the potentially power-infused relationship of teacher and student.

When in 1984 we began fieldwork in earnest, these issues were unresolved, but our conversation had begun. In July of that year we traveled from Bogotá north to Boyacá with the intention of locating separate field sites so that we might carry out a comparative study. Within a day we cast this approach aside and began collaborative work. Over time, our field discussions often concerned this relationship itself. To our surprise, control over an instrument of transport – the automobile – played a role in the conceptualization of our study, for a car became not only our means of transport but a mode of inquiry and a marker of "conversational communities." The use of an automobile, of course, permitted us to see rather fully the physical environment, its degradation, and the marginal conditions in which most of the rural folk live. It allowed us to make a truly regional study and to experience rapid ecological shifts; in some areas one can descend in less than an hour from a high plain at 11,000 feet where only sheep can graze to a semitropical environment filled with lush fruits. The roads are not always in fine condition nor so wide as one might wish, and we grew accustomed to changing tires several times a day as well as relying upon the more experienced of us for the driving. One evening in Boyacá, on meeting up with two Colombian social scientists, we were reminded of the power of the automobile as an instrument for gaining entry to many conversations. At that point in our research, we were engaging in twelve or more discussions per day; the two other researchers talked about their difficulties of travel and of feeling successful when completing one interview in a day.

From the outset, the car became a place for our discussions and facilitated the making of our own conversational community. After a field conversation, in which we both participated and took notes, we returned to the car (or a path or house) to discuss what we thought we had just heard or observed. Our talks were in Spanish and English and both; sometimes they simply concerned issues of translation, for we found that working in two languages helped us understand rural usage better. For example, part-way through the research one of us insisted that "*las utilidades*" (useful things) had an important place in the rural lexicon. He argued that it was applied to material things "used" in the house and that the question to be explored was how this domestic usage in a remote part of Colombia was linked to its textual usage by nineteenth-century "utilitarians" and to its later incorporation into utility theory as developed by neoclassical economists. The other pointed out that rural use of "*las utilidades*" might be evidence of the contemporary impress of the market world, where it is used for "profit," what a corporation retains after its costs of operation. As in other instances, we were both right and both wrong, but the discussion led us toward a better understanding. We found that for the people "*las utilidades*" refers to the usable returns that a house takes in from the land or from trade and then expends. If this usage is viewed historically – as one still preserved in Colombia but taken over and transformed by the corporate world and textual theoreticians some time ago – the several contemporary applications of the term can be seen to be interlinked. Incidentally, in modern North American usage, "utilities" refers exactly to the electricity, gas, and water that a house receives from outside and uses up inside.

But translation was only one of several tasks we undertook within our conversational community. More often than we would like to admit, each of us had missed something the other had heard, or heard the "same thing" differently. This was disorienting and humiliating, because it meant that "facts" were not external pillars of knowledge but partly constructed through our success in persuading one another, and our ability to listen, too. For example, one rainy afternoon we had a long conversation with an old man in a marketplace; each of us made notes, and we recorded the discussion as well. His oral history about haciendas centered on the differing rates of pay during the week, the "obligation" each tenant owed for use of hacienda land, and the way haciendas "enslaved" people. Afterwards, we found that our notes did not match, and our discussion about the "facts" became heated; this alone was disturbing, but the telling moment came when we listened to the tape and discovered that the man seemed to have said something different from what each of us claimed to have heard, and even the recording was not definitive. We never assumed that the "facts" we were collecting had an unimpeachable sturdiness, but moments such as this emphasized that we were listening to an unfinished discussion about which we might talk without end. So our continuous "review" in the car and elsewhere had for us an "interpretive" as well as a "verification" function, in some sense of those terms.

The car accelerated the fieldwork not only because it shortened the time between discussions but also because we could digest larger amounts of information communally than alone. And as we learned to manage conversational shifts between field and car, our conversations with the people became more probing. Frequently, we finished a conversation "on the ground" and began one in the car only to find that new questions were raised or that important ones had not been asked, so we would turn the wheel and return, sometimes more than once. The car allowed us to discuss immediately in "longhand" or to explicate to ourselves what had been "shorthand" or elliptical field discussions.

In time, we saw other advantages in having our own conversational community. Certainly, it quickened our energies – for as one might fail, the other carried on – and enhanced field conversations by giving each of us a few more moments for the taking of notes; and we could both facilitate the discussion by approaching complicated issues in different ways. We found also that joint work better drew out our different skills. One might know more about ecological processes and geography, the other about market goods. But there was a more intriguing way in which our community affected the work. One of us knew "Colombian culture" from growing up in it; yet this knowledge often came to be voiced only when the other did not fully understand a word usage or a practice in the field. The relevant "longhand" or implicit context might be a Colombian commonplace or a remembrance of what a grandparent or great-grandparent had said decades ago; so hearing the shorthand and discovering the longhand became a communal practice of our own. Eventually, we turned this process about and conversed in longhand about shorthand practices in the United States such as the transformed appearance of the "house model" in contemporary television programs. This dialectical drawing out and use of personal knowledge led us to wonder whether anthropology might not be nearly impossible for the single foreign researcher, who, lacking a lifetime of personal knowledge, could never fill out, make the cultural connections, or turn into longhand what we increasingly understood to be elliptical field encounters; and also whether it might not be impossible for the "native," for whom every verb and noun, every phrase and explanation, was too familiar to require conscious explication – or was an atavism, unconnected to anything else.

Still, in these uses of the car to make conversational communities, we were segregating the two discussions; the rural folk comprised one community of conversants and we another. In other ways, however, the automobile dissolved these boundaries. From the first day, we carried people in the car, and it was forever filled with produce and small animals; but the car in movement was not a useful context for "field" discussions. It did, however, allow us to juxtapose voices from different areas, for we frequently related to one group what another had said. There is much linguistic variation throughout the Andean region, and the people were interested and amused to hear of it, offering their commentary upon it. We became interlocutors between and among their conversations, which in other ways had been going on for hundreds of years. But we were also conversation makers in the sense that our presence and voices always made a new and enlarged community of discussants. With rare exceptions, the people welcomed us; and we explained our presence – in which they were always interested – as an attempt to expand our knowledge so that we could tell our home communities about practices existent elsewhere. This expansion of conversations and forming of new communities enabled us to carry out various functions. In the conversational community that we helped make, it was appropriate to frame the apt, the unexpected, and the infelicitous question, for we were interlocutors between conversations at home and in the field. This participation in a newly made community was also a way of "verifying" or "validating" our developing stock of information. Upon hearing our commentary, people agreed and explained, replicated what others said, or disagreed. Almost everything we describe was put to the "test" of conversation by the rural folk. As our experience developed, we also used our car conversation to predict responses that we thought a field conversation would bring. In the later stages of the research, the relation between car and field conversation became thicker, taking place in both at once. One time, high above an old hacienda, we sat in the car, with the doors open, surrounded by a dozen people only some of whom we could see and be seen by. We heard voices from in front and back, and they may only have heard a voice from inside. But the conversation, which captured everybody's attention, lasted nearly two hours and was outlined by a series of predictions we had previously made and continued to discuss as the larger conversation proceeded. One after another the connections of land, crops, and economic theory came to light, and our enthusiasm must have been enjoyed by the people, who stayed on and on. The physical context, with its merging of car and field, reproduced the merged content of the conversing community. Our attempt to converse, to understand, and to listen, as the rural folk often said, was a compliment to them; perhaps the interest from a more powerful context was a form of "validation" for their own way of life, which in so many other contexts is denigrated. One afternoon, as we were driving an older man to his fields and trying out a range of voices upon him, these aspects of merging and diverging conversations, the power to control and to listen, validation for one and for the other, came together in his parting words: "It is so nice to talk to intellectuals like yourselves who understand."

But as the car was bringing us more and more into contact with voices "on the ground," it was increasingly invaded by "voices in the air." These voices from written history – from the several textual communities of economic theorists – began quietly enough and sporadically; but they grew more intrusive until we were forced to revoice them from memory and let them enter the conversation. This breaking of conversational limits started as we listened to the people talk, for instance, about the "force of labor," gaining ownership of property through work, the "advance," "making savings," and seeking a "just price" in the market. Their carefully used words startlingly called forth the texts of Adam Smith and John Stuart Mill, of Aquinas and Aristotle, and of many others, so that these forced themselves upon the conversation. Eventually, for example, we were able to bring to conversations in the field various puzzles about which the Physiocrats had written and disagreed, for in certain respects the people appeared to be practicing Physiocrats. Still, what they said and practiced was never equivalent to any of the received texts. When we posed "Physiocratic questions" to them, their answers were not the same as the Physiocrats'. It was not clear to us then why the rural voice should echo texts, for clearly the country folk had not been trained in economic theory as it had developed up to the turn of this century. Yet it did seem that rural life and historical texts could illuminate one another, and so the relation of the two became a problem to be solved. This meant that the link between inscriptions of the past and practices of the present, between the Old World and the New, and between theorists of the core and practitioners of the periphery, had to be considered. We return to these several issues, but for us in the car at that time, the idea that bounded communities exist, that conversations have a completeness in themselves, had to be cast aside; and the number of participants in our discussions was vastly increased. In fact, our initial view of the car as a conversational container was exploded, and we were led to form several frameworks and hypotheses for analyzing the local situation. One of these concerns the long-term relation between the corporation in the center and the house at the margin.

HOUSE AND CORPORATION, CORE AND PERIPHERY

The house and the corporation are institutions or means of grouping, but neither is a total economic system. We focus on the house as opposed to the economy or the individual acts and decisions that are said to lead to a macrosystem, and we argue that the house economy is an institution of long standing, dating from Greek times and earlier.

The corporate means of grouping is also an institution of long standing, but a later development associated with the expansion of the market.

Both the house and the corporation are means for accomplishing material tasks. The house, smaller, is locally based and wholly or partly produces its own means of maintenance; it produces as outputs some of the inputs it requires. The house is never fully engaged in or dependent upon the market. Often, it is organized by kinship relations. It grows by increase in number of members and material means, but its expansion has limits having to do with its internal organization, control over information and technology, and the larger economy of which the house is a part. As it grows it tends to fragment, to replicate and repeat itself, or to be transformed into a corporation.

The corporation is enmeshed in exchange; it buys to sell in order to make a profit. It produces one set of outputs and sells these to purchase a different array of inputs so that it can undertake production once again. Normally, it does not reproduce its own material necessities. By altering its internal structure, the corporation can expand almost endlessly, and its continuity is hardly contingent upon the survival of particular members. In theory and law a corporation is never extinguished; it is characterized by "perpetual succession."

Both the corporation and the house fit various economic regimes, sometimes together. The house has flourished in slavery, city-states, empires, feudalism, seigneurial society, mercantilism, capitalism, and other political-economic contexts, while the corporation is found in capitalism, socialism, and the market. The house is known to us from Greek writings, while the Roman villa, fundus, and praedium had an impact on a broad area of Europe through the influence of Roman colonies and settlements; there were many subsequent forms of the house, such as the hide (England), the *huba* (Germany), the *mansus* (France), the monastic estate, the manor, the Great House, the great estate, and the hacienda. The corporation is a more recent creation; its growth is linked to the expansion of markets and the rise of profit making. As Braudel (1986) has shown, markets have long existed, along with trading for gain; but only in later European times, as markets expanded, technology changed, population increased, and wealth in productive equipment was accumulated, did the corporation develop as an important force in the market. According to Braudel (pp. 314–15), the first corporations were the twelfth-century guilds (*corps de métiers*) which controlled labor, production, and trade. Braudel endorses a typology that suggests a four-stage transition between the fifteenth and eighteenth centuries from house to corporation: material production began in the independent family workshop, shifted to scattered but interconnected workshops, was then concentrated in labor-intensive manufacturing, and finally moved to machine-based factories. Over the last several hundred years, the corporate form has displaced the house as the leading sector institution in most economies. Between the two, partly because of their differing capacities for growth and control of productive resources, there is an asymmetry of power. In the market, the corporation takes over the arenas of profit making and is dominant, consigning the house to the periphery of the competition and to undertaking fewer and fewer functions.

Both house and corporation were brought to the New World at the conquest and after.[4] Initially, the house as hacienda was dominant, but it was increasingly brought into competition with the mining venture and the plantation, both corporate forms. Today the hacienda has fallen into desuetude, squeezed between corporate farming on the one side and small householding on the other. But the house persists, exactly where the corporation cannot. The corporation possesses capital and tries to make a profit on it, but the profit margin defines its area of movement and control. The house is found at the margin and beyond.

The opposition we draw between house and corporation, then, is intended to cut through other historical sequences, such as slavery followed by feudalism and then capitalism. Similarly, there have been lengthy debates about whether Latin America after the conquest was feudalistic, colonial, neofeudal, or market-like. We focus instead on the two means of grouping and on their relative and historically shifting places in the market.

In conjunction with this distinction between corporation and house, we employ a model of core and periphery that itself has several applications. The core is the center of market activities. In this zone of profit making, there is continuous investment and reinvestment and a high frequency of transactions among units. This is the home of the corporation. At the periphery, which is the locus of the house economy, market activities are less frequent.

In Latin America this difference often has a spatial visage. At the core there is the industrial city, at the periphery the agrarian countryside; in the countryside the split is repeated between towns and rural areas, and in rural regions it appears again between larger farms or *fincas* and campesino houses. Yet, the relation between the two is dynamic and ever-changing, and inserts itself at all levels and in all spaces of the economy. The periphery lies toward, on, or beyond the margin of profit. In modern neoclassical economics, the "production-possibility frontier" – a metaphor – marks the boundary of profitable production given the resources available. It also marks the boundary of the neoclassical model itself or the domain of its explanatory power – the limits of its world making. For the neoclassical economist, beyond the production-possibility frontier there is either another market economy with which trade can be conducted for comparative advantage, or there is nothing but "savages" and "hunters" (as von Thünen once graphically stated [1966(1826):157]). We think, however, that in practice and in models there are many economies beyond the production-possibility frontier. In the Western context especially, the periphery of profit making and of the neoclassical model is the home of the domestic economy.

This peripheral space, whether in the remote regions of Colombia or in the center of modern cities and markets, is always contested. The space is opened by the practices, by the artisanry, of the house. In Latin America the contested region is the physical frontier, the new lands and forests initially tilled and felled by house units that have been expelled from elsewhere; in market economies the frontier region is the realm of consumption in the house, which is initially invented and improvised by domestic makers only to be invaded and appropriated by market goods of the corporation. The struggles at the periphery in Latin America re-present in a graphic way less visible processes in the core.

But corporate appropriation of resources and activities in the service of profit is only one of several asymmetric relations between house and corporation. In practice, their connection may consist of the use and appropriation of one another's remainders, although the corporate world sets the terms of the exchange and derives its benefits. Beyond this, the practices and voices of the house have often been inscribed in texts that are said to represent – to be from, to be about, and to be for – activities in the center. This appropriation, transformation, and textual amnesia centers around two focal metaphors and two changing models.

METAPHORS AND MODELS, THE HOUSE AND THE CORPS

The corporation and the house are modeled after two contrasting figures: the body and the house. These are metaphors – one organic, the other mechanical; one naturally given, the other humanly constructed. In rural Colombia, for example, a house is said to have a "base" or "foundation," which is its holdings of wealth. When the holdings are used to reproduce themselves, they are employed "from the doors inward"; when sold, they "move through the doors from inside to outside." The project of a house is to "support" and "maintain" itself; otherwise it will fall into "ruins." In these and other ways, the image of a physical house provides a means of formulating and voicing economic practices. It is a static figure in size and locale.

The corporate imagery is equally elaborate. The corporation is a single "body" (corpus, corps) that must have an "internal organ"-ization to "function" properly. It works best when it has an organizational "spirit" and is led by a "head," supported by a "right-hand man," both of whom use an internal "organ" to communicate with others if they cannot speak with them "face-to-face." But the corporation's "head" (or chair) should not be confused with the corporation's "capital" (head), which also comprises its "corpus" (body). The wealth of the group provides the "circulating" funds for sustaining the corporation's "members" and "arms," and even its "fundamental members," who are the "backbone of the organization." As a corporation grows, it "issues stock"; and though a corporation "never dies," a "sick organization" does go "belly-up."

Use of the body metaphor is not limited to profit making groups; there are legislative "bodies" (as well as legislative "chambers"), and the "head" of state may need to call upon the support of the "armed" forces or even the "armed arms" (*los brazos armados*) of the nation. The two metaphors of body and house not only flow outside the economic realm but invade one another, and this is also part of our argument. A corporation, for example, may have an "in-house" publication, and the corporation of great antiquity, or with pretensions to being such, may call itself a "House." According to modern mythology, many high-technology firms started in a "garage" or "basement" or even over an "Apple" on the kitchen table, but these beginnings are not very different from those of the cottage industries of centuries past.

The house and body metaphors are the starting points for the more elaborate and changing house and corporate models. Models often resemble metaphors, in which one figure is used to "see," "talk about," or constitute another. Like metaphors, models may be shocking, illuminating, or banal. They may be fiercely debated and contested or, like "dead" metaphors, fail to excite the imagination or rise to consciousness. Some are used in daily practice, others for heuristic purposes; some have a place in science, others are employed in human society, and still others cross between the two. Whereas a metaphor is suggestive and open, a model is a detailed working out or application of a figure. Once a metaphor has started a model, the latter may be developed quite variantly by different people.

There seem to be many kinds of economic and cultural models the world over (Gudeman 1986). According to some researchers, a script for entering a restaurant and ordering a meal is a model; maps and charts used to organize physical or social space are models; there are said to be models for logic, for legal reasoning, and for the pattern of emotive experience as well (Holland and Quinn 1987; Hutchins 1980; Johnson-Laird 1983; Schank and Abelson 1977). We think that all such models are the products of long conversations, fashioned by communities of discussants. Humans work and rework "experience," and therefore the "real world" is neither raw nor filtered but modeled and then debated. Models and their lexicons emerge through the agreement, argument, and reflection of humans engaged in practices and conversations, both verbal and textual. The model of the house economy in Colombia is the outcome of an extensive conversation that occurred over several thousand years and continues to take place in many lands.

The Colombian rural folk often explained their actions to us as "the way of doing things" (*el modo de hacer*). For them, practice is a process and so is a model: a model is developed through use. For example, in the process of modeling a corporation, the group comes to have a "head," "arms," "members," and "organs"; but it might have had "fingers," "joints," "muscles," "lips," and "hair." The "initial" body figure itself is formulated by use just as the model of an economic group is made by application of the figure. There is an open-ended and shifting quality to this modeling process of perceiving, playing with, and constructing similarities and differences.

Many models are simple or appear so because they are known by the use of shorthands or metaphors: "It is another Korea," "He is another Hitler," "Inflation is on the rise again," "The economy is a house." In each of these cases, the verbal shorthand helps clarify a new context by providing an instant frame for more detailed exploration. But this process of modeling is itself embedded within a larger sequence of practices. Modeling begins with a type of "search behavior" to find applicable figures from written history, personal memory or even dreams. For some, Vietnam was "like" Korea, but others saw it through the lens of the American War of Independence or the Civil War. Salient experiences such as epidemics and economic depressions seem to have a formative impact upon the interpretation of later times. We often explain political events by past viral epidemics or one war by another. For a group of people sharing a history, particular historical moments come to be persuasive in determining what is to be done. Similarly, the body and the house are compelling as models for their immediacy and continuity. This way of modeling has its economies; if certain models are common coin, search behavior can be shortened and a model more quickly brought to bear upon a situation. Still, the use of the same model again and again is compulsive or uninformed behavior, immune to learning.

Models vary in their generality. In many cases, a model is an evocative suggestion. The Colombian house model, for example, does not apply to the specifics of agriculture or pastoralism. It has to do only with the management of material activities, whether pastoral or agricultural, whether in the lowlands or at high altitudes. This is a strength, for if it covered specific techniques it would leave little room for new application. The model of the economy as a house has been used in widely disparate ecological settings and for divergent products and ways of producing; it has been employed by large and small families and within different political conditions and patterns of exchange.

But this broad and lasting use, or "hegemony," of the house model is only a local phenomenon. Certainly, the domestic model is not "logically" superior to other constructions of material practices, and in the Colombian countryside it is not deployed in all domains of life. The model often has to be brought into use with another one, developed by a different community of modelers. According to the rural people's model, the market is – or should be – a place for the trade of equivalents, but they know that this seldom occurs and that pure market participants enter to make a gain. The market is one context in which limits on the constructive power of the house model become apparent. Such model conflicts often erupt in violence or lead to the transformation and disappearance of one of them, but sometimes they persist longer than might be imagined. The inability of the house to control market transactions was recognized by Aristotle and later by the medieval Schoolmen. But the market is only one instance in which the limits and "incompleteness" of the rural folk's model become evident. Their model has mostly to do with land, foodstuffs, and everyday life – with where wealth comes from and how it enters the house and is controlled by it. To speak of the house model as "key" or "hegemonic," then, is to claim only that it has contextual importance, which implies that one ethnographic task is to detail its domains of application.

Models are made and remade through use. Never definite, never finished, they are experiments in living. In Colombia, from the Ecuadorian border to the north coast, there exist many verbal variations in the terms for meals, for exchanging work, and for the wealth of a house; these are evidence of historical shifts and transformations. But our experience, that in each area the rural people have a precise model lexicon and that these slightly varying lexicons are understood elsewhere, suggests – what is astonishing given the physical distances separating them – that the rural folk comprise a community of conversationalists.

These contemporary variations in models raise several issues concerning persistence and change. For example, according to the Andean folk, the human was created by God in his "semblance." In our terms, a semblance is a model or, more exactly, a metaphor. In fact, as the people explain, man was made by God in His image yet subservient to Him because lacking His ultimate power; man both is and is not God. He is Godlike. For the rural folk the human is a metaphor for the divinity. But this metaphor was far more common in early Western times than today. One of the epistemological shifts developed and argued by John Locke consisted in the severing of this metaphoric connection between man and God. We might call this Lockean revolution an act of "deconstruction," of removing the logos. For Locke, man had not made the world as God, so he could not know it as God. But man could study orderly nature and arrive at an understanding of it through his sensations and ideational associations; and what man transformed in the world he thereby possessed. In offering a different model of man, Locke was not so much renouncing a belief in the deity as expressing deep humility about man's place and capacities. In brief, he shifted the conversation.

In rural Colombia, however, the older model persists. For example, the people say that man possesses an object of nature because he "makes" it with the strength and might of God. This view, neither a Marxian construction of labor value nor a Lockean construction of labor right, seems to be an echo of the earlier conversation. The rural model, employing a metaphor connecting man and deity, is almost a conversation "displaced" from the past to the present. Should we, from today's vantage point, call it an atavism? We shy away from this designation but do suggest that the conversational continuity is linked to the persisting marginality of the rural folk, to the enduring influence of the church in the peripheral areas, and to the steadfastness of the house economy itself, which organizes and gives substance to an otherwise fragmented conversational community.

We argue, then, that the Colombian model provides a glimpse of, or window on, earlier conversations. Over time, conversations certainly shift, but new ones incorporate and appropriate from the old so that all conversations are thick with history. Part of our argument is that such an intermixing of conversations occurred with the house and corporate models. Discussants of the emerging corporate model did not create a totally new lexicon; they also appropriated, applied, and transformed parts of the house one. More closely viewed, this shifting of conversations has involved: a long-term institutional shift from the house economy to the market and corporate domination; the continual inscribing and transforming of practices in texts which in turn have had their influence upon later practices; and the use by theorists, not always with attribution, of folk voices. As Tawney once remarked with respect to the concepts of the just price and usury:

> These doctrines sprang as much from the popular consciousness of the plain facts of the economic situation as from the theorists who expounded them. (1926:36)

We propose that there has been a continuous movement from folk voice to centric text over long periods of time and across a variety of practices as the balance of power between house and corporation shifted, and we think that the Colombian material is illustrative of these transitions. If the thesis is correct, it has implications for the epistemology of economics, or theory of the center, for it suggests that economic theory has unexplored social roots; it has implications for the postmodern "textualists," who seem to have denied the place of human learning by eliding the complex field practices of anthropologists and other inscribers who have attended to the voices of the folk; and it has implications for the understanding of "underdevelopment" at the periphery, for what is now on the margin was once a wellspring of ideas for the center.

Chapter 2

THE STRENGTH OF THE EARTH

The earth and its products are the basis of the rural economy. "Without land, you have nothing on which to live," one man said, implying that both the earth and its fruits are the means for human survival. Commented another, "All value comes from the earth," and though the word "value" is infrequently heard, the sense of his statement is common. But for the rural folk the earth is not simply a material resource, to be used or neglected; it is the repository of the "strength" or "force" (*la fuerza*) that is drawn upon in agriculture and contained in a harvest: "Everything produced from the earth gives strength," as one person expressed it. Transmitted to the body by food crops, strength is expended by humans in helping the land to "give" more crops and provide more force to maintain the house. The strength of the earth itself, however, was created and is sustained by the divinity, and therefore the success and worth of human endeavors are also reflections of this other power. In the words of a discussant, "One lives from the earth and the will of God."

We think that this finding – that the house economy is naturally based and divinely underwritten – applies not only to the Colombian countryside but also to other areas of Latin America, for it is the product of a conversation once dominant in the Old World and brought to the Americas with the conquest. This set of voices is no longer hegemonic in economic centers, but in addition to persisting on the periphery it continues to influence contemporary orthodoxy.

A contemporary conversation: the land

Before considering the people's practices and voices, we shall set the stage with a textual conversation. This other conversation – about land tenure and soil usage – comes from written work on Colombia, and few topics have drawn such sustained discussion in the society. From the conquest, the formation of Indian reserves, and the imposition of *encomienda* through the *repartimiento, mita,* and the rise of haciendas, the dissolution of church and Indian reserve lands, the expansion of *latifundios* (large farms), and the emergence of debt peonage to the final growth of a property-holding peasantry, the struggle to gain control of land and command labor through its possession has been a leitmotif in Colombian history. The several, complex historical processes have left their signature on the social placement and physical location of the house economy today.[1] Historically, fertile areas located near urban markets have prospered, and Colombian plantations have exported crops such as tobacco, quinine, bananas, coffee, and flowers. Counterposed to this profitable corporate sphere has been the domestic economy in its several forms, from the hacienda to the small house, and there has been continual competition for land between house and hacienda and between these two and the profit-making organizations.

Rural land traditionally has been unequally divided between agriculture and pastoralism. Cattle ranching, especially in the Andes, is land-extensive and undertaken by few; agriculture is more intensive and practiced by many. According to Smith (1967:33), in 1960 over 75 percent of rural "exploitations" were devoted to farming, but these occupied only 30 percent of the land; less than 14 percent of the exploitations were centered on cattle, yet these covered more than 60 percent of the land surface. The small house economy is primarily a farming unit, although it may keep some animals.

The division between agriculture and pastoralism is closely linked to a skewed pattern of landownership. Again according to Smith (1967:34), in 1960 1.7 percent of the agropastoral producers held more than 55 percent of the land, while more than 50 percent had the use of less than 2.5 percent of the land's surface.[2] Similarly, Kalmanovitz (1982:62) reports that in 1960 only 6.9 percent of the rural holdings were larger than 50 hectares, yet these few holdings occupied over 75 percent of the farmed area; by 1970–1, landholdings of more than 50 hectares each had risen to 8.4 percent of the total and occupied almost 78 percent of the rural property. At the other extreme, in 1960 nearly 63 percent of the holdings were less than 5 hectares each and covered 4.5 percent of the farmland; by 1970–1 this had changed for the worse, almost 60 percent of the holdings being under 5 hectares each and these covering only 3.7 percent of the farmland (Fajardo 1983:110). Published information on rural holdings from the 1980 census is not yet available, but according to data for 1986 collected by the Planning Bureau in Nariño much the same pattern persists today. For example, in the municipality of Cumbal (see figures 1 and 2), the largest number of individual holdings falls within the categories of less than 1 and less than 3 hectares each, while the smallest number of holdings is found in the range of 15, 20, and 50 hectares each. Conversely, the total area covered by the few grand holdings is very large, while the area occupied by the small holdings is quite small; in Cumbal 82 percent of the holdings have 8 percent of the land. Each time we visited Cumbal, in the 1970s and the 1980s, intense land struggles, including "occupations," armed confrontations, and legal battles were occurring, for land shortage and unequal allocation is very marked there. Variations on the Cumbal pattern are found in many other municipalities of Nariño, such as Samaniego (see figures 3 and 4) and Consacá (see figures 5 and 6).[3] These patterns from Nariño, possibly more accentuated than in other departments, are broadly characteristic of Andean land distribution today.

Linked to this pattern of land concentration is another feature that Fals-Borda (1979) described some years ago for Boyacá: fragmentation of the small holdings. Given private holdings, equipart inheritance, and the pressing need to farm for subsistence, small lots are divided, subdivided, and then divided again over time. The resulting proliferation of *minifundios* (very small farms) and *"micro-minifundios"* seems especially pronounced in Boyacá, Nariño, and Cundinamarca, our principal regions of fieldwork, where the land frontier has long since been exhausted.

Smaller farms, according to Smith's (1967:53–5) 1960 census data, were generally dedicated to raising maize, potatoes, and wheat, while larger ones tended to produce cotton and rice for sale. For example, 32 percent of the potato harvest was produced on farms smaller than 5 hectares each, while only 7 percent came from holdings

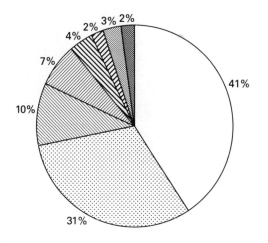

Less than 1 ha.
From 1 to 3 ha.
From 3 to 5 ha.
From 5 to 10 ha.
From 10 to 15 ha.
From 15 to 20 ha.
From 20 to 50 ha.
50 or more ha.

Figure 1 Number of holdings and plot sizes in Cumbal, 1986

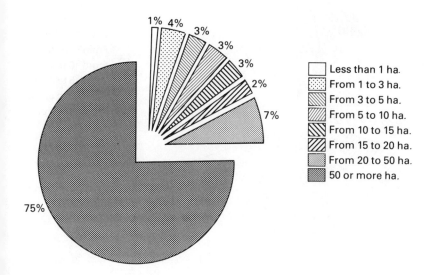

Less than 1 ha.
From 1 to 3 ha.
From 3 to 5 ha.
From 5 to 10 ha.
From 10 to 15 ha.
From 15 to 20 ha.
From 20 to 50 ha.
50 or more ha.

Figure 2 Plot size and total area in Cumbal, 1986

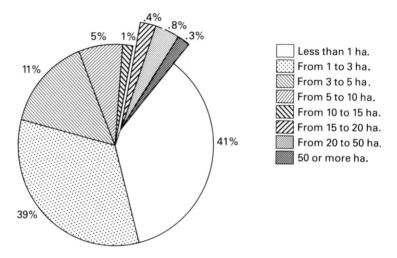

Less than 1 ha.
From 1 to 3 ha.
From 3 to 5 ha.
From 5 to 10 ha.
From 10 to 15 ha.
From 15 to 20 ha.
From 20 to 50 ha.
50 or more ha.

Figure 3 Number of holdings and plot sizes in Samaniego, 1986

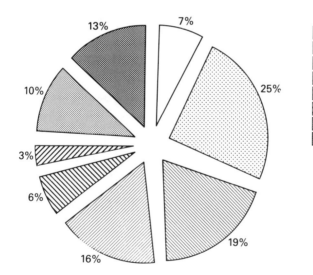

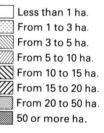

Less than 1 ha.
From 1 to 3 ha.
From 3 to 5 ha.
From 5 to 10 ha.
From 10 to 15 ha.
From 15 to 20 ha.
From 20 to 50 ha.
50 or more ha.

Figure 4 Plot size and total area in Samaniego, 1986

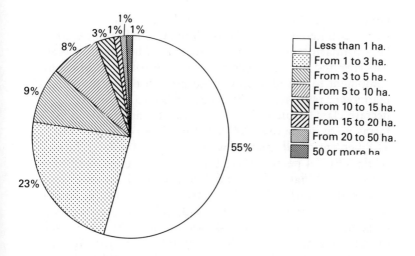

Figure 5 Number of holdings and plot sizes in Consacá, 1986

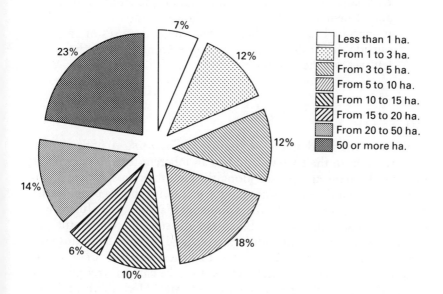

Figure 6 Plot size and total area in Consacá, 1986

larger than 200 hectares. For animals, a similar bifurcation was encountered. Sheep, hogs, donkeys, and mules were kept primarily on the smaller holdings, while cattle were concentrated on the larger ones. The distribution of capital equipment followed a similar pattern. Of the farms using manpower only, nearly 70 percent fell into the under 5-hectare class, while only 1.1 percent of "manpower only" farms were in the over 200-hectare category. By contrast, 41.8 percent of all tractors were found on the large farms, while only 7.4 percent were found on the many small ones.

In general, flat, valley land – at any altitude – is occupied by *latifundios*; these farms are also nearer sources of water, and the land can be easily plowed. Surrounding these better zones – on the slopes, in the rocky areas, and distant from water – are the *minifundios*, located on less accessible, less fertile, less usable land (Perry 1983:14). Sometimes this division can be traced to the formation of a hacienda centuries ago; sometimes it began when a hacienda sold off its poorer land or ceded it in settlement of squatters' or inhabitants' claims. Even today, when haciendas shrink, they hold onto their valley, irrigated, or riverbank land. The result, throughout the Andean area and elsewhere, is that the small house economy is located in marginal regions. The soil that the house uses often lies outside the profit margin; the house economy uses the leftovers of the market.

THE EARTH

Some rural folk say that it is the "nature" (*la naturaleza*) of the earth to give strength. In their view, land has an inherent feature or property useful to humans and passed along through the crops. Other discussants claim that the earth is not unique in this, for the sea provides fish, also a food of strength; still others point out that the successful growing of crops depends upon several factors – the sun, the temperature, the wind, and the weather in addition to the land. According to this view, the force of earth and sea is akin to "the elements" or "nature's powers." Yet different voices suggest that the earth's strength comes from rain, for nothing grows without water. Here there may be a metonymic connection with the divinity (assumed to be in the heavens), for, as an older speaker once argued,

Food gets its strength from the earth,
Earth gets its strength from water,
Water gets its strength from God.

Not all agree with this metonymic reasoning, though everyone concurs that nature's forces are ultimately the work of the divinity.

The earth, say the rural folk, was not randomly made, with humans its accidental and fortunate possessors. The forces of nature were created for humans, to be used by them. This implicit goodness of the earth is expressed through the notion of "giving." Over and over the people said, "the land gives" (*la tierra da*). After some time, we realized that the phrase was shorthand. It can be completed with the name of a crop, such as "the land gives maize." The land also gives "food," "a harvest," or "the crops," and only the earth "gives the base" of the house, meaning that all wealth comes from the land. More broadly, the rural folk explain that the strength of the earth is "given" by God.

This relation between humans and the earth is asymmetrical, for humans themselves are not repositories of force and so cannot give it in return. To obtain the earth's strength, however, human work is needed, for the earth gives neither by itself nor by divine will. Humans must "help" the land to give its products. As one person said, "Maize gets its sustenance from its roots and the work done to it, just as humans get sustenance from food." Once, in a discussion about humans and the land, we asked one man:

> "Do both produce?" "No," he answered, "producing is giving. Man helps the land; the earth produces the fruit."

Humans, it is said, aid and "compose" (*componen*) the land; they seed and "make the force" (*hacen la fuerza*) of the other work required. As one man stated, "Only the work of man can *move* the land . . . one helps the earth, and it gives its help." In most regions the easiest crop to raise is fodder; as the people say, the earth gives pasture almost by itself, yet humans are needed to manage (*manejar*) the crop, to cultivate and order or control (*mandar*) it. Sometimes a metaphor links the giving divinity and land with living things that bear offspring; just as the earth gives as does God, so animals "give" as does the land. The people say, for example, that a hen "gives" an egg or that sheep and goats "give" offspring. A man once cautioned us that it was "coarse" (*una grosería*) to say that a cow was "bearing" (*parir*); rather, one says that the animal is going to "give." According to this figure of speech, the human helps the earth to give as a midwife assists at birth. As we shall also see, animals "give" offspring only when the earth has "given strength" to them.

When humans properly assist the land, they are able to take (*sacar*) what it gives, a relationship of "give-and-take" from earth to humans. Thus, the rural folk speak of "gathering up" (*recoger*) and "picking" (*coger*) a harvest that is "left" (*dejar*) to them, and they talk about the earth's "plenty" as "arriving" or "reaching" (*llegar*) them. Agricultural processes are also discussed in terms of human exchange. Some speak of a "trade" (*un cambio*) with the land, while others say that working the earth is like trading with a neighbor. Either way, the connection between humans and the earth is modeled in relation to a human bond. But this trade with the land is also unlike that with a neighbor, for it is never measure for measure (*ras con ras*). Humans put wealth and work into the earth, while it gives something different and more in return; they expend seed, fertilizer, money, and labor, and the land returns food. The transaction is neither homogeneous nor balanced. Humans do trade with nature, but by using its already given force to gather more strength on which life depends. This relationship of mutual help – or reciprocity – and of trade favors humans and underlies all others.

Because the land has powers that lie outside human control, agriculturalists can never count upon getting a return. Agricultural activities are spoken of as "a luck" (*una suerte*), "a gamble" (*un juego de azar*), "a lottery" (*una lotería*), and as part of one's "destiny" (*el destino*). "What is luck? . . . It is what you don't control. Potatoes are a lottery." Often, the raising of a crop is said to be a "venture" (*una ventura*), a term capturing the notion of a chance, a risk, and an adventure as well. As one man, in a typical word play, said: "We agriculturalists, we are ad-venturers." All these terms are applied to crop plagues and bad agricultural prices in addition to the earth's fertility. Those who make earthenware jugs say, when their pots crack or burn in firing them, even when great care has been exercised to control the temperature, that this is a matter of "fortune." As the rural folk explain, "Luck is for some people but not everybody." Among themselves, humans allocate and control rights to natural resources but not the force these contain. For this reason, the people also say that the earth "gives the wealth of the house," as if the land itself were not already held by the domestic unit.

The rural folk often call upon God for help in agriculture. As seeding begins, a man ordinarily says, "In the name of the Lord and the Holy Spirit, may it come up well." Some add, "Blessed Saint Isidore, help me" or "Saint Isidore, farm laborer, bring the water and get rid of the sun." Saint Isidore is a widely revered patron of agriculture who, according to local history, prayed to God for rain and a limit on the amount of sunshine. When his pleas were answered, but the crops did not grow, he turned in puzzlement to the Lord, who responded that there had been no petition for wind. (In our conversations, the people mentioned again and again the need for wind to have the crops grow.) There are other verbal acknowledgments of God's power. In vows to saints, a common expression is "When God doesn't want it, his saint can't do it." Playing upon this, one man said, "When God doesn't want it, there are few harvests." One also hears "God first and then maize." These homologies, fashioned between a garden or harvest on the one side, and a manifestation of divine power on the other, recall and validate God's continuing and required presence. The people continuously engage in such acts of verbal modeling.

The land may produce an abundance (*una abundancia*) or a scarcity (*una escasez*). In times of abundance the harvest covers house expenditures with leftovers; in periods of scarcity losses are incurred. But there is much variation between the extremes, and all are expressed in terms of how well the land "gives." Some land is also said to "give more force" or to produce certain crops better than others. Thus, through the expression "giving," the people can attend to climatic change, marginal differences in soil fertility, and the land's varying crop suitability. Everyone says that the earth gives less now, and local conversations are dominated by the theme of scarcity. Today the land yields a smaller variety of crops and needs more help – "much more help" – from humans in the form of plowing, weeding, and pruning; the crops also need more fertilizer and irrigation. But the people also draw distinctions here. Use of insecticides and herbicides, they say, reduces the human work required but does nothing for the land's strength. Fertilizer is different, for it adds force to the land. Using the same comparison as the rural folk of Panama (Gudeman 1978, 1986), the people say that fertilizer is like ashes from trees in a swidden that are burned to clear a plot for seeding. As trees grow they store force from the land; when they are cut and burned this force is released, falls to the earth in the ashes, and strengthens the soil. In the past animal manure (*abono orgánico, abono negro*), which gets its force from the pasture that animals have eaten, was used to strengthen the soil. In the absence of forests today, and with the reduction in number of domestic animals held, chemical fertilizer (*abono químico, abono blanco*) has to be applied. But this fertilizer "burns the earth" and "takes away" its force. The worsening situation is not the land's "fault," for it is "tired" and needs to "rest"; still, one consequence is that the people must invest more and more cash now to have a successful harvest.[4] Even with use of purchased additives, the land sometimes "does not produce what it costs" because the price of fertilizer is so high, and from this deteriorating situation there seems to be no "salvation."

STRENGTH AND FOOD

Food crops as well as usable plants, such as trees for firewood or *fique* (henequen) for hemp, draw their strength from the land. Coal is also a repository of force, and any mine is a standing reservoir of strength varying from "little" to "much." Animals contain force but consume food to gain it, while their fodder gathers its strength from the land. Humans consume crops and animal products to gain their strength, and this, when turned to work on the land, yields more force.

The foods said to have most force vary by region. Outside Villa de Leiva in southern Boyacá, people claim that grains, peas, broad beans, and potatoes contain most strength; but in northern Boyacá, from Soatá to Capitanejo, maize is said to give most force. Elsewhere people identify beans, lentils, or wheat as having strength. Rankings of foods within a region are also discussed. "Maize, peas, and potatoes," said one man, "are powerful nourishments. Rice and noodles give less force." The foods said to contain most strength are usually what the earth produces best in that zone, although this is not the way the people voice it. For them, certain crops in a region are better able to use the land's force there (e.g., "potatoes are given better") and so contain the most strength as foodstuffs. The single expression "strength" is, however, used everywhere for the land, its products, and food.

Food (*la comida*) provides the human with nourishment (*la alimentación*), and it gives both energy and spirit or intention (*el ánimo*). One discussant summarized:

> In working you are using the strength of food. One uses up health and energy. So you pay for it yourself. When you eat you put back [*reponer*] this force. You eat and use up. This goes on and on in the body. But in bread, what strength do you get? People suffer when they do not have enough force to work; they are using up their health. You have to maintain yourself.

A young person has more energy and spirit, while older people produce less (*poco rinden*) because they have used up (*gastado*) their health. Within this life trajectory, force animates (*anima*) the body, which itself is a kind of reservoir that has to be maintained: "If one does not eat, where does the strength come from?" A person must continually replace (*reponer*) the force expended. The substances needed for living are also known as *víveres* (food supplies, provisions), a term deriving from *vivir*, "to live." Nature's strength is the substance of living, the human body its container.

Most of the foods raised or purchased first are said to be foods "of first necessity" (*de primera necesidad*). These, which contain much strength, are also known as "basics." As one person stated:

> Maize is basic, it provides all the force – for humans, chickens and pigs. It all comes back to maize. The basics are the support [*el sostén*] of one and the family, from breakfast to dinner to clothes. They are all products of the land.

WORK

By providing energy and spirit, the strength of food sustains work. The full expression for work is "the force of work" (*la fuerza de trabajo*), but at times a shorthand, "strength," "force," or "work," is used. When asking someone for help, a person says: "Will you assist me with strength today?" In this and other verbal practices, work is construed as a physical activity. But it is also the final using up (*gastar*) of the land's strength. One person explained: "You use up force in work; you don't see this strength, but you can see it in the work people do. Some people have more force to work." Another added:

> Maize gets its strength from the 'vegetables' in the land. Humans have to help put these there, and they use the force of work to do so. Their strength is used up; you do not see it. Force is spent in sweat.

The expenditure of strength in work is directly connected to rights of ownership. In general, ownership can be gained through purchase, gift, inheritance, or a lucky find, but in the first instance it is gained by work through the use of force. As a person said: "One is owner of what one works – the only thing." This mode of gaining property provides the model for other forms of acquisition. For example, when we asked how gaining ownership by work fitted ownership by market purchase, one man explained that money used to buy was itself earned by working, so ultimately a purchased item was owned through one's labor. When we then suggested that an inheritance surely was not the result of one's work, he explained that a person had to manage (*manejar*) and maintain the property or it would be lost and that the possession itself had been built up by work performed a generation ago.

Human work is unique in being able to create ownership; but physical work does not make rights of possession. Because it depends upon the use of strength, work itself is owned and controlled by the provisioning of its force. For example, the people say that whoever is paying and feeding a group of workers is the owner of their work (*el dueño del trabajo*). They explain that one is never owner of a human; and though a work owner can dismiss his laborers, tell them how to work or when to eat, he has no command over their actions outside the work context. A person is owner of the work alone, and this ownership yields possession of what that work produces. Thus, when house members work for themselves they own the results of their efforts precisely because they are provisioning themselves. To be self-sustaining is not just a matter of feeding oneself and of having command over one's labor but of gaining ownership of its results.

This construction brings the local model full circle. There is a flow of strength from the land to crops to food to humans to work that helps the land to give more force. Strength is secured from the earth and used up as humans gather more. Control over this process is established through the house, for by using resources of the house to sustain their work the people gain control over the results of their efforts.

Conversations: the earth, strength, and the Physiocrats

The several rural concepts are familiar yet distant from our own. The key notion, as we gradually discovered, is "strength." In 1984, during fieldwork in Boyacá, we had been startled to hear people speak of *la fuerza de trabajo*, which we thought meant "labor power." Our attention was also drawn to the fact that the exercise of labor yielded property rights, for this suggested to us that a rudimentary "labor theory of value" was being used: human labor, endowed with an inherent power, could create property through its exercise. The human world, therefore, must represent an accumulation of labor's power or "dead labor." As we further listened to the people, however, it became apparent that "force" or "strength" was a more appropriate gloss than "power" for *la fuerza*. Our notes also show that the people talked about the "strength of food," though we did no more than register the fact.

At this early stage, then, we faced the problem of translation and understanding. One way of interpreting the people's talk, it seemed, was to project our contemporary models on it. Perhaps this was a Marxian construction of "labor value," developed as a critique of the dominant corporate economy. Alternatively, by using the neoclassical idea that land, labor, and capital are all "factors of production," we could substitute our "land as a factor of production" (or "the land's productivity") for their notion of "the earth that gives," and our "uncertainty" seemed much like their several concepts of "luck," "venture," and "gamble." But in these "translations," many of the internal connections or longhands between their terms were being lost. For example, in their context, the expression "the earth that gives" is part of an internal conversation by which the connection between soil and humans is modeled in relation to social relationships and transactions with the divinity. Similarly, in the neoclassical model land is equal to other "factors of production" such as machines, fuel, seed, and human labor; but for the rural folk, the earth gives more than it receives, humans only assist in production, and tools do not give at all: "You cannot even see what goes in from the tools." From their perspective, our notion of "land productivity" shifts theirs substantially – by modeling the earth as a mechanism and obscuring nature's unique capacity for supporting life, by endowing equipment and humans with qualities that pertain only to the earth, and by obscuring humans' singular relation with the soil.

In 1986, during work in Nariño, we finally "heard" the people speak of the "land's force" itself. Then, upon returning to Boyacá in 1987 and starting fieldwork in the region of Villa de Leiva, we noted the full register of the word "force" – for the land, work, crops, and food. From our discussions in the car, it seemed clear that "force" was the same for work, land, and food and that the rural model did not privilege the three "factors" together or labor alone. The model was not Marxian but seemed to be a pre-Smithian view of the economy. With this "understanding" of their conversation, we posed new questions about the sea and fish, and with growing excitement we seemed to find that their voices verified our developing explanations. We carried the process further by first voicing what we thought might be their answers to questions on specific topics, such as how and why cattle grow. When these answers were voiced by a number of people, we thought we had reached rock bottom in their conversation: this was a Physiocratic, land-based model.

In accomplishing these steps, we had been listening to several conversations. Their "on-the-ground" talk, from Boyacá and Santander to Nariño and back, was the principal one. Our car conversation was a discussion about this conversation. But we were never alone, for there were also "voices in the air" – those textual authorities of the past, acquired by learning, never stilled in memory, yet dimly recalled when needed. When we decided to ask the folk about the "force" of cattle and of pasture, it was not a question formulated *de novo* but one based on our knowledge that such issues had perplexed the Physiocrats. In this complex way, voices on the ground and in the air, practices and texts, living history and the history of living, became joined for us.

As we attended more and more closely to the people's lexicon, therefore, it seemed that a "translation" of *la fuerza* would have to be worked through conversations shared in the past. In the late eighteenth century, the Physiocrats formulated a model which indeed bears a resemblance to rural Colombia. The Physiocrats were a group, a conversational community, who formulated one of the first total or holistic models of economic practices.[5] Influenced by Locke and often anti-Cartesian in tone, their writings had persuasive force in France right up to the Revolution. But with this political shift and the publication of Adam Smith's *Wealth of Nations* in 1776, their influence diminished. Still, much of their work presaged later developments in economic theory, and in many respects they were the first true writers on "the economy."

According to the principal Physiocratic tenet, only the land and the sea are productive of wealth. Mirabeau once said, "The land is the mother of all goods" (1973[1760]:120). Turgot spoke of "the revenues of the earth, a gift of nature"; of "the earth which is always the first and only source of all wealth"; of profits which "always come from the earth"; and of the land as offering "a pure gift to him who cultivates it" (1898[1770]:14, 44, 46, 89). Quesnay's voice was similar: "The sovereign and the nation should never lose sight of the fact that the land is the unique source of wealth, and that it is agriculture which causes wealth to increase" (1963c:232). This lexicon, indicating that the earth possesses a special fecundity, was widely shared among the Physiocrats and used in varying degrees by the Bullionists and the Mercantilists as well.

In the Physiocratic model, the land and the sea are the only places of "productive expenditure"; all other expenditures, as in artisanry and manufacturing, are "sterile." The Physiocratic distinction between fertile and barren spheres, and between productive and unproductive using up of wealth, was based upon the idea that only nature returns and restores more than it absorbs. Both leisure and human work constitute a "using up" or "expenditure" (*dépenser*) of materials already gathered. In the case of work, everything depends upon where it is used. The application of human effort to land provides a return larger than expenditures, while work in artisanry does not. According to the Physiocrats, the fertility of nature contrasted with the barrenness of other domains is the handiwork of the divinity.

The similarity to the rural Colombian model is striking. In both models land and sea are the source of wealth and this natural fecundity is the work of God. (With respect to mining, there is a difference; some Physiocrats considered mining a nonproductive or barren venture, while the Colombian folk see mines and forests as reservoirs of natural force.) Human labor, like that of a midwife, assists in the production of natural riches, but the work itself is not productive, being an expenditure of wealth previously obtained. According to both models, wealth is used up as it circulates through society, both workers and the idle rich living from the material stock already secured.

The two models differ, however, in their institutional focus. According to the rural folk, materials from the land flow to the house where labor is supported and foodstuffs are held. A principal task of the house is "to order well" (*mandar bien*) its people and material flows. In contrast, Physiocracy is focused on the nation and the flows that occur within it. But the Physiocratic state, in some respects, is modeled after the house, being the domestic economy writ large. For example, in rural Colombia, the fault for agricultural failure is attributed not to the land but to the weather and human management, even though the earth is the source of wealth. Two hundred years ago, Quesnay argued that the blame for a lack of foodstuffs lay not with the land or farmers but with the government, whose duty it was to organize all the activities of provisioning. By this same argument, he justified the position of the landowners, who received some of the fruits of the land. Idle they were with respect to securing wealth, but their task was to manage the nation and its flow of riches as did the head of a household. Still, in rural Colombia, all members of the house are expected to help, and the campesinos are not so forgiving of the landowners (*los ricos*) who can be idle because they are rich.

But there is another, more pointed difference between the two models. In Physiocracy, the conversation focuses on agricultural flows, from the land to humans and back to the land. These flows are measured in money – as in Quesnay's *Tableau économique* (1972[1758–9]) – and made commensurate through price. In Colombia also, the people talk of securing real materials, but useful things (*las utilidades*) are encapsulations of force, and this notion has no counterpart in Physiocracy or other texts of the time. Both models have a materialist emphasis, but Physiocracy is less reified, less abstract, for it does not invoke a notion such as "force."

Thus, recalling the Physiocratic conversation is enlightening but not conclusive with respect to the problem of translating and understanding the people's term "strength," for the Physiocrats measured agricultural flows by money. Yet, at times the rural folk appear to do so, too. One explication of "force," suggested to us by a man in Nariño, was precisely that it is like a currency. This discussant survived in a remote region partly by cutting logs and transporting them to a nearby town for sale as firewood. When we asked how this mode of livelihood fit his other practice of slash-and-burn agriculture, he explained that the forest was a "savings account" (*una caja de ahorros*); he drew on its strength to make a living. By contrast, with crops he had to plant and do other work before securing the force of the earth in the harvest. We laughed with satisfaction at his comparison, for he had used a concept from our model world – the savings account – to construct a metaphor in his own in order to make his comprehensible to us. We took pleasure in the surprise provided by his imagery, in having our world reproduced in his, and in the quick – shorthand – understanding we had achieved. His utterance also indicated a willingness to join in our conversation and an attempt at understanding. But our pleasure was short-lived, for we soon realized that we had misunderstood his metaphor; trees in fact are like crops, not unlike them, for both gather their strength from the land. The difference is that the forest, like a mineral deposit, is a standing reservoir of strength, while crops have to be raised before securing their strength in the harvest. A stand of trees is like a savings account in that it is accumulated, held for some time, and exhausted through use. As one person said, when we asked if a used deposit of coal would reproduce, "No, it is finished there, but you can find and get it [*sacar*] somewhere else." As we finally came to understand, our discussant's metaphor hinged upon the fact that the word "savings" has its own usage in the countryside. Savings of materials and money are made by the house through thrift and are kept as a reserve; such savings do not collect interest as in a bank and are liquidated by use. Our discussant had indeed been drawing a metaphor but one within his conversation, between household savings of money and stands of trees. Still, according to his metaphor strength is like money: force – being gathered, circulated, used, and saved – links the activities that depend upon it.

Should we surmise, then, that the rural Colombian idea of "force" is anterior to ours and to eighteenth-century economic theory? This would yield yet a different set of translations. Where the rural folk speak of the "strength of the earth," we talk about "land's fertility"; where they say the "force of labor," we talk about "labor power"; and where they speak of the "strength of food," we say "food value." They employ "strength" or "force" where we use "fertility," "power," and "value." Could it be that our terms have come from a European folk conversation? We suggest that European folk did indeed provide a wellspring of ideas for later cultures and economists and that there has been a long-term dialectic between folk practices and inscriptions, linking the models of the present-day Colombian folk and of Physiocracy, Marx, and others through a series of conversational shifts. A term such as "force" was probably used by European folk to indicate the divinely mandated lawfulness of nature. Such a concept was given a more specific land and agricultural rendering in the conversation of the Physiocrats and a labor turning in the texts of Marx; later, it was broken into the several terms, "value," "fertility," and "power," that we use today.

On a Whig version of history or a positivist view of economics – according to which analytical tools improve over time, hypotheses are verified or thrown away, metatheories are exposed, and economies are better understood as knowledge accumulates (Blaug 1978:7) – such conversational shifts are the stuff of progress. By this view, our modern conversation is more accurate than the folk one of Europe or the current one in Colombia. But is it? If, on the basis of historical connection, we can project our conversation upon theirs and translate their "strength" as "fertility," "power," and "value," then surely the reverse is valid, and our "utility" means something like their "force." Injecting their voice into our discussion makes us speak of the "force" of things and goods as well as "the inherent strength" of an object. It also makes us say that capital has "force" and so does money, which is very close to current linguistic usage. In fact, this easy substitution of their imputed essence for ours helps reveal some of the reifications in which we are caught. The words "utility" and "value," for example, have proven to be enormously difficult for economists to use (Robinson 1962). The *Macmillan Dictionary of Modern Economics* defines value as "the intrinsic worth of a commodity" and also as "utility," which in turn is defined as the happiness an object brings and the desire that it should exist. A Marxist would argue that these are mystifications. But a Marxist would hardly prefer the Colombian model, dismissing it as a form of Physiocracy, for in the Marxist view, value is created only by application of "labor's power." In response, the Colombian folk might claim that the Marxist constructs of "labor value" and "labor-power" locate in humans something that comes only from the land and the natural world. Over this fundamental point the two conversational communities would separate and the discussion would become heated, all the while enlightening the listener.

But considering the rural model only, the word *la fuerza* remains refractory, for all our proposed translations omit some of the connectives of their usage. And if our surmise is correct that the crucial Marxist concept of "labor-power" and the modern economist's concepts of "utility" and "value" are conversational carryovers from an earlier European notion about "force," then an explication of the rural term is all the more needed. This realization that the folk notion of strength is central to their economy and to the models of modern economists, and that we were still operating with a shorthand understanding of their conversation, led us to return to the field in October 1987.

FORCE AND POWER

"The force of the cultivation comes from God's power," explained a woman in Cundinamarca:

> The food you have in the house is this *strength* for working. On Sunday the food of communion gives spiritual *might*. One is material, the other is spiritual. You live from both – if you are a Catholic! Money does not have this *power*.

Other discussants also distinguished between material "strength" or "force" and divine "might" or "power" (*el poder*), while suggesting that both emanate from God. Similarly, they distinguished between "corporal" food and "spiritual" food just as kinship in the house and spiritual kinship through the church form an oppositional pair (Gudeman 1972).

In the beginning, say the people, God made the world with His will (*la voluntad*), and He is the owner (*el dueño*) of all that He made. God also made man – in His semblance – for which reason God is the "Señor" or "patron" of everyone. He "orders" (*manda*) all. This is His power.

Man, the rural folk explain, makes the world with the power of God. Humans are the administrators of what God gives and have to order (*mandar*) it well. "You work with the will of God and the Virgin"; without this, man can do nothing. Man gathers up divine power in his daily and spiritual food, provided by God: thus, the parallel sayings "There is nothing like God and the Virgin" and "There is nothing like God and one's garden." Agriculture is not simply legitimated by the metonymic association of rain with the divinity in the sky; the two are alike in offering provisions, corporal and spiritual. And they are ultimately the same: "One gets his strength from God just as maize gets its strength from its roots. But food also gets its power from God's will." A different discussant succinctly united the duality: "Jesus Christ gives sustenance for all." Christ's body, both temporal and spiritual, force and power, strength and might, earthly and divine, is reproduced through the daily work that maintains the house of man and the Sunday work that keeps the house of God.

This religious or cosmological construction of the economy as God's might is directly linked to the way property rights are created. Initially, we had understood ownership to derive from work alone, and we interpreted this as a Marxian conception. With further consideration, it became clear that despite the similarity in terminology – "labor-power" in Marx, "force of work" in Colombia – the Colombian folk concept was closer to the earlier Lockean conception of property, according to which the labor of the human annexes those portions of nature upon which it is laid. But our final conversations in Cundinamarca led us to realize that the folk notion of property was related to a yet earlier construction. The Colombian folk speak of human activity as "making" or "doing" (*hacer*), and it is this shorthand construction that ties directly into the longhand cosmology. Just as God made man in his semblance and owns him for it, so man owns what he makes. And just as God works with his goodwill, so humans in His semblance must work with spirit (*ánimo*), energy, hope, and belief that there will be good results. God "organized" the world in such a way that "to eat bread" man must work, although if God willed it "you could sustain yourself remaining in bed." By living and making in the semblance of God, by administering God's power, man is the owner of what he makes. As one person said, "He who rules (*manda*) is the one who made it." In the longer perspective, one cannot own after death, and everything is God's. But during a lifetime, one is owner of something for having made it, in the semblance of God.

In Europe it took hundreds of years to shift from conversations about God's power to make man and man's strength to make property to discussions about human making as a property in itself, then to talk about labor-power alone, and finally to a discussion of economic value and utility. Starting with the Colombian model and tracing these steps back through successive conversations helps elucidate the place of "strength" in the rural model today, just as a better understanding of this term may help illuminate the way conversational communities have transformed and used the verbal semblances of the might and power of God over the centuries.

Chapter 3

THE HOUSE

Both the house and the corporation are found in the countryside, but from the most distant and marginal zones to the edges of fertile plains near towns the house predominates. The arresting feature of the house is that its activities are modeled on the layout of the dwelling itself.

Rural houses take many forms. Some are constructed of sticks and thatch, others of adobe, wattle and daub (*bajareque*), tapia, or brick and cement. Shapes also vary; simple ones with a room or two may have a veranda on one or all sides, while more elaborate houses, with four sides and an internal patio, recall the Roman villa. Nearly every material activity can be witnessed inside and around a dwelling: sorting seeds and sharpening knives; drying a harvest of tobacco or coffee; eating, conversing, and tending children. A small garden usually surrounds the house, and frequently one of the major agricultural plots is located nearby. Houses may contain single individuals, married pairs, nuclear families, or larger agglomerations of kin and nonkin. Whatever its size or physical shape, the house itself provides a plan for the economic group.

The principal features of the house model can be quickly summarized. A rural economic group is known as the "house" (*la casa*). It has a "base" (*una base*) or "foundation" (*un fundamento*), which is its wealth. It also has "doors" (*puertas*), as is signaled by the expressions "from the doors inward" (*de puertas para adentro*) and "from the doors outward" (*de puertas para afuera*). The people use shorthands to talk about material transactions of the group: goods are produced by the house and kept "inside" (*de adentro*), pass "from inside to outside" (*de adentro por afuera*), and come "from outside to inside" (*de afuera por adentro*). Any shift of the house's base through the doors, from inside to outside or outside to inside, is termed a "movement" (*un movimiento*), just as people themselves are said to move through the doors.

A house has two projects. Its first is to "maintain" (*mantener*), "sustain" (*sostener*), "support" (*soportar*), or "keep" (*guardar*) itself.

These frequently used words are themselves employed in two contexts, each evoking or implying the other. The physical aspects of a house must be "maintained," and the members of the house must be "kept" or "sustained" with food. "We work to support ourselves," said a man in Nariño.

> We need foods. They come first, but support includes clothes; otherwise you are like an animal. These are the house expenditures.

Normally, when people speak of "maintaining a house" the physical image is taken to mean supporting the members with food, but this social application implies the need for keeping up the dwelling. The model works from the physical to the social to the physical, conjoining the two.

An elaboration of the house model is used when the group hires outside laborers. A house usually feeds its "outside" workers and is said to "support" them. But a special terminology is employed for one of the meals served late in the day: the repast is said to "buttress" (*apuntalar*) the hired workers, to "prop them up," just as a buttress on the outside of a building gives it extra strength. In the people's precise usage, the food is an "auxiliary support," limited in time and scope, given at that moment in the day when the strength to work is ebbing; and it is an "outside" support, being provided from without the worker's domestic group. The elaboration of the house figure playfully models the limits and purposes of the household obligation and practice.

The second project of a house is to "augment" or "increase" (*aumentar*) its base. The rural folk try to expand both the wealth of a house and its physical foundation. To accomplish these two goals people try "to keep" or "hold" (*guardar*) household products (*la base*) "inside the doors"; they practice "householding" and "housekeeping." The figure of a physical house is consistently and creatively used to model the parts and the project of the economic group.

A conversation: models and metaphors

In the house model a figure from the built world – with foundation, supports, and doors – is used to talk about and organize material practices. Between physical house and material processes there is no a priori connection, but through the model, physical houses are turned into economic centers, while economic units are realized as houses. The model is built around a metaphor.

The domestic metaphor in Colombia is, as we have suggested, a key one, for it has a central place in structuring material activities and helps shape other domains of discussion. For example, the expression about the doors of the house is used to express political control of information. The government voice that speaks "from the doors outward" provides information for public "consumption"; this is filtered news, though not necessarily false. The political voice that speaks "from the doors inward," however, offers "inside" information for private "consumption," as does an "in-house publication." In this "government-as-house" metaphor, the doors mark the edges of the controlling group and signal its ability to control the flow of information. The political expression is a projection of the "economy-as-house" metaphor. Thus, one figure (the physical house) is used in a metaphor (the domestic economy) that itself is applied within a new domain (the polity); information flow is modeled after wealth "movements," which are modeled after human movements through the doors of a house. By such projections models invade each other, and conversations become ever thicker over time. Within a culture, however, some figures seem to hold a persistently central place, and the "polity-as-house" example suggests something of the persuasive power that the "economy-as-house" metaphor still has in Colombia.

In the domestic metaphor itself the figure of a house is not fully exploited. The metaphor does not utilize the roof or walls, although the existence of both is implied by the expression about the "doors." A metaphor seldom, if ever, consists of a point-for-point mapping from domain to domain. It seizes upon certain characteristics of a figure, leaving others aside for later elaboration or oblivion. In discourse also, the house metaphor is not a totality. Only by the fiction of inscription or within an extended conversation does it appear as a whole. Normally, the metaphor is used in bits or is called forth by parts, the naming of a house feature serving in everyday conversation as a shorthand for the whole and for an economic function. The word "base" implies the physical house, the house economy, and the wealth of the group.

The rural folk, of course, do not speak of a domestic

metaphor, and what an outsider might term "figure" (the house as physical structure) and "application" (the house as economic organization) are mixed together. This is part of the model's persuasiveness. For example, according to the metaphor, land and crops are part of the foundation and fall within the doors of the house. But the people also say that one leaves the house to work on the land, that one has work outside the house, and that one brings the crops to the house for storage: "You bring from outside what you gather up from the land." In the one usage, the crops and land are inside the house; in the other the land is outdoors and the crops are brought from outside to inside. Clearly, the various parts of an economic "house" are not always held within the physical house, and certainly they are never kept underneath it as a foundation; conversely, an existent structure may contain people or things that are not part of its economic organization. But in conversation the two are intermixed and cause no confusion.

There is more to the several uses of the word "base." The people say that the base as wealth does not include the physical house itself. For example, a day laborer may possess a house on its foundation without having a base, and it is possible to have a base of wealth without having a dwelling. In such instances, the economic or "figurative" application of the term contradicts its "literal" or original use. According to some views on metaphor (Beardsley 1981; Henle 1981; Ricoeur 1977), when figurative use contradicts literal application a metaphor is in play, and this seems to be true of the case at hand. "Base" does and does not mean the physical underpinnings of a house, and it does and does not mean the undergirdings of an economy. Its use for the latter depends upon its use for the former yet denies it.

HOUSE CONNECTIONS

A house has two arenas of contact with the larger world, the land and other humans. New wealth moving into the house normally consists of agricultural produce or pastoral products. We initially thought that because land and cattle are part of the base, new crops and progeny must be "inside the doors," too; it seemed inconsistent to claim that they came from outside to inside. The rural folk explained, however, that crops and cattle (via pasture) depend for their growth on the earth's strength, which is never owned. The "giving," therefore, comes from "outside," and wealth "moves into the house" from agriculture or pastoralism. This wealth is then used up or expended, which diminishes the base.

The house's connection to the material world is marked by a gender difference. A woman is said to perform "domestic work," a man "material work." The construction fits the household way of getting things from the land and using them up inside. The male works principally in the fields, the female primarily in and around the house.

A household also engages in material exchanges with other humans outside the doors. Any movement of labor or goods into the house is termed an "entry" or "entrance" (*una entrada*) as well as a "gain," while a movement out is a "departure" (*una salida*). When a man trades labor with another, he says he is "gaining a peon" (*ganar un peón*), and when he works for someone else he speaks of "leaving to work" (*salir a trabajar*).

In transactions that involve a movement of the base, the people have different expectations for the earth and the market. With market transactions, they try to recover their initial position, not to make a gain. Market trade involves movements in which a material good leaves the house and is traded for money and then the money is used to purchase a different item, which reenters the doors. The aim of the movements, from inside to outside and outside to inside, is to "replace" (*reponer*) the base. Money is a means of transfer, and the house is engaged in what we term the base→money→base' circuit.

The word "replace" is used similarly with animals. Sometimes an animal, such as a calf, is obtained to be raised for sale. When the animal is sold a young one may immediately be purchased. This is "replacing" the animal, meaning having what one started with a year before. Replacing the base, however, means being able to purchase a young animal plus the equivalent volume of food given to the old and its caretakers during the previous year. Anything that remains above replacement of the base is "an increase" (*un aumento*).

Replacing the base through trade is an uncertain process, for price changes are beyond the control of the rural folk. As one person voiced it, "You expend today and wait until tomorrow to see if you can replace it, and if it doesn't come, what then?" She continued, "Often you use up what is inside for outside without knowing what will happen – that is occurring now. To go forward, you have to have more inside for the future. But money cannot be replaced inside like the base."

In addition to moving the base through the doors to change it, processing of the base takes place inside the house. For this the terms "return," "maintain," "keep," and "hold" are used. After the harvest of a crop, one portion is set aside for "returning to" (*volver a*) seeding in the next year. This is not a replacement of the base, for the entire harvest is already part of it; rather, the earmarked volume (and its planting) allows the base to be "maintained." Similarly, within the house, the base may be shifted from one form to another to hold it better. For example, the foundation is "kept" by feeding maize to chickens or a hog. If the maize were sold to purchase animal feed, then the people would speak of "replacing" the base through market trade. Of course, maize physically leaves the house when it is fed to chickens and hogs or taken to the fields for seeding, but according to the model the crop does not "move through the doors." To distinguish this second way of shifting the base from the first, we label it base→base'. The two circuits are alike in that they begin and end with base, but the base→base' circuit, as opposed to the base→money→base' one, keeps processes within the house and does not require the use of money.[1]

When the doors are closed or allow entries only, the house is engaged in the base→base' circuit and is self-supporting. In many respects, this is the project of the house. We were often told, "I am working to sustain the place" or "I am maintaining the food plate." A frequently used phrase was "I am working to live, to eat," and some said, "The land gives for living, for maintaining, nothing more." The people do not speak of goals or finishing points but of what they are doing or what "it is necessary to do" (*hay que hacer*). When a house has "increased" and accumulated sufficient wealth to maintain itself, its owner or someone else may finally say, "It is done" (*está hecho*), but this does not mean the work is finished, for continuing management and effort are always needed.

Goods that flow into a house from the land are used first for maintenance. We translate the frequently used verb, *gastar* as "expending," "using," or "using up." An "expenditure" [*un gasto*], said one person, "is all that you consume." One uses up one's work in the fields, uses up health and energy in work, and uses up food to restore the body's strength. (Ultimately, all are expenditures of force.) Money too is "used up," although a money use, unlike a material use, is a "cost" (*un costo*). The people also distinguish the general use of the word "expenditure" from its house application by employing the lexical modifier "of the house" (*de la casa*) for the material expenditures that a house makes to support its members and activities. When the goods or useful things (*utilidades*) that come to the house are directed to self-maintenance, they are "expenditures of the house" or "uses from the doors inward." As one woman said, "One uses it up for the house, but in order to avoid buying."

The rural folk are normally thrifty with goods, but sometimes the base is used without being replaced. One morning in northern Boyacá a woman who was shelling maize for animals in the house patio explained that two weeks previously she and her husband had purchased a dozen small chickens to "replace" grown ones that had been sold. Along with the chicks she had purchased some pigeons, for she liked to watch them, and they were being fed with maize, too. The pigeons, like the chickens, were an "expenditure of the house," but unlike the chicks they were a "luxury," as they ate but were not for consumption or sale. They did not "return" the base.

A part of the base is also lost through waste. Spoiled food, disposed of beyond the walls of the house, is said to be "lost to use" or "thrown away" (*echado a perder*). Once or twice in its lifetime, however, a house may lavishly use its resources by entertaining others or celebrating the passage rites of a member; this is known as "throwing the house out the window" (*echar la casa por la ventana*). Rather than moving part of its base through the doors in an orderly trade, the house throws its entirety "inside out" for public display.

The flow of goods in the base→base' circuit may quickly turn negative, for a house uses up base to undertake agriculture; and if the earth does not return the expenditures, more goes out the doors than comes in. The balance is always precarious. But with declining productivity of the soil, ever more fertilizer must be used, and the money for this is gained by selling something from inside. Say the people, one can no longer "keep the base inside the doors."

Labor patterns fit these constructions in various ways. The rural folk say that the base is expended to "support work" (*mantener el trabajo*), and the work is intended to yield more base. Members of the household, who are supported by its expenditures and work for it, "help" the group, for they "help the earth" to produce. Help is performed "inside the doors." For example, "children help but do not collect from one. They are inside help." But help is not performed exclusively by house members, for hired laborers are also used. If outside laborers are paid with cash already held inside the house, both their cash cost and their labor are "inside the doors." If the money is borrowed, however, their cost is "outside the doors" while their labor is "inside help." Outside workers also may be fed during the day, which is a "house expenditure" from "inside the doors," unless the food has had to be bought with borrowed money, which makes it "from the outside."

Thus, the two movements of the base, toward the earth (base→base′) and toward the market (base→money→base′), are alike as ways of maintaining the house but also different, for market trade requires that parts of the base leave house control before returning.

Linked to this difference in use of the base is a distinction made between crops "for eating" (*para comer* or *para consumir*) and crops "for sale" (*para vender*). The distinction applies to the uses of a harvest; but it also sorts different crop types. Some crops, such as herbs, fruits, and yucca, rarely leave the house for the market; these are raised for eating inside the doors. Crops such as maize and potatoes are raised principally for eating, but portions may be for sale. Still other crops, such as sugarcane, are raised almost entirely for sale; however, when sugarcane is locally refined into the brown sugar cake known as *panela*, a portion of the harvest may return to its owner in processed form. Finally, tobacco, onions, and coffee are grown only for sale; they are raised inside the house but move through the doors for money. The rural folk note that they do not control the price of a harvest for sale: "In tobacco the campesino serves to cultivate it [*beneficiarlo*] but he does not put the price on it." With respect to raising a new and more costly variety of tobacco, one person said:

> Where does this money come from? Where does one get the money to raise it? Blond tobacco doesn't even give back the base that has left the house. With tobacco you cannot replace what you have used up.

The opposition between "for eating" and "for sale," thus, is an elaboration upon the distinction between "returning to" and "replacing" the base. It has to do with diverging movements and uses of crops relative to the house, with varying control over them, and with varying power to determine the size of their returns.

Other expressions also serve to place the house within the market world. In most rural towns there is a weekly market, and the people talk about going to market "every week" (*cada ocho días*) or "every two weeks" (*cada quince días*). The marketplace itself is situated in the town plaza, which is usually near the church and government offices. The rural folk speak of the market by its location, "the plaza," and generally any market activity, including purchasing at everyday stores, is known by the shorthand "going to the plaza." The market is a place rather than a conceptual entity, with the circumscribed town locale forming an opposition to the bounded house in the "countryside" (*el campo*).

The people say of an active market that it has much "movement," therby modeling it as a place where the "inside" wealth of many houses is traded. But they also distinguish between the aims of a house in the countryside and those of a "business" (*un negocio*) in the market. In English, "business" comes from "busy-ness," and in Spanish "*negocio*" comes from *negar ocio* or "negating inaction." This is marketplace activity, the "busy-ness" consisting in buying and selling and buying again. For the people, a *negociante* is a trader or "intermediary" (*intermediario*), who makes purchases and sales to gain money. We term this set of transactions the "money→base→money'" circuit. It is quite different from the house one. As one person explained, "The land gives for sustaining oneself, but the market does not give useful things." A harvest is sold to purchase a needed item, not for profit.

This difference between market and house activity is linked to an opposition between "making savings" (*hacer economías*) and "making money" (*hacer plata*). Use of the base→base' circuit is closely tied to "making savings." As the people say, if nothing goes out the doors, one is "making savings" or "being thrifty." They add that "making savings" means replenishing or "returning" something within the house itself. A principal example is self-sufficient agriculture, for if a house's foodstuffs come directly from its base, and the holdings are "returned" through agriculture, then the provisioning process is contained "within the doors" and money is saved. In contrast, "making money," the intent of a business, is accomplished through trade. The opposition is between two projects and two circuits of exchange. One of them starts and ends with money in order to have an enlarged sum; this is "making money," or money→base→money'. The other begins with material holdings and their uses in order to maintain and augment them within the house; this is "making savings," or base→base'.

But the two circuits are intermixed, because trade to replace the base involves the use of cash, the base→money→base' circuit. For the people, money always comes "from the doors outward," while what is traded for it comes "from the doors inward." Trade, interlinking the house and business, is necessary to secure salt and clothes; but a house has no assurance of being able to replace its holdings once it is engaged in the market. Today, a house is even less able than before to provide itself with the materials needed for agriculture; yet purchasing inputs to transform them and sell the product (money→base→base'→

money') is precisely what the rural household is unable to do. The land available for farming is either marginal or fully "off-the-margin," and when it occasionally does become profitable (often through the initial colonizing activities of the rural folk) the house is usually squeezed off it by market actors (LeGrand 1986). The house cannot persist as a pure market participant but is increasingly forced to attempt to do so, with the result that it must lower its consumption or raise its work input. As one person observed, "There is no margin here."

Conversations: circuits, the house, and the corporation

The people's distinctions between "from the doors inward" and "from the doors outward," the house and business, crops "for eating" and crops "for sale," the house and the plaza, and "making savings" and "making money" find corresponding voices in the texts of economists. For example, in the first volume of *Capital* (1967[1867]), Marx makes analytical use of the difference between two exchange cycles that he labels the "commodity→money→commodity" circuit and the "money→commodity→money'" circuit. The first involves the circulation of commodities in which a sale is made in order to buy, money serving only as a medium of exchange. His examples are drawn primarily from the world of the peasant, who is said to enter the market with a commodity, such as a harvest, which he exchanges for money that is then converted to a different commodity, such as clothing. For Marx, the peasant producer engages in market exchange to fulfill limited material goals. Transactions come to an end with their accomplishment. In contrast, the second circuit is typical of the capitalist producer. The profit maker exchanges money for a commodity that is held or transformed and then sold for more money. The capitalist starts with money in order to expand it; purchase is made with the end of sale. The commodity bought can be a good that is then sold, as in mercantile capitalism, or a raw material (including labor) that is transformed into something else, as in industrial capitalism. The money→commodity→money' circuit never reaches a conclusion, for each end point is a new beginning. The money circuit is the dialectical completion of the commodity circuit. One has to do with exchange that uses goods, the other with uses of goods in relation to exchange.

Marx's discussion is in fact an elaboration of earlier writings by David Ricardo, Adam Smith, and the Physiocrats. In the *Wealth of Nations* (1976[1776]), for example, Smith distinguished between "value in use" and "value in exchange," and this was taken over by Ricardo (1951[1817]). John Stuart Mill, who in some respects carried on the Ricardian tradition, also discussed the distinction (1929[1848]:437), but after his summary volume it fell by the wayside with the marginalist revolution and the rise of neoclassical economics. The analytical division between use, value, and exchange has remained a central theme only in Marxist economics.

But this capsule summary of the textual history of use and exchange foreshortens the conversation. Two thousand years before Smith, Aristotle had drawn an opposition between the oeconomic and the chrematistic, and it is this distinction that profoundly influenced the subsequent textual conversation from Roman writers through Aquinas and the Scholastics right up to the early modern theorists. The opposition is also relevant to rural Colombia today. In the *Politics* (1946), Aristotle developed the distinction by pointing out that a shoe has two "uses," one "proper" to it, the other not; a shoe can be worn by its owner or it can be exchanged for something else. The first use leads to the "acquisition" of shoes solely for the satisfaction of limited needs, the second to "acquisition" itself as a boundless goal. Aristotle saw "exchange for use" as a function or feature of householding while "exchange for gain" was the goal of retail trade. But the context of his discussion is important. Aristotle was examining the relation between the domestic economy and the market, and his discussion of use and exchange is situated within a consideration of the household as a unit in "political society." He was not writing about capitalism, the market, or the economy itself. Marx (1967[1867]:152), while using Aristotle's distinction, situated his discussion differently. He located both exchange for use and exchange for gain within capitalism and omitted the institutional connection that Aristotle drew between the house economy and exchange for use. Marx, concerned with the world of capitalism, left off a discussion of householding as an economic process, replacing the household group with "the peasant" as actor or participant in the capitalist and business-dominated market.

This is a long and complicated conversation with many mediating voices, both written and verbal. Marx, certainly versed in Aristotle and other early writings, shifted the conversation for his purposes. These changes aside, we surmise that he and his conversational predecessors were influenced by distinctions made by European folk and that it would have made little sense for them to deploy these distinctions unless they had first been voiced in social life. As seen from Colombia, for example, Marx appropriated part of the domestic model in order to construct a critical view of capitalism: his critique – from notions about the force of labor to the importance of exchanging for use versus exchanging for gain – was influenced by the world of the peasant house. Yet this was not simply a one-way movement from practice to text, for the living culture of European folk had been inscribed in a different form two thousand years earlier by Aristotle, and his inscriptions had their persuasive effect on succeeding practices and conversations as they did on Marx. There has been a continual oscillation of models from practice to inscription to practice. Our suggestion is that the house is a folk institution of long standing and for this reason has been a source of ideas for inscription ever since Aristotle. Furthermore, as a European institution, the house model early on became a component of Latin American life, where it has since developed and changed. Colombian rural life and the inscriptions of European theorists are part of the same conversation.

But if the similarities with Marx's views help illuminate the campesinos' conversation, the differences are illustrative, too. For Marx the word "commodity," even when used in the context of the commodity→money→commodity circuit, implies something made for sale and gain. This is the more evident when the Spanish term for "commodity" is used, for *la mercancia* is derived from *mercado*, "market." In Marx the commodity→money→commodity circuit starts and ends with commercial or market items. By contrast, the Colombian rural folk speak of getting needed "provisions" (*las provisiones*) and of trading the base or foundation, not of securing market "commodities." The rural model of exchange takes the perspective of – as Aristotle suggested – the house and not the market. From the Colombian folk perspective, Marx's discussion subsumes the house project within the market model. Also, the rural people model two circuits involving the house. One takes place solely within it: this is the notion of returning to seeding (base→base'). The second, in which base materials move from house to market and back, is replacing the base (base→money→base').

This difference between the folk and economists' models returns us to the general, institutional distinction between means of grouping: the house and the corporation. Our view is that European history has witnessed a broad movement from a house to a corporate economy. This movement has not been without reversals, and many economic formations, such as slavery, feudalism, and mercantile society, have served as the larger matrix for the domestic economy. But the house has persisted throughout, counterposed in later history to the corporation (Bloch 1966; Braudel 1986; Duby 1968, 1974; Postan 1972). The initial written division between householding and gain, adumbrated by Aristotle, was continued by a variety of Roman authors, such as Cato (1933), and, as Tribe (1978) has shown, found its way into the early texts on "the economy." At times, the "domestic economy" meant the household itself, and at other periods the house model was applied to the state, the entire nation being seen as a self-sufficient household. From the fourteenth century onwards, the corporate mode of organization developed and expanded, but the transition from the one to the other was not a simple function of time's arrow. Historians, for example, have been discovering that self-sufficient economies existed on the "frontiers" of North American economy and society during the nineteenth century (Clark 1979; Faragher 1986; Hahn and Prude 1985; Merrill 1977; Pruitt 1984); these house economies developed or were reproduced "after" the historical rise of the corporation and yet before its "arrival" in an area. Everything depends upon the market and the way in which the two means of grouping are linked to exchange.

A corporation – like a house – must always provide for

its necessary expenses, funding them perhaps from a past accumulation. But a corporation is not self-reproducing in a material sense, for it exchanges part of its product to secure its necessary means; and it operates on the assumption that sales, by more than covering purchases, will generate a profit. The corporation is surrounded on its input and output sides by buying and selling, or market exchange. In addition, corporate profit is a social phenomenon in that it is partly distributed to those who own the corporation as property; it cannot be fully kept "inside the doors." The balance sheet of a corporation makes public its ties with others, as assets and liabilities. These are the current yet enduring exchanges it maintains on the input and output sides. In an older but felicitous terminology, assets and liabilities were known in English as active debts and passive debts, while in contemporary Spanish they are *los activos* and *los pasivos* – apt expressions because they recall both Mauss's (1954 [1925]) well-known argument that debts of exchange link humans and groups and Leach's (1954) claim that social structure is a system of lasting debts. The balance sheet of a corporation – its "double-entry bookkeeping" – displays these debts by focusing on their momentary conjunction within the corporation itself. The market participant is enmeshed in persisting exchanges, developed in the past and projected into the future, in which buying is a means for selling. A breakdown of trust with loss of confidence in the future undermines this network of ties, yielding business cycles of the Keynesian and Kondratieff variety. More generally, if debts "make" the market world, their liquidation unmakes ties and produces autarky. The house, unlike the corporation, has no assets and liabilities, no enduring relationships. It does not need debts to "make it work." Quite the reverse; if the house did exchange or buy in order to sell, it would undermine its project of survival. The house is not susceptible to economic cycles, for it represents a distancing from the economic intentions of others, although it is vulnerable to ecological changes. A house can enter the market to sell some of its product if this represents the amount above what is needed for reproduction, for then changing market prices have no effect on the perpetuation of the unit, determining only the volume realized in trade. In the market context, the house takes its place in opposition and relation to the corporation.

But the interconnection of these two models is always complex. The house has occurred separately and before the corporation; and it has been prompted by the market economy, on the edges and beyond the border of profit. In European history there has been a dialectical tension (in both inscriptions and practice) between the "body" model and the "house" model. Clearly, in market societies the house model has been shrinking in scope, particularly in recent years. Yet we still use much of its lexicon: "housekeeping," "householding," "maintaining a house," "housewife," and even "kept woman"! The recipes of domestic economy, including ways to be thrifty and the art of home baking, that used to be so avidly taught in land-grant universities, are the remnants of this once vibrant way of life. In the United States, "fast foods" sold by corporations and bought in the market have replaced the slow foods that used to be prepared in pots on the stove, but the house economy is still alive in many parts of Latin America today.

Chapter 4
THE BASE

A house's most important component is its base (*base*) or foundation (*fundamento*). This is the wealth of the house, and through it necessities are met. "The base," said one man, "is what permits you to work; it is for living, and a defense for meeting heavy obligations." As many explained, the base is what you need to be able to start work; one works with the base and on it, and one is supplied by it. A house relies on good management, hard work, thrift, and judicious trading in the marketplace, but its existence depends on a proper foundation, accumulated over time.

When the people describe a base, they mention a variety of material things. Land is primary, for it is the earth that gives. A base also includes seed or accumulated harvests, tools, and animals: it is "the land, tools, seed, fertilizer, and even the drugs for animals." The size of base a house requires depends on its expenditures; a house with more people and animals must have more on which to work, to live, and to create future supplies. A potter says that his base consists of sand or clay, molds, a place in which to work, an oven, and some money to purchase other productive materials. Cash is part of the foundation, but money alone does not make a base. One man, who had built an impressive small farm, explained that for eighteen years he had worked for an *hacendado* (hacienda owner), had been paid a good salary, and had accumulated funds in a savings account; however, the wages and money savings did not constitute a foundation ("*no daban la base*"), and he had left because the owner had never allowed him to farm some of the hacienda's land. Until he controlled land and the tools to work it and was managing his own labor, he lacked a base, despite the cash he had accumulated. The base must be in a form that supports an independent life.

The term "base" and the practices surrounding it are distinctive to the countryside, but there are continuities between it and the contemporary notion of "capital." We suggest that in the course of the long transition from house to corporation, the house voice and practices concerning the base were used and transformed for the nascent model of capital. This is especially evident in late eighteenth- and nineteenth-century theory. As time passed, however, corporate capital increasingly took a different form from house wealth. We think that the difference concerns their degree of liquidity and that today it has much to do with the distinction between wealth on the periphery and wealth in the profit centers.

A conversation: translations and conversing communities

In English, the term "holdings" seems to capture best the rural word "base," but this translation emerged only slowly through the interplay of our car and field conversations. During 1984, when we first heard the term "base," we understood it to mean that a young man had to have a proper personal foundation in order to marry – that he had to have the character, experience, and skills to take on the responsibility of supporting a house. Later we understood "foundation" to mean the starting point for building up wealth. Separate from this, we began to develop the view that the house model was common to both campesinos and hacendados in the countryside. These different issues were pursued in April 1987, when we again found that "base" was frequently used by the rural folk. In trying to understand the range of the word's uses, we found it helpful to use the English term "holdings," but we soon noted that there is no exact way to translate "holdings" back into Spanish. Shortly, however, it seemed that *"la hacienda"* was an appropriate gloss; for example, the *Ministerio de Hacienda* is best translated as "Ministry of Holdings" or "Treasury" (it has nothing to do with housing, which is the concern of the *Ministerio de Vivienda*). This sequence of translations, from the Spanish *base* to the English "holdings" to the Spanish *hacienda*, drew upon our divergent personal backgrounds and emerged as we shifted conversations from field to car to field to car; but as these initially separate conversations were drawn together, a different discussion reached closure. *La base* and *el fundamento* were now connected to *la hacienda*, and this helped to confirm our view of the domestic model's pervasiveness in the countryside, from small house to large. To this point, we had understood the word "foundation" to mean personal character, skills, and an initial fund of productive materials. After these discussions, we began to "hear" that a "foundation" is part of a "house." As the house metaphor emerged for us, "base" became shorthand for the entire model, while our initial understanding of the word "foundation" to mean character and skills retreated to the background as an implication or secondary application.

Another part of this same conversation bears upon our argument that the house model is used by both small and large holders. One campesino strategy in managing the base is to make savings by diversifying and raising animals as well as crops. The hacendado does much the same. In many cases hacendados own land in two or more ecological regions and use products from one to supply workers in the other without having to make use of the market; like campesinos, hacendados make savings by avoiding the cash circuit and "internalizing" what would otherwise be an "external" exchange. All this fits linguistic usage. Throughout Colombia the word "*hacienda*" is applied to large landholdings, often fifty hectares or more. The rural folk frequently call their very small farms "*fincas*," although outsiders label them "*minifundios*." The term "*hacienda*" comes from *hacer*, "to do or make" – it is a "making." But, as we have remarked, the smallholder in Boyacá who had left off working for an hacendado and used his cash savings to make a diversified small farm said of his effort: "Now it's done" (*está hecho*), meaning that he had the necessaries for sustaining a domestic economy. The hacienda is the house economy on a grand scale and "in the making."

As part of the long history to this conversation, the Latin origins of some of the key terms are relevant. For example, the word "foundation" or *fundamento* comes from the Latin *fundamentum*, meaning "foundation," "groundwork," or "base." But the English "foundation" is also rendered in Latin as *fundus*, which likewise means farm estate or landed property. In turn, the Latin *fundus* is the origin for the Spanish *fundo*, a term used for "farm" in Colombia's eastern plains, and for *minifundio*, the word employed by government and academic observers. The Latin *fundus* also has a different derivative in the Spanish word *fondo*, which in areas of the Colombian countryside is another term for "base" and "foundation" as well as personal capital.

MAKING THE BASE

A base, say the campesinos, is something they maintain for the future. It is a "savings" (*un ahorro*) that could be used now but is held for coming years. They add that cash is hard to keep and soon disappears, so it is better to save it as a material product.

In rural areas the term "*finca*" is used both for smaller holdings and for the underpinning or foundation; as one man stated, "the *finca* is everything – animals, land, all that you have." When harvest after harvest is poor, the people say "the *finca* is being lost" (*uno va perdiendo la finca*). A traditional idiom expresses it well: when a person leaves substantial collateral for a loan at the bank or just a small deposit for a soft-drink bottle at the store, "he pledges the *finca*."

The people have other ways of speaking about the base. A man often talks about "the work I have," meaning what he is doing now and the work awaiting to be done. When he completes the work, it becomes part of the foundation; as one man said, the base is work "already obtained" (*ya conseguido*) or work done. Another added that to have work, one has to have a base, and what a person is working on is the result of past labor. So work is performed within a temporal stream, and when the people speak of a harvest in the fields as "the work," they mean that it is past work, what they are doing, and something that will require work in future. (In both Spanish and English a factory used to be called "the works" [*el obraje*], being a place where people worked and the physical result of their work, and we still say of something in process that it is "in the works" [*en obra*].)

In some rural areas the word "reserve" (*reserva*) is a substitute for "base," but it seems to be a transition term between the house and the corporate lexicons. On the one hand, the reserve is something put aside or postponed in use. A cow is a reserve, for it can be sold and the proceeds turned to other uses. But a reserve is also what one puts into work and hopes to take back out. For example, a sharecropper and landowner together provide the base for an agricultural venture. When a costly cash crop such as tomatoes is being raised, the sharecropper must have ready money (*la plata disponible*) to defray his obligations, and this is his reserve. The sharecropper's reserve starts as money, which is converted to real items and then returned as cash. This money may subsequently be used to purchase an animal (reserve) that is held until cash is again needed. "Reserve," then, is used for both material things and money, with the implication that each may be converted to the other as well as put into use and then taken out (*sacado*). It is a term that crosses between the goods circuit (base→money→base') and the money circuit (money→base→ money').

When the people of a region are even more fully enmeshed in cash-cropping and the market lexicon, other terms supplant "base." In some zones, the rural folk talk about "the principal" that goes into a crop. Sometimes land is secured through a pawning arrangement, and for this people will say that they have put up "principal" for two or three years in order to have use of the land. The crop return (*el rendimiento*), they add, is "like the interest" that a lender gets on principal. In regions where the word "principal" is used, the associated terms "funds" and "resources" (*los recursos*) may be employed. Occasionally, we heard "*el caudal*," which in the city means "capital" or "money funds" but in rural areas has the older sense of "wealth" or "holdings," in short, the *hacienda*. The broad contrast, again, is between house and corporate uses, but, as we argue, many terms from the lexicon of the former have been appropriated for the latter.

In talking about the base the people use active verb forms such as "working," "maintaining," and "sustaining." A base is used, and each is a unique constellation of items which, aside from an inheritance, has been made by a person or couple. A base reflects local practices and knowledge, past decisions, and work, and it seldom has the same value for an outsider as it does for its owners: what a person can receive for sale of his or her base almost never compensates for what can be saved in money by using it. It is a life – the crops growing and gathered, the trees and bushes selected and planted, the tools bought or made, the animals chosen and raised. Each base is a different human project or "making" (*hacienda*).

Starting a base is a major challenge. As a group of people once said, "This is the grave question. You can't begin on your own; you have no funds and no place to put your 'strength' and your account." The central problem is obtaining access to land, which, despite its marginal condition, is relatively expensive and unequally distributed. Because entry costs are high, we inquired of successful campesinos how they or others were able to begin. The many personal accounts we gathered seemed rather like folktales, perhaps suggesting how and where our own folklore originated. Parental gifts sometimes provide an initial base. A young man may begin by working on his father's or his wife's father's land, putting in three days a week at low wages in return for usufruct rights that he exercises during the remainder of the week. Sons may begin by sharecropping with a parent or parent-in-law under favorable terms, the one providing work and the other land and seed. This sharecropping pattern is also found between unrelated younger males and older men, being a way for the older people to recruit labor and the younger to get started. Alternatively, and this account was heard only from older males, some began by working a small piece of hacienda land. One man started working on an hacienda in the 1930s; in return for laboring one week in four, "the obligation," he was allocated a plot of land for his personal use. We heard no accounts of successful people who had begun solely as wage laborers; the relatively successful had gained early access to land, although this alone did not guarantee prosperity. The general aim was (and remains) to move from sharecropping to renting to owning land and then to seeking sharecroppers or renters as the land holdings grow.

To build a base, a young man must work ceaselessly from sunup till dark, but the work of the woman is crucial, too. Some females take in washing to earn cash, others bake bread for sale or run small stores. Often, the remunerative work of the woman provides the daily foodstuffs, thus freeing the man from wage work and allowing him to devote his efforts to building up the base. "What she earns serves for the market, so one does not have to take out from inside to outside." The young pair also has to be thrifty and to save. It was said repeatedly that the man has to avoid spending cash on drink and that one has to run a household well: "He who doesn't know how to run his holdings will spend what he doesn't have; he who works is able to succeed at pulling it all together." As the people explained, by economizing, working hard, securing an abundant harvest, and selling part of the crop, a couple can accumulate some holdings and put its savings into animals. Everywhere we heard stories about individuals who in their twenties had begun with one head of cattle or a sheep and built a herd. One woman said that she had taken a ewe in payment for a store debt "and from there the sheep went on multiplying." People also explained how they began with chickens and moved to raising hogs, then goats, sheep, and finally cattle. A successful house also tries to retain this diversity. But because larger beasts require pasture, having access to land is an important element in pastoral as well as agricultural success. Some young people are allowed to pasture a cow or two on parental land or in an area granted as part of their sharecropping arrangement.

In the local accounts, building a base may also involve use of resources from a town. One woman explained that in the early years of her marriage she had run a store, which she referred to as a "little business" (*un negocito*). Some of the cash earned was used to purchase a small motor-driven wheat mill, which provided more revenue, and over time she and her husband had been able to acquire cattle. Using the cattle as collateral, her husband had secured an agricultural loan; he had then sold the cattle and used both that money and the loan to buy land, thereby extricating himself from being a sharecropper. Eventually, the couple had repaid the loan and had enjoyed further success. This general pattern of turning a small accumulation into animals, using the animals as collateral to gain access to money, and investing the money in land was reported by many others. We also recorded instances in which minor officials or persons with low-skilled jobs in a town built ties to the countryside by supplying funds for sharecropping or by purchasing bits of land. For them, this was a form of diversification and a way of making a base.

Given that each base seemed to be dependent upon the existence of a prior one, we inquired about the chronology of accumulation in human society itself. Once, finding ourselves in a group of nine adults, we asked where the first base came from. After a silence, one discussant responded that they understood our question but had no answer; another added, in a typical turn of phrase, that our question made them feel as if they had no base. We asked again: "If it takes a base to make a base, where did the first base come from?" A third then offered a response that was later repeated by others. Adam and Eve, he said, were in Paradise and were given an initial base by God. With the first sin, they had had to leave the Garden, but they had taken seeds with them, and these had provided the starting point for a new base. This second base was worked by two brothers, but a base had to be started again after the Flood. From these beginnings humans have inherited and have been able to build bases over time. Tellingly, biblical history is about the starting of a base; it charters the first and explains its continuance through a sequence of events. But perhaps the Colombian conversationalists are not so different from our own. Adam Smith, for example, constructed his theory of supply, demand, and market pricing by beginning with "that early and rude state of society which precedes both the accumulation of stock and the appropriation of land" (Smith 1976[1776]:53); von Thünen did much the same in his argument about land, rent, and the agricultural margin, outside of which hunters roam and barter hides (1966[1826]:157). These and other theorists have substituted the state of "nature" or of "primitive society" for a momentous act by the divinity, but the implicit argument that there exists a precultural or pristine state from which one can and must trace a present institution is much the same (Kuper 1988). The argument justifies a model by the authority of history or logic, all the while denying the constructed nature of the world it would legitimate.

A base is scarcely ever static. With a good harvest, it grows. But a growing base is not inevitable, and most people aim first to "keep" what they have. If a person loses his foundation everything is lost; a couple can borrow from a friend but usually must seek its living in a new area. Stories about losing a base were common. One man detailed the decline from his grandparents' to his generation. He recalled that his grandparents had had plenty of land, food, and animals; they had even hired outside workers. His parents lived less well, for they owned a smaller amount of land that was deteriorating in quality, but they maintained a base that they worked on their own. Our discussant had experienced several crop failures and had been obliged to sell part of his base for survival. Now he did not have sufficient land to raise even a few crops for eating, and he was sharecropping someone else's land. Though he had children in their teens who assisted, he was up half the night watering the tobacco being jointly raised – a fact which suggests that hard work alone does not ensure that a base can be maintained or expanded.

A contemporary problem for everyone is the rising entry costs in agriculture. Because of the need for purchased additives, it takes money to grow even a house crop. One must have a "good" base for this, and many say they are not "capable" of producing the costly crops; others are losing their bases in the attempt, and interest rates are too high to be payable by the crop return. But a deteriorating ecology, lack of competitiveness on the margin, and the rising cost of inputs are not the only reasons for current diminution of the base. Electricity has been brought to many homes in the countryside, and to pay for it people are finding that they have to sell part of the base, usually an animal; for electricity to enter the doors, some part of the base must exit.

A *conversation: transforming the base*

These local histories of the base suggest that house economies differ in capacity to sustain themselves. Domestic groups are not homogeneous in size or stage of development. The question of "peasant differentiation" and of "class structure" in the countryside has received considerable textual attention, principally by Marxist-inspired writers who have developed or examined theses about the penetration of capital into the countryside, its

effects upon small-scale producers, and the relation of
peasant producers to capitalist forms. An early elaboration
of Marx's views was provided by Lenin in *The
Development of Capitalism in Russia* (1956 [1899]).
Making use of the rural-council statistics collected after the
1861 reforms, Lenin paid special attention to the themes of
progressive rural differentiation and of "disintegration" or
"depeasantization." His thesis, which was dialectical in
character and presented in opposition to the populist
Narodniks' (Hart 1988), had several parts (p. 174):

The rise of property inequality is the starting-point of the whole process, but
the process is not confined to "differentiation" at all. The old peasantry is
not only "differentiating," it is being completely dissolved, it is ceasing to
exist, it is being ousted by absolutely new types of rural inhabitants – types
that are the basis of a society in which commodity economy and capitalist
production prevail.

Lenin's views have remained important, not least because
he offered a processual, dynamic view of the peasantry and
had a persuasive effect on later writers. But Lenin may
have underestimated the possible transformations in a
house economy itself while ascribing to commercial capital
the singular power to change the form of domestic units.
For example, he argued that without investment in
production and industrial capital, "the whole of the
peasantry would represent a fairly even type of poverty-
stricken husbandmen" (p. 187). He was surely correct in
linking differentiation among the peasantry to
decomposition, but the two are not identical. We see the
process of "decomposition" in the light of the long-term
relation between house and corporation, and this involves
institutional dynamics as well as the complex interplay of
practice and texts. Sometimes the corporation preserves a
space for the house – in the informal economy (Hart 1973;
de Soto 1989) or in small-scale business – and sometimes it
does not. But the interconnection of the two must be
separated from shifts in the house itself and its base, which
are also temporal processes.

The local folk do not often make invidious distinctions,
but in discussion they will draw an opposition between
"the poor" (*los pobres*) and "the rich" (*los ricos*). It
usually applies on the one side to agriculturalists and on

the other to landowners with cattle. Agriculturalists have a
small amount of land devoted mostly to crops; they expend
the strength of their work in an uncertain venture. Rich
cattle owners use the force of the earth to grow the pasture
on which their animals live, and they do not have to sweat
for their living. (At other moments, the verbal category
"rich" may also be applied to town or city dwellers.) The
category opposition between campesinos and cattle owners
is modulated by the idea that people can be more or less
"well off" (*acomodado*), and this is a local recognition that
some houses have a more ample base. Within the domestic
economy there are shifts from one base position to
another, and though these transitions may be connected to
the use of outside resources, they do not signal a
decomposition or transformation of the domestic economy
itself. The rural people recognize at least five positions of a
house in terms of its control over labor, food supplies, and
land. The five are often moments in the life cycle of the
domestic group but are not reducible to that temporal
sequence.

In one of these positions, the house has sufficient labor,
food, and land to maintain itself. The land may have been
obtained by inheritance or purchase or may be rented or
(infrequently) pawned. The house supplies its own labor
(sometimes indirectly via work trade), and it has sufficient
food to sustain its working and nonworking members.
Such a balanced state is rarely permanent, for there are
advances and declines in the base over time. But the
position provides a useful marker for understanding the
others and their interconnections.

In another position, the house has command of labor
only. The laborers work by the day for others, receiving
cash, cash plus food, or remuneration in kind. Day
workers (*jornaleros*) cannot sustain a house over time. We
consider later the details of work and its remuneration;
here we underscore that the house economy is not a source
of permanent wage labor, nor does it comprise a rural
proletariat. On the margin, work for cash or kind has to
be done in conjunction with other house projects if a group
is to sustain itself.

A house may, alternatively, have command over labor
and food but lack sufficient land on which to expend its

work. Its workers may therefore undertake some wage labor, migrate, or enter into sharecropping arrangements. The labels for these contracts vary – in Boyacá they are called *aparcería* or *en compañía* – and their terms are locally negotiated. Typically, in sharecropping one unit provides the land while the other provides the labor and its food. The product, which may be received in agricultural goods or in cash, is divided equally. But there are always negotiations over who provides the seed, fertilizer, and other necessaries of the production process, and depending on local conditions the output division may also shift from an even split to two to one in favor of the landholder or cropper. Whatever the terms, a house in this position – and it may shift even in the course of a year – has insufficient land to fulfill its project of self-maintenance.

The position of sharecropper defines a complementary one, that of the house with more agricultural land than it can use. Such a house enters sharecropping arrangements by putting out land. A key feature of sharecropping is that it obviates the need for control of money funds. Typically, it is a practice on the profit margin and beyond. But in rural Colombia today it is not always undertaken between the more and the less well-off. For example, a house with an elderly or incapacitated senior laborer or one headed by a widow may have to enter into a sharecropping transaction in order to gather a return from the land it controls.

A further position is an intriguing variation on the others. Sometimes a house with insufficient land has workers but no food, or food but insufficient workers. Two such houses may together engage in a sharecropping arrangement with a third house that has command over land, one providing the labor and the other its food. In combination they make up a unit for the sharecropping transaction. The agricultural product is first split in half with the owner of the land and then divided in half again between the two parties. This arrangement is known as "*sacarruin*."[1] We heard the term principally in Boyacá, and it appears to be a contraction of *sacar de ruinas*, "to get out of ruins." According to this startling elaboration of the house metaphor, a domestic unit that commands only labor or only food is in ruins; it joins another in ruins to pull itself out of this condition. As the people explain, "Such a house has no base or luck; it may lack a cook and food." To have to engage in *sacarruin* is unenviable but sometimes necessary in the hope of becoming a (full) house.

The term "*sacarruin*" in fact is applied to other variations on sharecropping. Sometimes two sharecroppers, neither having sufficient workers or food to undertake the contract alone, both provide labor and food, each receiving 25 percent of the return. For this and the preceding case the people say that the product is divided "from four, one" meaning that the "*sacarruinero*" receives a quarter of the product. Occasionally, a landowner provides both land and food to a single *sacarruinero*, who offers only labor. In this case the return is divided "three to one" in favor of the landowner, though it must be added that we found confusion in distinguishing "from four, one," "three to one," and "four to one." The latter form of product distribution occurs when the landowner offers even more inputs, has fertile land, or is able for a different reason to set favorable terms with the *sacarruinero*.

We find, in summary, five positions in the balance of land, food, and work:

1 The house with wage laborers (*jornaleros*)
2 The house with food or labor only or with insufficient food and labor to enter alone into sharecropping (*sacarruinero*)
3 The house with food and labor but insufficient land (sharecropper)
4 The house with sufficient food, labor, and land to undertake agriculture (self-maintaining house)
5 The house with more land than it can use, which employs sharecroppers (and some wage laborers) and is well-off

All houses attempt to keep animals, but only those with sufficient land can eventually make the transition from agriculture to cattle raising. In this respect, the five positions represent the house project – to move from wage labor to pastoralism by expanding the base. Certainly, there are shifts in positions over time, and a house usually combines several positions at once. Position 5, which can turn into the large *finca* or hacienda, is more an intention than a frequent reality. It also links a house most closely with the market.

Conversations: forms of capital

In today's lexicons, the word "base" might be rendered as "the means of production," for controlling a foundation is a way of providing and maintaining the resources needed for production. The foundation also serves as a "rotating fund," being put into an activity and then retrieved to be held for a time and used again. By contrast to the modern rotating fund, however, the base does not finance the ventures of different people; it stays within a single house. The base is also like "working capital" or a "working fund" as opposed to a permanent investment in that it supports work that produces an immediate return. As one artisan said, he had to cover his "running costs." But again, these funds are kept within the house, not put out to others, and there are some other constructions in written theory to which the base is more closely linked.

Contemporary economists often draw a distinction between *stocks* and *flows*. A stock is the sum of goods existing at a moment. In most economies such "moments" do not actually exist; rather, a stock is a model of a corporation's stationary state, measured as a quantity of goods. A flow is a movement or using up of goods as the business functions, a rate or quantity measured *in time*. This economist's distinction between stocks and flows is rather similar to the anthropologist's opposition between the synchronic and the diachronic, between stasis and change. One is associated with a moment of time, the other with a period of time. But stocks and flows do not have to be viewed as disparate, and in a useful discussion the economist Georgescu-Roegen has offered the intriguing view that "a flow is a stock spread out over a time interval" (1971:223). A flow can be accumulated into a stock, and a stock can be turned into a flow and used up over a period of time. For clarity, Georgescu-Roegen also distinguishes a *fund* and its *services* from a *stock* and its *flow*. A fund, unlike a stock of materials, is relatively durable; it lasts beyond a particular production period. During the time of production the fund, for example, a piece of equipment, offers a service but is not used up. Cement in sacks is a stock; it is used up as a flow while a building is being constructed. Once built, the edifice is a fund that offers the service of housing; this service lasts as long as the building (fund), but in the interval the fund does not decrease in size.

This double opposition can be usefully applied to the Colombian countryside. The people use a base as a stock with flows. Agricultural land is a "fund" in that it lends "services" over time, but most of the people's land has not been permanently improved, and most of the other holdings of a house are stocks. Agriculture is a good example of the stock→flow→stock pattern. A crop of potatoes or maize standing in the fields is a stock. While the crop is being harvested and carried to the house it constitutes a flow, but the foodstuff stored within the house is a stock. This stock is subsequently used up as seed and food, and the flow of materials supports the work leading to the accumulation of the next stock. We often saw potatoes being harvested over several days, carried to the house, and placed in a large pile. Subsequently, they were divided into stocks for seeding, for eating, and for sale, all of which became flows. A crop moves from flow to stock to flow, and so on, and the base as a compilation of various crops consists of many overlapping stocks and flows; it is a rotating stock constantly being put to use and then returned.

From this perspective the base itself might be seen as a composite of time-dated stocks (Stock$_1$, Stock$_2$, Stock$_3$ . . .). The base does not actually mirror these stocks, for it is a single reserve. Each stock comes from the earth through the application of labor supported by food, but the flow of food comes from earlier stocks that were also the result of what the land gave. Ultimately, therefore, a base resolves into stocks of force gathered from the land. This force varies over the years, however in good times it yields more than enough and builds the base.

But a base consists of more than stocks and their flows. The people make use of some funds that lend services, though in unexpected ways. Animals are especially interesting. Chickens and hogs are not raised to make money; because maize, food scraps, and spoiled crops are fed to them, they are a kind of "stock holding," holding a base and its waste and disintegrating parts. In times of need, they can be converted to a stock of money or directly (through butchering) to a flow of food. They are held as a "reserve" stock that can be converted to a usable stock or flow and then back again. But the reserve stock is not a fund, for it does not provide services (except that chickens lay eggs). Cows, by contrast, are an intriguing combination of stock and fund. Like hogs they are a stock holding of food and are sold in times of need; but they also supply milk, which is a flow and a service, so they are a fund, too. Oxen also are an accumulated store of food, but they are kept solely for the service of pulling plows; unlike cows, oxen are equipment, almost a pure fund. Yet, some *campesinos* make a stock holding out of this fund by acquiring young oxen, feeding, training, and working them, renting out their services, and then selling them when they have grown to full size and replacing them with a pair of young oxen. Animals have both stock and fund, flow and service functions in the countryside, and they differ in their purposes from chickens to oxen. Most animals, however, are kept as stocks, and even with cattle the fund function is not highly developed.

This leads us directly to a relationship that Georgescu-Roegen does not consider: the balance in an economy between stocks and funds. We argue that a key feature of small house farming in the Colombian countryside is the high ratio of stocks to funds, and we suggest that this is a general characteristic of farming on the profit margin. Campesinos who accumulate a base and become wealthier do not so much change this ratio as escape its context of use. But to see this we must consider a third opposition, that between *fixed* and *circulating* capital. This distinction has even greater currency among economists than the previous ones to which it has a likeness. "Fixed capital" is capital or equipment that has a relatively long life or lasts beyond a single production process. It does depreciate, but the replacement or amortization cost per year is a fraction of its total. Fixed capital is similar to a fund that lends services, although if a stock lasted long enough it might also be viewed as fixed capital. "Circulating capital," also known as "liquid," "working," and "rolling" capital, is used up in a short period of time, often a single production period. It covers wages and raw materials. This capital that "turns over" is similar to a stock and its flow, though a short-lived fund might also be circulating capital.

Several features of the rural folk's base are notable in light of these distinctions. First, the base consists primarily of real materials or tangibles rather than money. Set on the margin of the "money market," the rural house has little command over cash and participates principally in the base→base' and base→money→base' circuits rather than the money→base→money' one. The domestic economy uses "real property."

The campesino house, like houses everywhere, contains both productive and nonproductive assets. But idle wealth is small, and some holdings, such as pigeons, directly lower production, representing expenditure with no return. In general, the campesino house has a high proportion of usable to nonusable holdings. By contrast to houses in the market world, it uses most of its assets to support production, elsewhere undertaken by corporations. Still, compared with businesses, the campesino house has relatively little command over productive capital, such as raw materials, equipment, or money. Rural houses are small holdings, which is coordinate with the fact that they are located outside the margin of profit.

Houses in the countryside have a high proportion of circulating to fixed holdings or stocks to funds. Goods are used up in a relatively short time, while little fixed wealth is produced. Land is a durable holding, but it is not produced by the people and remains largely unimproved, except perhaps for a yearly plowing. Also, if a house is not practicing agriculture, it is usually involved in artisanry, repairing, or small-scale selling, all of which are characterized by a high circulating-to-fixed-holdings ratio. The rural house does produce what we term "capital" or wealth, but what it produces is foodstuffs and raw materials, which are stocks or circulating riches, and the fixed capital it obtains (by trade) is small compared with these circulating holdings. Savings from a harvest do go into animals and the purchase of land, but such expansion serves principally to increase the volume of circulating wealth. In the countryside, the ratio of fixed to circulating holdings and the amount of fixed capital going into production change little over time. Only a shift from house, with its project of saving the base, to corporation, with its project of making money, changes the ratio. The house produces and lives on circulating wealth.

But this balance between circulating and fixed holdings might be expected in a zone of marginal profit, for this region *is* the margin because it lacks infrastructure and an accumulation of farming equipment. The "off-the-margin" pattern has several implications. If a house does produce "net capital," that is, holdings above expenditures needed for sustenance, this usually leads to replication or expansion of the existing group. Because a house produces the means of maintenance or circulating holdings, it can only reproduce what this supports, which is another house. Thus, one form that rural accumulation takes is numerical increase of house members; another is the addition of a new house by intergenerational transmission; and when a house does buy more land, it often makes use of it by engaging a sharecropper from another house, who supplies the work and seed from his circulating holdings. In the countryside, "net" or extra capital is mostly used in the same organizational form as before, for what a house produces in excess is the means for human sustenance and labor.

In place of expanding the domestic group, the net or fresh "capital" of a house may be kept in animals as a hoard. This Colombian practice may be likened to that of the European peasant who kept gold under the bed or in the walls of his house – also forms of "housekeeping." In Colombia such hoards are known as the "advance" (*el adelanto*), but while this practice gives the holder future security, the holding itself is a reserve stock or *idle* circulating capital. It does not transform a stock to a fund. Hoarding converts perishables (*lo que se echa a perder*) to durables (*la base*) but does not transform the productive pattern itself, serving only to ensure continuance of the house over a longer stretch of time. Yet such hoarding or "keeping" is exactly the project of a house, being what the people mean by "making savings." The only exception to this pattern of rural reproduction, expansion, and savings occurs when a house is able to shift from agriculture to

pastoralism, for then livestock becomes a fixed and
profitable holding. To a large extent, as we have
commented, this is what it means for a house to transform
itself into an hacienda. But this transition, which requires
control over substantial holdings, is the path of only a few,
and the hacienda also tends to expand its pastoral holdings
rather than continuously shift its circulating-to-fixed-
holdings ratio. In general, lacking command over fixed
capital, the house is not a locus for reinvestment, growth,
and transformation. It does not exhibit capital
"deepening," or develop roundabout, prolonged processes
of production. New holdings do not change the means of
grouping from house to corporation; rather, the house
continues to live on an annual round and hoard for the
immediate future.

But the house is situated within a larger economic
system, and in this context a considerable amount of
capital, both fixed and circulating, may be produced.
Depending on the society, cathedrals, palaces, pyramids,
and other monuments or irrigation systems with canals and
reservoirs may be constructed. The house may share in the
production and use of these concentrations of capital, but
they are controlled by larger organizations. In the case of
Colombia, this external sphere consists principally of
corporations and the market. Fixed funds generally do not
enter the countryside except under control of a
corporation, which traditionally has taken the form of an
enclave organization or plantation. A corporation may
make a longer-term investment in the rural area, as in
coffee trees, bananas, or irrigation ditches, because it has
access to fixed commitments; however, use of these
holdings is not extended to the house. The rural folk gain
access to fixed capital only by exchanging their circulating
holdings in the marketplace. But terms of trade in the
market for heavy and motorized tools militate against a
pronounced shift in the circulating-to-fixed-holdings ratio,
and the fixed holdings that the people do obtain –
machetes, hoes, axes, shovels, and plow points – are often
made by small-scale artisans. With the exception of the
machete, the rural folk themselves make the handles and
yokes for the steel tips, and when a handle breaks it is
locally repaired. The life of the metal tools is relatively

short; although durable compared with the previous wooden implements, they are almost circulating capital. In any case, relative to its total holdings the purchased tools do not represent a large injection of fixed capital into the house. (In the larger economy of Colombia itself, the ratio of new to replacement capital and of fixed to circulating capital is probably not so high as in Europe or the United States. But our argument is focused on the place of the house within this economy.) The house obtains fixed capital by exchanging its circulating holdings, and so long as the terms of trade are unfavorable and the volume of circulating wealth produced is not large, houses cannot burst out of the circulating-to-fixed-holdings ratio generated in agriculture.

From this perspective, the house is linked to the market through its production and use of circulating capital as opposed to the larger system's use and control of both fixed and circulating capital. For the larger system also, profit "in the marginal zone" is obtained primarily by securing and controlling liquid capital; the articulation between the house and the corporation occurs at the level of circulation. Businesses entering rural areas have traditionally profited by gaining command over exchange rather than production. Profits are made by truckers, middlemen, brokers, and merchants such as store owners and itinerant sellers in the plaza. Viewed differently, fixed capital has not yet intruded into the productive space occupied by the house; conversely, the countryside producer has to rely upon his control of circulating wealth. In the peripheral areas, business profits are made by having command over fixed and circulating capital in exchange, leaving the marginal producers to the use and production of circulating wealth.

The voice of theory in the historical conversation

To help place the house term "base," we have used several verbal categories from the modern textual conversation about the corporation, and not simply for the purpose of translation. We think that the two conversations are linked, for in several respects the corporate lexicon emerged from the practices and voices of the house. A retracing of this development not only elucidates differences between the house and corporation at the margin but illuminates some of the ways in which the house model was appropriated and transformed by theorists of the center. A look at this conversational transformation also helps us understand better the beginnings of certain theoretical problems in textual economics.

The distinction between fixed and circulating capital has been drawn by economists for several centuries. In his *Principles of Political Economy*, which was first published in 1848, was being reprinted well into this century, and served as the basic text in economics for more than fifty years, Mill (1929[1848]:91–100) provided perhaps the most thorough and thoughtful discussion of the distinction, but Smith had earlier given it currency (1976[1776]:294–301), and it was implicit in Quesnay's (1972[1758–9]) even earlier distinction between "original advances" and "annual advances" in agriculture. The general opposition is also echoed in Marx's (1967[1867]) distinction between "variable" and "constant" capital, although there is an important difference between his and the other inscriptions. For Marx, "variable capital" includes wages only, while "constant capital" covers machines plus the raw materials used in production. (By contrast, circulating capital in most texts includes both wages and raw materials.) Marx's "reclassification" of the traditional division fits his general argument that value is produced solely by labor. Only labor, in Marx's view, expands in value during production, hence it is variable. Because the remaining portion of capital, consisting of machines and materials, is only reproduced in value, adding nothing new in production, it is constant. These several ways of classifying the components of production are summarized in table 1.

Turgot, who followed upon, elaborated, and shifted the conversation from Quesnay, is especially interesting for his mixed and complex discussion. In *Reflections on the Formation and the Distribution of Riches* (1898[1770]: 43–63), he began with the assumption that the earth – and only the earth – may produce a "superfluity" above needed expenditures. This extra sum was termed "moveable

Table 1. *Models for classifying holdings*

Quesnay	Smith, Mill, neoclassical economics	Marx	Processes
Annual advances	Circulating capital (wages and raw materials)	Variable capital (wages)	Stocks and flows
Original advances	Fixed capital (equipment)	Constant capital (equipment and raw materials)	Funds and services

riches" (*richesses mobiliares*). In both French and Spanish, "moveable" has the double meaning of household furniture and liquid property. Turgot himself offered several examples of moveable wealth – furniture, houses, goods, tools, cattle – and suggested that this wealth provided the advances or capitals for undertaking all other economic activities. In effect, he commenced with a house model of "capital," that is, a liquid base accumulated from the land. For example, asking who provides the means of subsistence and raw materials for a tanning operation, he answered, "It will be one of those Possessors of *capitals*, or of moveable accumulated values" (1898[1770]:53), and then reiterated that the earth provides the first superfluity, which must be accumulated and placed in reserve. Like Quesnay, Turgot distinguished between "original" and "annual" advances, but he focused on the second, liquid form and described how moveable capital had continually to "pass through a crowd of different hands" (p.52). His emphasis was upon the "course of their [capitals'] circulation" (p. 55). At the end of his discussion, however, Turgot provided mixed voices. He continued to talk of "moveable wealth" and of "moveable accumulated riches," "values saved and accumulated" by household thrift from the land (p. 62), but he also identified these accumulations with money, whose "circulation . . . maintains movement and life in the body politic, and which is with great reason compared to the circulation of blood in the animal body" (p. 63). In effect, he employed two metaphors or models – the house and the body or corps – within one conversation. He began with a house model of accumulation but ended with a body model of exchange, and he did so with the intention of persuading the reader that circulating wealth in the latter derived from the earth and good housekeeping in the former. This juxtaposition of two voices, the attempt to derive the one from the other, and the emphasis upon circulating as opposed to fixed wealth suggests, indeed underlines, that Turgot's text was transitional. It illustrates how the one voice drew upon the other in its early stages of formulation.

Quesnay, though focusing on agricultural flows, gave greater weight than did Turgot to "original" as opposed to "annual" advances (1972[1758–9]), but it was Smith, himself influenced by the Physiocrats, who introduced the terminology of fixed and circulating capital. Even so, his division was inflected by the house voice. Smith claimed that the difference between circulating and fixed capital lay in whether it left its owner, circulated, and returned to him or yielded a "profit without changing masters" (1976[1776]:295). For example, he argued that the farmer's seed is a form of *fixed*, not circulating, capital:

Though it goes backwards and forwards between the ground and the granary, it never changes masters, and therefore does not properly circulate. The farmer makes his profit, not by its sale, but by its increase. (p. 296)

Clearly, this is opposite to our use of the term "circulating" for the holdings that a house controls; and Ricardo firmly dismissed Smith's distinction between exchange and nonexchange as the basis of the difference between circulating and fixed capital. But Smith's discussion is interesting exactly because it takes the perspective of the house economy, which either holds wealth within its doors as fixed capital (base→base') or "moves" it through the doors as circulating capital (base→money→base'). Smith, at least in this part of his discussion, did not fully constitute the exchange sphere itself (money→base→money') with corporate actors. Instead, he provided a house construction of the two forms of capital. Still, this was mixed into his broader and new conversation, for he also held that all fixed capital is derived from and supported by circulating capital (a point voiced again but differently by Marx), and he saw implicitly that fixed and circulating capital differ principally in terms of their durability or temporality, the issue so keenly elaborated by Ricardo.

If we can find a house voice still embedded in Smith's division between the two forms of capital, Ricardo marks an important shift in the conversation. Ricardo began the *Principles* with a simple labor theory of value that followed the general lines of Smith (Ricardo 1951[1817]:11–30), but he also perceived that time or capital must enter the picture. In brief, he saw that the ratio of circulating to fixed capital, the turnover time of fixed capital, and the turnover time of circulating capital could vary by industry, all having to do with differing payback periods between investment and return (Schumpeter 1954:636). Once such differences among industries or corporations arose, prices would diverge from simple labor quantities unless the ratios of circulating to fixed capital happened to be the same across all industries. Thus, Ricardo was much perplexed by what has come to be known as the "Ricardo effect": that a rise in wages, via its effect on lowering profits, causes the relative prices of high-fixed-capital products to fall and the relative prices of labor-intensive (or circulating-capital) products to rise:

Every rise of wages ... would lower the relative value of those commodities which were produced with a capital of a durable nature, and would proportionally elevate those which were produced with capital more perishable. (pp. 39–40)

This perception set Ricardo on his vain search for an "invariable measure of value" (pp. 43–7). A similar issue lies at the core of the Marxist problem of transforming labor values into market prices.

From our perspective, the interesting point about these puzzles and problems is that they arise only when there is a rise in fixed capital itself and when the conversation shifts from the house to the corporation enmeshed in exchange. In Smith and even more in Turgot, the discussion of fixed and circulating capital contains both the developing voice of the business undertaking and the remnant voice of the house. Clearly, in the eighteenth century, with its technological advances and marked developments in the durability of productive equipment, the ratio of circulating to fixed capital was changing, and there was a continuing transition in institutional dominance from house to corporation. But only with Ricardo is the house voice stilled and the corporate voice installed in the textual conversation. True enough, Ricardo does start with a simple labor theory of value, but within a few pages he has complicated this; the clear temporal division between circulating and fixed capital is not made before Ricardo, and the complex relations among changes in wages, prices, and profits is not examined before his written voice. With Ricardo's shift, the focus on and discussion of fixed capital in relation to prices becomes central. By contrast, in the house conversation the relation between the labor value of an object and its price is not considered problematic; rather, it is an ethical question of securing a "just price" or "fair trade." The house possesses primarily stocks and not funds, circulating and not fixed capital. It provides the circulating means for labor's maintenance and the circulating means for exchange that are produced by that labor, but it is not a receptacle for the deepening of capital. Questions about the value of capital and its relation to price are crucial only to the profit making corporation, with its perpetual succession.

Thus, a consideration of the Colombian model leads us to listen again to the long textual conversation on capital. Roughly, in the period from the Physiocrats (1750s) through Smith (1776) to Ricardo (1817) this discussion evinces an important transition. The textual discussion starts with the house voice but transforms it. This new talk then raises a different set of issues, especially the relation between quantities of labor needed in production and the price of goods in exchange. This latter question, of course, is central to Marx, and the conversation has carried on in its own way since. But for the Colombian house the problem is precisely the older one of securing a "just price" or "fair exchange" for the circulating base it trades.

THE BASE IN PRACTICE

Alfredo and Isabel Villa, along with several members of their family, live on the high plain (*el páramo*) outside the southern town of Cumbal. Alfredo, now sixty-six, worked on haciendas in his youth and also lived in the town but for the past fourteen years has been residing with his family in a remote area of the plain. He speaks of the pleasures of the countryside, with its clean water, tranquility, and lack of stealing. Alfredo is the "servant" (*el sirviente*) on the *finca* of an absentee landowner; his brother works for this man elsewhere and helped him make the initial contact. The owner keeps thirty-eight head of cattle, and Alfredo's job is to pasture the animals, make and clean irrigation ditches, repair fences, and perform related tasks. The owner visits the property at least once a month, and while Alfredo is not obligated to work a set number of days, he is expected to finish whatever needs to be done. He considers himself fortunate, because the landowner is "rich" and does not worry much about this property. Land values in the Cumbal area vary widely, from 2,500,000 pesos (about $12,500 at the 1986 exchange rate) to 40,000–60,000 pesos (about $200–$300) per hectare; the land of this *finca* is at the lower end of the range.

Alfredo does not receive a cash salary for watching over the *finca* but is allowed to use its resources in a number of ways. He may farm the land for his own benefit. In this very remote area, he practices slash-and-burn agriculture – cutting down the forest, removing the larger wood, burning the remainder, and farming a plot up to three times in succession. When the final harvest has been taken, he leaves the stubble in the field for the animals and sometimes adds pasture grass. These last practices are for the landowner's benefit, being a way for him to make savings. By allowing Alfredo to farm, the landowner has his pasture prepared at no cost; in effect, he exchanges the temporary use of his fixed holdings for work that would otherwise have to be remunerated with circulating capital. He keeps his *finca* going according to the same principle by which Alfredo operates – thriftiness in the use of money. Alfredo, for his part, does not own land – he has no "land fund" – but gains access to the earth's services through the unpaid work he performs for the hacendado.

Alfredo's house is maintained primarily by the potatoes he raises. In his words, with the potato he "has a base for house expenditures." Alfredo usually raises three harvests per year, and there would be more if he could arrange for more labor "help," but there are few workers to be found in the area. His agricultural methods are inexpensive, as he does no plowing, does not use fertilizer, and relies mainly on the hoe, the machete, and a curved wooden stick (*un garabato*) used for pulling back the brush. The three potato harvests cover the house's consumption needs and provide some amounts "for sale." The house consumes about a sack or quintal (one hundredweight) every two weeks ("one uses it most, one expends it most"), but it does not "keep an account" of its potato expenditures.

Since moving to the area, some of Alfredo and Isabel's family have grown to adulthood, but a teenage daughter and young son still live with them. Alfredo has also built sleeping quarters and a kitchen next to his own for a grown son who has married and had a child. The son's house keeps its own budget or expenditures apart (*los gastos aparte*), but the son also uses the land of the *finca*. He and Alfredo often work together, splitting expenditures and dividing the harvest (*a medias*). In effect, the son gains access to land through his father, and he uses some of his father's tools and pack animals as well. In return he undertakes some of the more difficult work in their joint ventures, such as carrying heavy sacks or doing extra errands. Alfredo and Isabel have given some of their animals to the other two children "so that they may have them" and care for them. The daughter, for example, raised and sold a small mule to defray the monetary cost of serving as a godmother.

A major source of cash for Alfredo, who never works as a wage laborer, is the sale of firewood. When he cuts down the forest, he leaves the larger stumps and roots in place for burning but pulls out the larger timber. This he cuts into firewood and loads on his packhorses for hauling to Cumbal. The journey in and back takes a full day, but Alfredo makes it every Saturday, as the town's demand for cooking fuel is unceasing and its nearby wood supplies have been depleted. Alfredo spends two or three days a week preparing, hauling, and selling firewood, and sometimes he hires a worker to help cut or load. For himself, however, he does not "count the hours" or "bill the time" spent on firewood collection: "Who pays me? No one but the forest itself." His work time is supported by material expenditures of the house.

A further benefit that Alfredo receives on the *finca* is the right to pasture cattle, and in recent years he has been able to increase his own holdings substantially. Eight years ago, in a major and unusual development, a dairy was built outside Cumbal. It supplies several cities to the north, and this had made for a steady demand for milk. In the past several years Alfredo has been able to send out milk daily, and the returns have added considerably to house income.

With this background we can consider the holdings and flows of Alfredo and Isabel's house (tables 2 and 3). The primary foodstuffs are potatoes, which are raised with few monetary costs. Most of the other foods are purchased every Sunday in the Cumbal market. Other house expenditures, for clothes, utensils, sundries, tools, and instruments,

Table 2. Monetary purchases of a house

	Quantity	Weekly	Biweekly	Monthly	Bimonthly	Annual
			Cost (in pesos)[1]			
Food						
Sugar	5 kg	$450.00				$23,400.00
Chili pepper	6	$50.00				$2,600.00
Barley		$200.00				$10,400.00
Rice	2 kg	$180.00				$9,360,00
Plantain				$300.00		$3,600.00
Salt	½ kg	$100.00				$5,200.00
Achiote	10				$50.00	$300.00
Flour	¼ kg		$170.00			$4,420.00
Cabbage	2	$40.00				$2,080.00
Clothing						
Clothing M						$6,500.00
Clothing F						$6,000.00
Clothing F						$6,000.00
Clothing Ch						$5,000.00
1 Hat	1					$4,000.00
2 Caps	2					$400.00
1 Watch	$\frac{1}{5}$					$500.00
Household items						
12 Pots	2					$2,600.00
10 Plates	2					$250.00
10 Spoons	4					$480.00
12 Cups	4					$480.00
3 Containers	1					$300.00
1 Grinder	1					$200.00
Miscellaneous						$1,000.00
2 Flashlights	1					$500.00
1 Radio	$\frac{1}{5}$					$600.00
Kerosene	4 liters			$100.00		$600.00
Candles	1 pack			$180.00		$1,080.00
Batteries			$300.00			$7,800.00
Starter						$2,000.00
Powder						$2,000.00
3 Shotguns	$\frac{1}{7}$					$1,000.00
5 Blankets	2.5				$5,000.00	$30,000.00
4 Beds	$\frac{1}{7}$				$1,400.00	$8,400.00
1 Trunk	$\frac{1}{20}$				$750.00	$4,500.00
1 Coleman lamp	$\frac{1}{12}$				$400.00	$2,400.00

Table 2. *Monetary purchases of a house*

		Costs (in pesos)[1]				
	Quantity	Weekly	Biweekly	Monthly	Bimonthly	Annual
Tools						
6 Hoes	2					$4,000.00
6 Machetes	2					$1,600.00
4 Axes	$\frac{1}{2}$					$900.00
7 Shovels	1					$800.00
6 Cutes	1					$1,000.00
2 Sickles	$\frac{1}{5}$					$80.00
2 Sprayers						$3,000.00
10 Sacks	2					$500.00
6 Baskets	3					$600.00
2 Carriers	$\frac{1}{5}$					$200.00
4 Horse trappings	2					$3,000.00
2 Saddles, etc.	2					$2,000.00
1 Cart	$\frac{1}{6}$					$4,000.00
1 Tongs	$\frac{1}{20}$					$25.00
1 Iron bar	$\frac{1}{20}$					$25.00
1 Hammer	$\frac{1}{20}$					$10.00
1 Drugs	4					$20,000.00
Total						$207,532.50

[1] 1 peso = U.S. $.004 (1986)

are made as required through the year. Here, especially, the house attempts to be thrifty. These cash expenditures amount to over 200,000 pesos (about $800), and they are met in several ways. The sale of potatoes through the year produces about one-twentieth of the needed amount. Nearly one-quarter of the cash costs are covered by the sale of firewood. Leaving aside the milk cows, the remaining portion of cash is gained by sale of animals. Guinea pigs, chickens, and most of the piglets are kept for house consumption. As the cattle and sheep reproduce, however, a few grown ones are taken to market. The younger ones are kept so that the base stays largely constant from year to year, with the cattle "increase" (*aumento*) being sold. Alfredo is fortunate in having unlimited access to the force of pasture so that he may keep animals and garner a return from their sale. But the truly unusual feature of Alfredo and Isabel's situation is the return that they are able to make on the sale of milk; this cash flow effectively covers all monetary costs, while the returns from other ventures have allowed

Table 3. *Returns on the base*

No.	Item	Unit value	Cash					In kind			
			Daily	Weekly	Annual	Aver/day	%	Quantity	Value	Day	%
4	Milk cows	$120,000.00	$980.00		$274,400.00	$751.78	70.25	1 liter	$14,600.00	$40.00	21.89
4	Calves	$8,500.00			$17,000.00	$46.58	4.35			$0.00	0.00
11	Sheep	$6,000.00			$12,000.00	$32.88	3.07			$0.00	0.00
4	Pigs	$2,000.00			$1,000.00	$2.74	0.26			$0.00	0.00
3	Piglets	$800.00				$0.00	0.00			$0.00	0.00
6–10	Chickens	$500.00				$0.00	0.00	8 / year	$3,000.00	$8.22	4.50
25	Guinea pigs	$600.00				$0.00	0.00	3 / month	$21,600.00	$59.18	32.38
6	Horses	$15,000.00			$18,000.00	$49.32	4.61				
5	Firewood	$225.00		$1,125.00	$56,250.00	$154.11	14.40			$0.00	0.00
2	Houses	$17,000.00									
	Potato harvest										
	January	$0.00			$0.00	$0.00	0.00	(2 sacks)	($2,000.00)	($5.48)	
	March	$6,000.00			$6,000.00	$16.44	1.54	7 sacks	$7,000.00	$19.18	41.23
	July	$5,950.00			$5,950.00	$16.30	1.52	22.5 sacks	$22,500.00	$61.64	
Total					$390,600.00	$1,070.14	100.00		$66,700.00	$182.74	100.00

them to increase the base. If the cash returns from the four milk cows were eliminated, the house would be in deficit and would need to sell some of its base and shrink expenditures. Similarly, if the home consumption of milk from the cattle were eliminated, the monetary value of the in-kind return from potatoes would constitute over 50 percent of house expenditures, the rest being made up of small-animal consumption. With the advent of the dairy and a slight development in the transportation structure, cattle have become – for Alfredo – a fund that renders a return rather than a stock(holding) or reserve that can only be turned into a flow. Without the dairy, cattle would serve as savings, agriculture would constitute the predominant source of food, cash would have to be gained by one or another activity, and the base would be characterized by a high ratio of circulating to fixed holdings. The shift in this ratio over the past several years and the change in monetary flow experienced by Alfredo and Isabel's house suggest how a judicious development of the larger marketing structure can lead to a better utilization of rural holdings, making it possible for some of these to move inside the margin of profit and become a fixed fund that lends profitable services.

Chapter 5
THE ADVANCE AND THE INCREASE

As our conversations shifted endlessly between car and field, ways of talking about time increasingly captured our attention. Voices from the distant past continued to intrude upon our car conversations, but in the fields and houses the people talked mostly about the daily round of meals and the weekly market. Our attention was also drawn to the way the rural folk placed the base within a time framework. They spoke of "replacing" the base and "returning to" agriculture, which seemed to imply a repetitive, cyclical notion of time. But they also explained how a flow of goods – after being "gathered" from the land – was "used up" in the house in order to "maintain" it, and this seemed to imply an unfolding view of time. The more we conversed, however, the more another difference emerged between car and field. Both of us were accustomed to hearing about the "progress" of technology, the "rise" of productivity, and the "growth" of the national product. This was not part of the local conversation, in which the acquisition of new seeds and fertilizer meant replacing failing ones and forestalling scarcity. The rural folk had given us narratives about the origin and long-term development of the base as well as personal accounts of success and failure in the short term, so "economic change" was part of their lexicon. But their discussion revolved about changing the size of the house through engaging sharecroppers or spawning a new one, not changing its form. Eventually, it became clear that two important expressions for placing the base within a temporal perspective were the "advance" and the "increase." Both have to do with ensuring stocks for future uses.

GETTING AHEAD

The term "advance" (*el adelanto* or, less often, *el avance*) usually refers to the amount from a harvest above what will be needed to supply the house in a later production cycle. "It is making savings for tomorrow," as one person said. Another explained:

When the harvest comes you put aside some for house uses: for the seed, the people of the house, the outside workers, the tools – all that you need for working, including clothes. This is what you need to work and live. The rest is to advance. You keep this as a reserve in a hog. When you have a need and a scarcity of money, you sell the animal and use the money to buy what you need to maintain yourself. The advance is a reserve for working in the future, because when you have a harvest that is lost, you have *this* harvest there in the advance. With a reserve you can withstand more failure. How much you need depends on the house expenditures you have.

In general, the base has two parts. One segment provides the expenditures for the coming production cycle. This is the stock for the flow of house uses (*los gastos de la casa*). It repeats the cycle and maintains the base. Whatever is not needed to return the base comprises the "increase" (*el aumento*). This is the advance. "Getting ahead" (*adelantar*) means that a portion of the base can be held in abeyance to sustain the house in coming years. "The advance from one year," said an agriculturalist, "is what you need to work in subsequent ones." The advance represents a house's control over the future.

The people provide many examples of the advance. Any animal, such as a chicken, hog, or ox, is an advance. The advance can be lost if the animal dies or if the proceeds are immediately expended when it is sold. A harvest gathered in one year for use in the future is an advance, as are portions of the seed and food held in the house. A man may spend several years accumulating the materials needed to build a house; on the site of construction, a sand pile grows, bricks are added, then roofing materials appear, and so on, until all the requisites for construction are in place. They are accumulated and advanced from one time period to subsequent ones. The rural folk add that one has to "defend" advances so as not to lose them and the effort they represent; advances, in turn, "defend" one's future work.

Sometimes the people use the word "savings" (*ahorros*) for getting ahead, because the savings made in one year are an advance for the future. For example, they often say that with tobacco one is always paying off debts, rather than saving, so that nothing is left: the cash crop "gives no advance." The advance, then, is a savings or supply for use in the future that is built by making savings or being thrifty in the present.

LIVESTOCK

The general term for any addition to the base is "increase" (*el aumento*). The word is used principally for animals, which grow and multiply. An abundant harvest also increases the base, but the crop excess must be turned into something else to constitute a lasting increase. Animals serve as a reserve of wealth: "If you sell an animal, you lose the 'advance.' But the animal is a defense, to be used for heavy obligations." The animals kept vary both by ecological region and by how well they store and augment the base. Most smaller ones are holdings only and may even constitute a drain on wealth; others provide this savings function and expand in value (*se valoran*) as well. Animals do not "give" an increase in themselves; rather, "the advances of the animal come from the maize," which gathers its strength from the land. Some animals store this strength; others store it and transform it into work; and some augment what they consume by growing, multiplying, and yielding products.

Chickens are ever-present in the patios and sometimes in the kitchens of rural homes. They forage, are fed kitchen scraps, and are supported from the house maize supply. No one keeps them to secure an increase in value, for at best "one comes out even." As one person said, "The hen is small, it doesn't cover anything." Eggs are house-consumed, and the animals usually end up in the kitchen pot. Chickens are sold only when no petty cash is available.

Other small animals, such as rabbits and guinea pigs, are less frequently encountered in the countryside. Rabbits are kept in a cage and fed greens until they are large enough for eating. Guinea pigs run loose in the kitchen, eating scraps and throwaways until they reach consumption size.

Hogs, say the people, are a "savings box" (*una alcancía*). They are kept loose or tied up at the house and require neither pasture nor much work. They are fed scraps, such as unsalable tomatoes and damaged potatoes or sugarcane, the objective being to feed them "from the doors inward." Hogs are efficient in "making do" with the refuse of the house and are an economical way to hold wealth already produced. Said one person, "What you lose in maize you gain in the animal growing," or, in the local voice, "You get out what you put in" (*lo comido por lo servido*). Hogs are true "piggy banks." They are of a useful size in relation to what most houses can provide, their consumption needs vary, they can be sold at any time, and their numbers can be expanded. In addition, because they are kept at the house, which is usually occupied, they are "safe holdings." (Rural potters, incidentally, make clay piggy banks that are sold in town markets.)

Sheep, goats, oxen, and cattle all require pasture; they are not animals of the patio. Sheep are found at the higher altitudes, though not in great numbers. They are raised for their growth, their reproduction, and their wool. The latter is sheared in the home, where women also card and spin. Oxen are kept for various reasons. Some people raise, train, briefly use, and then sell their beasts; a portion of the cash received is reinvested in a young pair, and the remainder constitutes the increase. Others keep oxen strictly for plowing. An ox-team owner can also earn cash, for there is a lively market in rentals. The daily charge for a team is approximately 60 percent above the human wage, and the oxen can be leased out alone or with a plow and driver. Some people own a single beast in order to trade use of it with another owner, an effective way to make savings. When a person has rented or traded for oxen, he must – as owner of their work – feed them during the day.

The most desired animals are cattle. If a person has sufficient land, their carrying costs are low, consisting principally of medicines. As the people explain:

> The land gives pasture; that is the harvest for landowners. Having pasture for cattle is like using maize in the house for humans and hogs. The pasture contains force, and that is what the cows use. They produce, they give, using the strength of the land.

Cows have various advantages. They give milk, which is consumed in the home or, in certain areas, sold. They also reproduce or multiply. Cows increase the base by giving offspring and milk and by gaining weight, all of which are the result of eating pasture that takes its strength from the land. Growing the pasture requires little effort, and tending cattle is relatively easy, being a task undertaken sporadically by children or adults through the day:

> With cattle, sheep, and goats, one is not losing time, money, or health. And they give. One's time is a use of the base, and animals take one's work also. But there is less suffering and personal ruination. Cattle take less work themselves and for their pasture which gives them strength. Thus, the rich – who expend less work – have cattle living off the earth. This is better than cultivating, advancing they go.

As the people repeatedly state, agriculture is for the poor ones; the rich dedicate themselves to cattle – and to lending money.

Sometimes keeping cattle and goats does not require the possession of pasture land or usufruct rights to it. In the rural areas people frequently pasture their cattle "off the margin." The animals are tethered or left free by the roadside where there is a strip of grass between the vehicle passageway and a fence that marks the beginning of private property. Goats, similarly, run loose on the edges of private holdings. In these cases and many others, the fodder has no monetary cost. The land is extramarginal in that it falls outside the profit margin of the market system. For rural folk the use of such market leftovers is one way to make savings. Cows feeding by the side of the highway and goats running loose are signs of the presence of the domestic economy.

In general, animals are storehouses of force or crops, and in raising them the people are changing the base from one form to another or from a less to a more durable holding as well as increasing it in size. They argue that when selling prices for their crops are poor, it is better to feed the harvests to animals, thus keeping them "in-house" and making savings. If an animal is sold and house needs are not overwhelming, a part of the cash received is used to purchase a young one; this "returns" the animal to its condition before foodstuffs were added. The amount above this can be used to buy more animal feed or to meet other necessities: this is the advance. More generally stated, a harvest of maize in excess of current expenditures is fed to an animal that grows and may be sold; the amount received above replacement cost of the animal represents the original maize saved or the increase of the animal – the strength advanced – and it can be used to maintain agricultural work in a new cycle.

This method of handling animals implies that time is modeled in several ways. There is, first, the irreversible growth of animals. The people, however, treat this as a reproducible pattern to be fueled by the crops, and they try to do it again and again. These growth cycles serve to maintain and sometimes to enlarge a house's food stock by advancing it from one period to the next, which, in turn, is a linear or stream notion of time. As the base increases, the advance sustains more cycles into the future.

THE ADVANCE AS METAPHOR

"Getting ahead" is a metaphor that employs the figure of a moving body. The imagery is common to many cultures. As the human body moves in space, time passes; thus, body movement in space is often a figure for the passage of time. But the body moves "naturally" in one direction only, so going forward spatially also comes to mean going forward in time, while going backward in space reverses time's arrow. In Colombia, the rural folk speak of any unfolding activity, such as planting maize or life itself, as a forward movement. This also conveys the qualitative sense that forward is betterment while backward is not.

The Colombian time as space metaphor has other implications. A worker and the people of his house need to be supported by a flow of goods as they move forward in time and space. The advance is the stock of goods that must be in place ahead of their passage in order to supply them. By the side of the path of life are provisions to sustain the people of a house, and these are consumed as they pass. But their work produces further supplies, and these latter are either "thrown forward" (*echado para adelante*) or "thrust backwards" (*echado para atrás*) depending on who supplies the current provisions. Stocks of goods are continually produced by work, but those who have an advance stock on which to live draw on it as they move forward and consequently are able to defer the outcome of present work in order to advance it farther along the path. This is "getting ahead." Those who have no supplies in place are moving forward and producing a stock but must be sustained by a base they did not create. These workers are obliged to replace the used stock, which, as they move forward, falls behind them. The products of their work must be "thrust back." In shorthand, a laborer may also say he is going "backwards" or is "behind" (*atrasado*), meaning that his personal progression is ahead of the stock he is creating. Such a person is in debt; as the people say, the debtor has "nothing for working," while paying interest on a loan is a way of being "behind."

Some workers are neither behind nor ahead. The day worker receives cash and food for current consumption in return for his efforts; in the precise folk lexicon, he "comes out even" (*sale al ras*). Also, someone who farms successfully but cannot build a reserve "comes out even." Neither case is satisfactory, for the worker is not building an advance with which to defend himself.

This trope of the forward movement of people and the forward and backward thrusting of holdings is connected to the economic status of the house. The rural folk often discuss whether their current supplies are sufficient to "reach" (*alcanzar*) the next harvest or "fall short" (*faltar*); the use of this figure of spatial distance in discussing the house food supply fits the larger metaphor of getting ahead: a house is always moving forward in time, and its project is to "throw" a reserve or stock of holdings ever farther in front of its own passage, but sometimes this advance does not "reach" far enough. As the people also explain, "getting ahead" means that the stock inside the house is increasing, while "going backwards" means that the base is growing smaller so that eventually the flow of current support will have to come from outside the house. The first process indicates that gains are being made, and there is a movement of goods from outside to inside; the second signals losses or a movement from inside to outside.

But the advance is more than the placement of a stock relative to human passage. The central issue is whether the stock providing maintenance is owned by the house or by someone else. The house that provides its own advance maintains itself and remains independent. By contrast, if someone from "outside the doors" supplies (*suplir*) the advance or the food with which to work, then the workers are not only "behind" but in "slavery" as well. When the beforehand payment is made in money, it is spoken of as a "wage advance" or "advance payment" (*un anticipo*), and the folk explain that haciendas, by supplying such advances, kept people in "slavery":

> They supplied in advance [*suplían adelante*] a load of potatoes or wheat, having one in slavery there. They also said, "I advance [*anticipo*] you the money" . . . so that I could work. For nothing, for nothing, one worked every day, deducting what they supplied to eat.

Today, some people use these same terms when sharecropping tobacco. The sharecropper, because he possesses no stock of crops for eating, usually has to secure food money from the landowner and the tobacco company, and with the harvest he is just able to pay off this advance. The sharecropper of tobacco is in "slavery" and can never get ahead on his own.

Viewed in terms of both historical and contemporary contexts, the people's voice can be seen as having been forged in opposition to the holders of the means of subsistence. When the rural folk provide their own advance, they are substituting house control over needed provisions for the wage and supply advances of outsiders. Maintaining command over an increasing stock that supplies a flow of food for work is the house's project.[1]

A conversation: the advance of economists

The concepts of the advance and wage advance were of special interest to the classical economists of the late eighteenth and nineteenth centuries, who paid close attention to temporal process and accumulation in the economy. Their formulation of the productive process was largely abandoned with the rise of neoclassical economics and the development of a more static view of the economy at the turn of this century. The particular concept of a wage advance or "wage fund" also proved difficult to justify given the rising power of laborers. The leavings of the concepts, however, have proved influential, and no one has asked where they originated or why they were so persuasive. In our view, the advance as a theoretical notion for the corporate economy was a projection from the practices and voice of the house. The concept was inscribed in the eighteenth century by economists who were attempting to model the impact of accumulations of wealth on the economy. Eventually, the notion of the advance was replaced by that of capital, but the original idea of advancing wealth from cycle to cycle continued to have a forceful impact on topics such as justifying the taking of profit. Our contention is that the concept of the advance – seminal in the sense of stimulating and giving rise to a collection of later voices – was taken over from folk culture and transformed and inscribed by a reflective stratum. Some of the historical linkages between the formal and the folk can be suggested by bringing the Colombian voice into conversation with the economists.

One reason for the classical interest in advances follows from the nature of physical production itself. Aside from plucking fruit in the Garden of Eden, a production process always takes time and therefore stands in need of a prior stock on which the laborer can live while working and "waiting" for the harvest to ripen or the manufacturing output to emerge. A productive process also consumes raw materials and tools. In the terminology of the classical economists, the preexisting stocks of food, materials, and tools constitute the advances on which production draws. But someone has to provide these stocks, and according to the same classical models this is what capitalists do: the advance is one form of capital. For example, it was argued, by economists such as Senior (1938[1836]:59, 89, 129, 185) and Mill (1929[1848]:68–70, 461–2), that advances of capital are built up through "abstinence"; only by forgoing consumption of funds is the capitalist able to advance them to others to support their work. The theorists reasoned that profit is the reward for this abstinence.

A different line of thought leads from the advance to both wages and the temporal functioning of the economy. A large part of the advance is used, or was used a century and a half ago, to cover the cost of labor. Because this suggests that a stock of money must exist and be earmarked for wages even before production begins, some classical economists deduced the existence of a "wage fund." The wage fund is a preset amount, used for workers' subsistence, that is paid out during production. The volume of the fund in relation to the labor supply determines the wage rate. While they are being remunerated, however, workers create tools and instruments as well as final consumption goods, and consequently the size of the wage fund also determines the rate of new capital formation. On this argument, the magnitude of the wage advance as well as its augmentation or diminution from period to period helps set the long-term growth of the economy; the volume of the wage fund – accumulated by the capitalist – is central in determining the functioning of the economy. In his early writings Mill (1929[1848]:343–4, 362, 457–8) developed and defended this theory; later he recanted his position but summarized it as follows (p. 992):[2]

The theory rests on what may be called the doctrine of the wages fund. There is supposed to be, at any given instant, a sum of wealth, which is unconditionally devoted to the payment of wages of labour. This sum is not regarded as unalterable, for it is augmented by saving, and increases with the progress of wealth; but it is reasoned upon as at any given moment a predetermined amount. More than that amount it is assumed that the wages-receiving class cannot possibly divide among them; that amount, and no less, they cannot but obtain. So that, the sum to be divided being fixed, the wages of each depend solely on the divisor, the number of participants.

How is this nineteenth-century conversation connected to the contemporary voice from Colombia? Again, it is useful to return to the Physiocrats, for they actually began the textual discussion. Turgot, as might be expected, provided a transitional voice between house and corporation (1898[1770]:51):

All labours, whether for agriculture or for industry, require advances. And I have shown how the earth, by the fruits and herbs which it produces of itself for the nourishment of men and animals, and by the trees whereof men have formed their first tools, had furnished the first advance of cultivation, and even of the first hand-made articles that each man might fashion for his own use.

Turgot argued that all advances ultimately are supplied by the earth. But while he began with this adherence to Physiocratic principles, he shifed to talking about the "advance of capitals" in enterprises and finally dropped the term "advance" to speak solely of "capitals." His textual discussion (pp. 45–65) thus covered the "house advance" for agriculture and corporate capital as well as a mediation of the two.

Earlier, in the *Tableau économique* (1972[1758–9]), Quesnay had outlined several uses of an advance: to prepare land initially, to pay for equipment, and to underwrite current expenditures on labor. He distinguished, as noted, between "original advances" (*avances primitives*), which start an agricultural process, and "annual advances" (*avances annuelles*), such as seed and food. His examples are very close to those offered by a Colombian campesino who stated that the advance is "the food, the seed, and the equipment one is using to till the land."

In both Physiocracy and rural Colombia, the advance is said to be "expended" or "used up" (French *dépensé*, Spanish *gastado*) in working the land, which is the sole productive element in the economy. This view led Quesnay to hold something like a wage-fund theory, even though he did not believe that labor was a productive factor (1963c[1766]:233, 242–3). He argued (1963b[1766]:209–10) that labor alone

cannot increase the wealth which the nation annually spends, since it is itself limited by the measure of this wealth, which can be increased only through agricultural work and not through the expenditure involved in artisans' work. Thus the origin, the principle, of all expenditure and all wealth is the fertility of the land, whose products can be increased only through these products themselves. It is the land which provides the advances to the cultivator who renders it fertile in order to make it produce more . . . No matter who the worker may happen to be, it is necessary that the land should have produced in advance what he has consumed for his subsistence: thus it is not his labour which has produced this subsistence. Nor has the consumption of the subsistence produced anything either, since this consumption is only a destruction of wealth produced in advance by the land. The worker who sought to do more work in order to increase his wages or his consumption would do so in vain, for he cannot extend them beyond the produce which are at present available.

Quesnay here wove together the several notions that land is the sole productive agent, that it provides an advance, and that labor is an expenditure of this advance. This "land fund theory" is different from Mill's later emphasis on the productivity of labor and the singular importance of the wage fund, but Quesnay's model did lead him to the view that economic growth is determined by the size of the advances and that the several advances should be sufficient to provide the largest possible product (Quesnay 1963c[1766]:233, 242–3). He envisioned that economic growth or decline would occur as the advance was directed to productive or sterile activities, although for illustrative purposes he assumed an intermediate situation "in which the reproductive expenditure renews the same revenue from year to year" (1972[1758–9]:i). A government, he claimed, had to ensure that proper "distribution of expenditure" was made, and accordingly it was possible to "calculate the effects of the good or bad leadership of a nation" (1963a[1766]:161). This general model, in which the earth's products are distributed in society and then partially return to the land as seed and labor for the next harvest, is much like the Colombian one according to which the land gives back the base used up in agriculture and this flows through the house which by good management can return to farming.

There are, however, some important differences between the economists' models and the Colombian one. The annual advance in Physiocracy and Mill's wage fund defray the costs of the forthcoming production cycle. These are akin to what the rural folk mean by setting aside "house expenses" (*los gastos de la casa*) for "doing it again" and different from their use of "advance" to mean the stock put aside for future use. In Colombia the "advance" normally refers to that part of the base held for subsequent periods, not to the productive means that are immediately required. This folk notion of the advance in fact is like the Physiocratic concept of the "net product," what remains after expenses for the next cycle have been reproduced (Quesnay 1963c[1766]:243). In the Colombian house model, then, a contrast is drawn between expenditures for reproduction and the advance for the future; in the "subsequent" Physiocratic model the contrast is between the "advance" for expenditures of production and the "net product" that remains. Good housekeeping in the Colombian model assumes sufficient expenditures for reproduction and keeps the advance; good leadership in the Physiocratic model directs the advance toward productive as opposed to sterile expenditures.

This difference is linked to a second one between textual and folk uses of the "advance." For Mill, the advance or wage fund represents a sacrifice of consumption by the capitalist who supplies it to someone else. In this construction, the advance is a form of corporate investment that occurs within an exchange economy. By contrast, in rural Colombia the advance is self-supplied by the house that uses it, and such working funds are neither borrowed from nor put out to others. The Physiocrats' notion of the advance, then, was probably appropriated from the house model but given a different turning in their conversation. Quesnay was interested in growth of the national economy, so the "advance" came to mean immediate expenditures on productive or sterile activities rather than an expanding hoard kept in reserve for future consumption. Subsequently, Turgot's transitional text exactly displayed a shift in terms from "advance" to "capital." After him, capital came to be seen as an advance and an investment, hoarded from the past through abstinence; this view, developed and elaborated by Smith and Ricardo, reached its conclusion with Mill, who argued that there is a preset wage fund that determines the dimensions of the productive process – "industry is limited by capital" (1929[1848]:66). This was an argument that he had finally to abandon, but by this time house and corporate conversations had taken quite separate courses.

The voice of Marx must be added to the discussion, for Marx also outlined a reproductive model of the economy that involved the use of advances. The idea of a wage fund also corresponds closely to Marx's notion of "variable capital." According to Marx, advances are provided by capitalists, who use them to control the labor process. Variable capital, provided by the capitalist, buys labor-power, the worker's unexercised capacity. Labor-power, purchased and controlled by the capitalist, is put to use and realized as labor. Ultimately, the value of this active labor, or of what it produces in materials, is larger than what was expended upon it as labor-power, and the difference is surplus or profit. This extra sum is gathered up by the capitalist who owns the variable capital that provided the initial advance for the wage. A crucial part of Marxist economics thus hinges upon the idea that advances exist and are controlled by capitalists. In *Capital* (1967[1867]), however, Marx pointedly added that the capitalist never actually advances the wage to the worker beforehand; rather, work is performed and the laborer is paid in arrears. The notion of a wage advance is thus a fiction of economists, for in practice the capitalist holds his money until a work period is completed, and this adds to the profit he gains. (In the context of *this* conversation it is worth remarking that in one contemporary model the classical assumption of a wage advance is finally turned around.) In a model of a reproducing economy influenced by the Physiocrats and perhaps even by a house model, Sraffa [1960:10] assumes that

> the wage is paid *post factum* as a share of the annual product, thus abandoning the classical economists' idea of a wage "advanced" from capital. We retain however the supposition of an annual cycle of production with an annual market.

Sraffa's *post factum* wage, as it happens, bears a close relation to the campesinos' notion of "house expenditures" that are taken from a harvest to cover the costs of the next cycle before the advance is laid aside.

Like Marx, the Colombian country folk are very cognizant of the importance of controlling a base, meaning having command over an advance or, in Marx's terms, controlling the "means of production." But Marx was writing about a corporate system, so we need to look closely at the differences between their conversations. To apply Marx's notion of command over "variable capital" (or the wage fund) in the rural context, we would need to expand it and go back to the Physiocratic idea of "advances," for the rural house provides the food as well as the seed and equipment it will use. This is a total advance, like the one outlined by Quesnay. Control of this advance is central as in Marxist theory, but there is a difference here, too, for a house advance is self-provided rather than supplied by someone else. In this respect the domestic economy is rather like an involuted capitalist relationship as pictured by Marx. It might by argued, in illustration, that a dialectical reaction to capitalist control over the means of production or the wage fund produces outside its border the self-sufficient economy; conversely, it could be maintained that Marx's model – with its "base" and "superstructure" – is but a dialectical completion of the house. Thus, for Marx, paying in arrears rather than beforehand is a capitalist trick for increasing profit. But this is not the way the campesinos view it. When someone else provides the wage advance, it is to allow the worker to purchase necessities to support his labor. The rural people consider such advance payments to be a form of slavery, for it makes them indebted to someone else. Their view is exactly the opposite of Marx's, who thought that a true advance before work was more just. Yet, the peasants' terminology is sensible in terms of their own practices and temporal metaphor. To be paid in advance is a form of slavery because it means that as one is laboring one is using the product of that work to replace – or "thrust back" – the stock owed to someone else. The people's solution, again, is to try to provide their own advance from the house; then they can be paid in arrears by others, yet not be in slavery to them or in arrears themselves.

Chapter 6

WORK FOR THE HOUSE

One afternoon in Boyacá, a man stood in front of his house and, pointing to the surroundings, said, "It is work, all work, every bit of it." Work is crucial in continuing the material flow of strength from the earth to the crops to the house and back to the land. The people's efforts turn the force of food into labor which aids the land. But work alone is not sufficient, for without human spirit and will nothing would be accomplished (*no lograría nada*), and everything depends upon the might of God and the consumption of His strength contained in the crops. Elliptically, therefore, work is also spoken of as "force," shorthand for "the force of work." The term links work not only proximally to food but distally to the divinity.

The people most frequently talk about work as "help" in the sense that work assists nature to produce, and in return the earth gives its help as base. But any work for the household is help, whether or not directly connected to the land. If children tend cattle or a flock, their work is help. All of a woman's work in the kitchen and elsewhere is help, and so is the man's work in the fields. Work received from "outside the doors" is also help; as the people say, one "helps another to work," and a no-interest loan of seed, tools, or oxen is also a help, for it enables the recipient "to place his work in the base."

The people work hard and continuously – a fact they recognize. Workdays are long, the labor is unbroken and tiring, and few persons can be found resting during the day. Saturday is a regular workday, and many work on Sunday. A large portion of our conversations, for example, had to take place in the fields. We were cordially treated, but our discussants continued to drive teams of oxen, wield hoes, harvest crops, and perform other tasks, and they worked in all conditions from chilling rain to brisk winds and burning sunshine. Sometimes a discussant would take a break to talk with us, but invariably this was interrupted so that she or he could attend to righting a sack, shooing an animal, feeding the workers, weeding a crop, or undertaking some other task. The loads of potatoes, maize, and other crops that men carry from the fields to the house are staggering. But their efforts are not motivated by the desire to accumulate. They are driven rather by the need for survival, "for living, for sustenance, nothing more." As one man said, "We have no extras, so there is no time to rest or for a vacation." The people, of course, vary in the effort they exert. One night, in northern Boyacá, a man worked in a group stringing tobacco leaves until 11:00 p.m., when his spouse served the laborers a plateful of potatoes; she and he then retired (as did we), but he was awake by 4:30 a.m. and weeding in his seedbed by 5:15 a.m. Sometime after 7:00 a.m. other men came by to lend their assistance for the day. Meanwhile the woman had arisen, prepared her husband's breakfast, begun cooking for the remainder of the day, tended their animals nearby, fetched water, and cleaned the house patio. This couple is unusual in its restless efforts, others not starting so early or leaving off sooner, but most people are guided by the work that needs to be done; and what needs to be done in the marginal conditions of the countryside is a very great deal.

The rural folk say that one has to have "enthusiasm" for work and that it "takes away one's health." They talk about needing to "feel capable" to give the effort that certain tasks require, and they speak of their own limits. But above all they talk about "suffering" in work and say that those in poor health suffer more. Crops are said to exact different degrees of suffering; maize, yucca, and beans, in that order, are easier to raise, while sugarcane, tomatoes, and tobacco are harder. The planting of tobacco gives rise to most misgivings. As one man pointed out, he was up all night for weeks in succession irrigating the growing plants when water was available and then weeding them during the day. A person "suffers much" in tobacco; it is, some say, a penitence and a sacrifice, especially given its returns. But one suffers in all the crops, particularly when "there is no strength" to replace the force used up in the work. "If you are working without the strength to work, you get sick, you can die; you are using up your energy and health." Yet, it is even worse to be idle (*de balde*): "You don't recover anything, it's lost; you go backwards." This discussion leads again to the local definition of the "rich":

> The rich live from their money, the poor from their labor. It is the poor who have to work and suffer. The rich are the ones just eating and not working. They have cattle that live off pasture, take little work, and yield money; or they lend out money at interest.

But despite this critical perspective and emotive construction of their physical labor, the people work with good humor. It is rare to hear them complain as they labor. Within a work group, there is talk and joking; in gender-mixed groups there may be friendly competition between the sexes and in the search for puns and sexual innuendos. Work in a group gives moments of levity, while alone it is quietly and steadily undertaken. The rural folk do not draw back from a particular task with the complaint that it is too onerous, nor can they afford to do so.

The skills of the people, males and females, are diverse. Women undertake a variety of food preparation tasks, but they also strip henequen to make rope, weave baskets, make clay pots, card wool, spin thread, and more. The female has principal responsibility for raising children, which is explicitly recognized by everyone as work. A woman's work is ceaseless; one rainy afternoon we watched a woman sort and load potatoes into sacks. The moment this was finished, and even while the men were loading the sacks onto horse-drawn carts, she sat down and began to spin thread. Women sometimes labor in the fields, where, as the men say, they work "equally" (*por parejo*). Young women still in their parents' home may help by seeding, weeding, harvesting, sorting, or doing some other agricultural task; we have seen them undertake all stages of the onerous labor in tobacco, and some engage in work exchange with other houses. Young men, beginning at the age of twelve or so, work for the house and for cash wages. At the outset, they receive a part-wage, but by fourteen or fifteen a male earns the same as an elder. Certain tasks requiring quick hands are best done by children. Tomato plants, for example, are tied to a horizontal string above them; accomplished eleven-year-old artisans grab a plant, loop and tie a string to it, then loop and tie this string to the horizontal one in less than two seconds. The adult male has many skills, learned at an early age and then developed and quickened by working with others. Aside from caring for animals, adults know about diseases in animals and how to cure them. A man can make almost any kind of house, from stick-and-thatch to adobe and tapia; he knows how to find and prepare vines for binding walls and fences. As the people say, it is an advantage to do something oneself, for then it costs no money and one makes savings. The odd-job, many-job rural folk make "within the doors" what would otherwise have to be purchased. Because houses, foods, tools, and agriculture are much the same everywhere, the people can use their accumulated knowledge and skills in many places. The campesinos "reproduce" the market and its specializations not because they "precede" it or are "traditional" in their ways but because use of their skills saves money. Of course, this monetary savings is made at the cost of using their own labor, which keeps them working continuously. The ever-working, many-skilled campesino trying to make savings is the obverse of the specialized market trader attempting to make money.

Work is closely linked to ownership. The term "owner" (*dueño*) is applied broadly. An owner has the right to use and manage his property. The operative words are to "order" (*mandar*) and to "dispose" (*disponer*). One may be an owner of land, crops, animals, tools, a house, stored goods, or cooked food. Ownership is singular or shared and may be conferred by market purchase or by gift, but it is principally gained by working. Work itself, as we have observed, is owned, and a work owner gains rights to the product of the labor he owns. He or she has control over both the activity and its results.

In the house, ownership of things and work is shared equally by adult female and male. The initial appropriation of material objects occurs in the fields, and in this sense the labor of women does not normally initiate ownership. But women prepare food that sustains the field work, and all their other tasks help maintain the house. A man may come home at night to be served food by his spouse, or she may bring food to him in the fields, but the people see nothing servile in this. His work is said to be "heavier" but no more important than hers. The people often use the metaphor of a "team of oxen" to describe a married pair; sometimes one, sometimes the other exerts more force, but unless the two work together and pull in the same direction nothing will be accomplished. The work of both maintains the cycle from fields to house to food consumption to work.

This equivalency of male and female work emerges in various ways. Decisions about household property are made jointly. Before an animal is sold or a major purchase is made, the couple ordinarily discuss it, because the property belongs to both. A woman's work in the fields is considered the equal of a man's, and, though it occurs infrequently, she can exchange a day's field labor with a male. In addition, if a woman of one house does a day's cooking for a single man in another, her household receives a day of field labor in return. Within a house, male and female are seen as combining or pooling their equivalent labor rather than exchanging it. The genders work together (*trabajan de ambos a dos*). The woman and man are a pair, providing strength to each other, the man by his material efforts in the fields, the woman by her domestic efforts in the kitchen. Their work is interdependent, and each has rights to the joint product.

By keeping work "endogamous," the house creates property, makes savings, and builds a base. When house members work for themselves, they own the results of their efforts precisely because their force is house-maintained; by provisioning its members the house gains command over their labor and creates ownership of the results. Only in this way, with their lack of capital and inability to compete in the market, can the rural folk accumulate private property. As the people state, "Food rules" (*La comida manda*). It is understandable, then, why the campesinos say that a day worker "cannot live." His work is intermittent and his pay low, but, above all, he is not building a food reserve with which to provision himself, gain rights to his own labor, and accumulate a base. By his practices, the day worker signals his lack of access to a previously accumulated supply. To preserve and control the one resource – labor – with which they are endowed, or to be self-sustaining, is both the people's project for living and a reaction to the power that outside possession of private property confers. In order not to give labor rights to others, the house must supply its "force of food." This is both a way of making savings and the project for an economic group that lies on and beyond the margin of a market economy.

A conversation: the force of labor

The expression "labor-power" seems not to have been inscribed in Western literature before Marx. We have suggested, however, that like terms may have been common in European folk conversation and had their beginnings in the notion of divine might, projected upon and reflected in nature as strength or force, then severed from its origins to be used for the human alone. But whatever the semantic genealogy, Marx was part of a long conversation, and it is useful to examine the ways in which his voice and that of the rural folk combine and diverge.

One difference is partly a matter of word usage. Marx distinguishes between labor and labor-power. Labor-power, for Marx, is the human poised or equipped to work; labor is the effort that a human exerts when working. By contrast, for the campesinos the strength of labor is what the human consumes before working, what he has at the onset of work, and what he expends in it. The rural people do not draw a difference between labor-power and labor as does Marx, and they apply the term "force" to the human in action. These differences are connected to a more profound one.

To clarify, we return to the distinctions between stock and flow, fund and service. A stock is an accumulation of materials, a flow is the use of these over time; a fund is a "permanent" entity, while a service is the use of the fund over time. For the rural folk, the "force of work" is the energy stored in an individual and expended in work. This force comes from food and ultimately from the earth and God. It is not a historical cumulation that includes the skills and training of a worker but a physical quantity. The people speak of good and bad workers, the "knowledge" one needs for work, and the "spirit" one must have to work; the "force of work" is different from these and must be accumulated and stored beforehand. It is a "flow" into the person that is "stocked" and then used up in the flow of work.

This marks one difference from Marx, for whom labor-power is "the aggregate of those mental and physical capabilities existing in a human being, which he exercises whenever he produces a use-value of any description" (1967[1867]:167). Labor-power is a set of capacities that differs by historical period and individual training; it includes both physical and mental skills and lasts beyond a particular usage. In the opinion of Georgescu-Roegen (1971), labor-power as defined by Marx is a kind of human "fund" that renders a "service," labor. But Georgescu-Roegen claims that in the midst of his conversation, Marx converted his model of labor as "fund" to labor as "stock" so that he could reduce the "services" of labor to a "flow" of energy. By means of this shift, Marx was able to make commensurate what workers receive in wages and what they offer in labor. Labor-power and labor both became flows – one into the worker, the other from him – and Marx could then show that the difference between intake and output was appropriated by the capitalist. In Georgescu-Roegen's view, the human being "is degraded to a mere stock of energy for the sole purpose that the material means of production may also be denied the quality of agent" (p. 234).

But within the larger conversation that we are

examining, the interesting point is that Marx's rhetorical "degrading" of human labor from fund and service to stock and flow brings it closer to the Colombian model, though differences remain. For the Colombian folk, the "force of work" is the stock of energy a worker gains by eating and uses in work. In their lexicon, this force is "expended" or "used up" (*gastada*), but significantly the word covers both moments of the flow. In Marx, there is a difference between the two moments of labor-power and labor; these can be measured in volumes of goods, but the material volumes are reduced to quantities of labor. For Marx, labor is the source of value and the irreducible denominator. In the Colombian model, however, the human uses up force that can be traced to food, then to land, to nature, and finally to God's might. For the rural people, the capacity to work productively is not given in their being; rather, labor signifies force that comes from God. Because labor does not create value, there is no inherent value difference between the food expended when the worker eats and the work he or she expends when laboring.

We offer the suggestion that Marx "listened" to his economist predecessors, specifically Smith and Ricardo on labor value, and "heard" a folk lexicon on the power of labor, transforming it to his purposes. By contrast with the Colombian folk, Marx offered an antideistic, humanistic view of the person, yet he accomplished this by proposing, as they do, a materialist – or stock-versus-fund – model of the human.

TRANSACTIONS IN LABOR

Within the house, work is performed as a "house expenditure" and is unpaid. Outside the house, there is a labor market. In the countryside there are no labor halls, there is no written communication about the wage rate, and some of the people live hundreds of miles apart. But there is a labor market. For example, as one moves outward from a town or fertile zone toward a marginal area, the wage rate tends to drop; and the wage, though lagging inflation, rises over time and is fairly consistent from region to region. In 1984, around Soatá in northern Boyacá, the cash wage was approximately 250 pesos per day (plus meals). As one moved away from this center, the cash wage declined. Far to the north and east of Soatá, outside the small town of San Miguel, it was sometimes possible to find employment with other rural householders, but the going wage was 180 pesos per day. This was the lowest rate we encountered in 1984. By 1987 the cash wage around Soatá had risen to 400 pesos per day, but because the inflation rate had been at least 25 percent per year this did not represent increased purchasing power. In the same year, the daily wage in rural areas just outside Bogotá was nearly 1,000 pesos per day.[1]

The labor market is mostly for day workers (*jornaleros*), and the rural folk say that labor is "scarce." Laborers can be found to work for a day or two but not continuously. Even rich hacendados offering wages as "high" as 700 pesos per day are said to be unable to draw workers. The problem of attracting and holding workers is an old one in Colombia and elsewhere (Deas 1977; Brush 1977), but the theoretical problem it poses is that unemployment (or subemployment) seems to be coupled with labor scarcity, and this should not be; if unemployment is high, then labor cannot be scarce, and if labor is scarce, then unemployment should be low and wages should be high. As one talks to the people and listens to their explanations, however, this phenomenon becomes less puzzling. Partly, it has to do with temporal swings in labor needs; at peak times, when harvests are ripe, both haciendas and houses need and compete for labor. This is not the whole of the story, however. The people do not find, nor have they ever found, that the wage is sufficient to support a house. As they say, the wage worker at best "comes out even"; they prefer owning, pawning, renting, or sharecropping land, whatever the returns, to working for a daily wage. For them, wage work is to be done occasionally, in order to secure money for market purchases. It is performed by the younger people in a house and by single older males but has little attraction for the senior householder who supports a family.

A higher wage might "clear the market" and build a permanent labor force. But in the extramarginal zones no landowner can offer a higher wage, for raising the wage lifts the money costs, and this lowers the rate of profit still further or makes the finished product less competitive. If profit making units are to persist beyond the profit margin, the wage rate cannot be competitive – often it does not even purchase the basket of goods needed to sustain a worker and his family. For the smallholder, therefore, participation in the domestic economy of maintenance is the only recourse, and much the same pattern, magnified, is expressed by the haciendas, also marginal relative to the market.

When the rural folk do work for one another, they are remunerated in several ways. Occasionally, in northern Boyacá though not in Nariño, workers are paid in kind with wheat or potatoes. The volume of produce paid varies with the market prices of labor and the commodity so that the produce payment is roughly equivalent to the money price of labor. For example, when a sugar-mill owner makes *panela* (brown sugar), from six to twelve extra pairs of hands may be needed. For this short-term help, payment is made in *panela*; in fact, people work to obtain the necessity without having to pay cash for it. Both sides are financially better off because the costs of transport and marketing are eliminated: the volume of *panela* a worker receives is slightly more than he or she could purchase with the daily cash wage, while the amount the owner gives over is less than if it had to be converted to cash to make the wage payment. Ultimately, the *panela* "price" at which labor is remunerated is locally negotiated and falls between its selling and buying prices on the market.

In the past, especially on haciendas where in-kind payments were more frequently offered, a harvester was given an extra amount of the harvest itself. In maize, this was called the "Twelve Apostles" (*Los Doce Apóstoles*), and at the end of the harvest each worker selected six pairs of cobs. Also, during the harvest, when food is served to the workers, they may be fed in the harvest crop itself. Workers in wheat eat wheat cakes (*arepas*), while workers in potatoes eat potato soup. These perhaps are shorthand or representations of the day's project for the workers. Both the food serving and the harvest bonus are comparatively small payments.

Cooked foodstuffs have a more important place in the remuneration of labor. Hired workers usually earn cash or cash plus daily meals. These alternatives have various names depending on the region. In some areas, the distinction is known as work that is "free" (*libre*) or "at full cost" (*a todo costo*). Without food a worker might be paid 500 pesos a day or "at full cost," while with food he would be paid 300 pesos or "free." The worker is "free," say the people, because he does not have to go to market and feed himself, and he is "at full cost" when he has to bear the burden of feeding himself. In other regions the distinction is known as "little day" (with meals) and "big day" (cash alone). In much of the rural area the payment in cash plus food is encountered more often than its alternative, and the Colombian census bureau categorizes salaries throughout the country as with and without food (DANE 1987:157–73). The people explain that serving food to workers is more convenient and efficient, for the laborer may be working some distance from home, while the spouse of the work owner will have to cook anyway. But this seems to be a rationalization or an incomplete explanation, for some workers carry food to the fields or are served by their spouses there. The preference, like in-kind payment of *panela*, seems advantageous to both sides. For the worker's part, the value of the money plus meals is slightly larger than a cash payment alone; it would take more than the monetary wage offered to purchase (and cook) the same foodstuffs and still have the same remainder in cash. For the work owner, the payment in food and money is less expensive, for he can use food from his house stock. Even when food has to be bought, its cost is lower because of bulk purchase, though a house supplies as much food as possible from "inside the doors." Said otherwise, a house tries to make the food payment a material expenditure (*un gasto*) rather than a money cost (*un costo*). By serving food instead of paying a full wage, a house makes savings, substituting the work of the female and the base of the house for cash outlays. It incorporates the outside worker within its economy; as one person explained, serving meals is "as if the worker were from the house." Seen this way, the expressed distinction between the two forms of labor payment assumes a new dimension. The worker paid entirely in cash is "at full cost" (*un costo*), because the work owner cannot substitute a material expenditure (*un gasto*) for part of the money cost and so make savings in cash.

This practice of substituting meals for money is encountered outside agriculture, too. For example, workers in the small sugar mills who are paid wholly or in part by *panela* are fed during the day. We found the same practice in towns. In areas where bricks are made for sale – by mining clay, then mixing, drying, and baking it over several days – the full-time workers are paid in money plus daily meals. The owner's house is usually on the plot where the clay is secured, and he may have some crops on the land. The brick producer is trying to make money through the manufacture and sale of bricks; he pays for inputs and sells the output. But he uses the domestic model of making savings by substituting an expenditure of food for a money cost.

This pattern of using food payments is practiced in more extended ways. One cattle owner, with pasture several days' walk from his house, employed a young man to oversee his herd. They worked "by shares," with the young man receiving one of every four newborns. The owner also provided raw food, and though the worker's family had to cook it, the owner was insistent on providing foodstuffs rather than cash. He was ensuring that the worker had sufficient force to work, and with his double in-kind payment he avoided all monetary costs.

Because food sustains the strength of work and laborers are scarce, most work owners take some care to offer ample meals so that their laborers will feel satisfied, put in a good day, and leave with the desire to return another time. There are standards about the food that should be provided, although the number of meals varies by area, the content varies by ecological zone, and the expectations seem to have changed over time. In some areas, people claim that three meals used to be served but now four or five must be provided; and if only four are given, they should be large. In other regions, people say that less food is served now. In these respects, the food serving appears to be market-sensitive, though less than the cash wage.

In most areas, the rural folk speak of a food serving (*comida, alimentación*) jokingly as "a hit" (*un golpe*) or "a time" (*un tiempo*), although there are separate terms for the meals, too. For one region of Boyacá the five meals are as follows:

Breakfast. This meal, served at the beginning of the workday, may include hot chocolate or coffee, a broth of barley, maize, or potatoes, and bread; sometimes a mixture of ground maize and milk (*una mazamorra de maíz*) is served.

"Nine-thirties" (*mediasnueves*). This lighter repast, served after a few hours of work, consists of chocolate or a sweet drink (*guarapo, agua de panela,* or *agua de miel*) and a roll, or it may be composed of coffee with a wheat cake (*una arepa*) or a plate of potatoes.

Lunch. The main meal, usually served before noontime, includes beans, greens or potatoes, and perhaps maize. Sometimes a slice of meat is added. This is usually a "dry" meal in that no soup is provided.

"Elevenses" (*onces*). This snack, despite its name, is often served in the afternoon. It may consist of a roll or wheat cake with coffee or chocolate. If lunch is omitted, this meal is larger.

Dinner. This meal is usually served between five and six, after the day's work is completed. It may consist of potato soup and beans or soup and coffee. When only four meals are served, dinner is omitted, to be taken at home.

In practice, the meals are often simpler. We were often invited to share a main meal that consisted solely of a plate of potatoes or of rice garnished with a hot pepper sauce. But the quantity served is always ample whatever its nutritional value.

The fourth meal served is also known as "*el puntal*" (from "supporting beam"), which, as we have remarked, is a metaphoric projection of the house figure, the purpose being to "shore up" the force of work. The use of the term "*el puntal*" is not encountered in towns and cities, although in Bogotá people do speak of having "elevens" in mid-afternoon.

Unlike a payment in kind, which is raw food of a single type, such as wheat, barley, maize, or potatoes, to be taken home, the food provided to workers is cooked food ready to eat. It is not a general exchange good that can be put to various purposes; it has one use only, which is to be eaten.

Serving meals to workers lowers their cash cost; trading work with them eliminates it completely. Labor trade is found throughout the rural area, as it is in much of Latin America and other parts of the world. In rural Colombia it occurs only in agriculture. For one-time ventures such as building houses, a person invites many people to work for a day and eat amply. But labor trade consists of a transfer of equal effort between two or more persons. Usually, men trade work, but women do so occasionally. The work is measured by the day, with participants receiving like amounts for the effort expended. A group of two or more moves in sequence from plot to plot until all the credits and debits are balanced. The harvesting of domestic crops is facilitated by the gathering of a workforce, but today the trade is used most often in cash crops such as tobacco. This use of a nonmonetary transaction within the market context is due to the cash saving it permits; trading labor, by transforming costs to expenditures, is a way of making savings. Still, according to discussants and documentary sources, the practice of labor trade preceded the raising of crops for sale; even with crops for eating it was a way of avoiding money costs.

In addition to the type of crop, size of plot helps determine whether labor trade is used. If a man has only a little work, he does it alone, and if he has sufficient labor in the house he will deploy this first. But once a plot exceeds half a hectare, outside labour may be needed. In the crops for eating, four to five men form a useful group, for this allows them to spend a day or two on each plot in succession; but sometimes just two persons trade labor. The people who trade have approximately equal needs, with minor differences being adjusted by adding household labor and hiring day workers. Labor trade is not often used when plots exceed a hectare and a half or when there are great differences between participants in work requirements.

The owner of the labor feeds the workers and is in charge. Often, the owner brings a few extra tools, although each worker should have whatever is necessary, whether a hoe or a needle for stringing tobacco. The experienced owner tries to set an example by working steadily and well himself, "so that they know how to do the work." He directs the work but not by issuing peremptory orders. The people say that trading labor is pleasant, an antidote to boredom, and yields more than could be accomplished alone. The social nexus transforms and enhances the work of the individual.

The trade itself is set within broader social relationships. Because it is a delayed transaction, a loan to be repaid, the exchange must be underwritten by confidence and trust. Labor trade is always undertaken with neighbors, kin, or friends, for it is said that one can have little confidence in a stranger. Some explain that if one advanced wages to a stranger, he might not reappear to work off the loan. For him the advance and its liquidation would not be set within an enduring network of personal bonds.

The social relationships surrounding labor trade serve to sanction and control the work effort. In wage labor, a man may arrive late, spend time smoking cigarettes, or leave off early. But there are few inducements to underperform in the trade of labor, because a person receives back what he has given, and the enduring bonds of which the transaction is a part allow social sanctions to have full effect. When one man arrived late to a tobacco-drying session, he was greeted with "joking" remarks, such as whether he was really coming to work and whether his shortened evening contribution should be counted as a repayment. The participants in the trade are never anonymous market actors trying to gain short-term benefits. For this same reason, however, some of the hardest workers in the countryside say that trading labor and food is a constraint on their output compared with what they can achieve by themselves or by hiring others for cash.

The practice of labor trade is itself constructed by use of the house model. The expressed categories of the house and its doors, of the force of work and of food, of female and male, of uses and gains, and of ownership and control are all put to use in this relationship that links one house to another in the countryside. The exchange of labor is a creative and metaphoric application of the house model.

The verbal categories for the trade are revealing of the way it is put together. One series of expressions for the transaction comprises a substitutional set. The series is heard throughout the rural area, but within a region only one term is employed. Use of an expression outside its normal area elicits a nod, a querying look, a laugh of recognition, and finally a denial that it is the appropriate term. The expressions we recorded for labor trade include:

"returned hand," "loaned hand," "returned arm," "loaned arm," "arm for arm," "back for back," and "rib for rib."

Each refers to a body part; all are shorthands for the upper body that is used in field labor. Other verbal formulations include "lent work" and "lent force," "worker trade," "trading strength," "force returned," and "in trade." In addition, the transaction can be expressed in terms of "help"; one person says to another, "Ay, compadre, help me and I will return it to you." The exchange is also voiced in terms of time, as in "time returned" (*el tiempo vuelto*).

The various words highlight different aspects of the transaction. All are lexical modifications of terms used for house labor – force, work, help, time – and for movement through the doors – trade, loan, return. The people draw upon and "detach" work – as it were – from "inside the doors" to see it as traded between houses. The terms also formulate the transaction as an exchange of identities ("back for back," "work traded," "time returned," "hand returned"); a house receives back exactly what it has given. Thus, when talking about labor trade, the people speak of "replacing" the work, the term used when the base is traded for an equivalent. This exchange of identities is implied also by the word "loan." In the countryside no interest is charged on loans, while a loan of a tool, animal, or seed is paid back as it was borrowed. A rural loan is a delayed trade of equivalents. Also, both a rural loan and labor trade are termed "help." The word "help" often refers to assisting the land to give crops or force, but the people say that "everyone needs the help of others." To receive work one must lend it, because other houses need one's help just as one needs theirs. "Helping one another" (*ayudarse unos con otros*) refers to the help that one house offers another in its project of helping the land or assisting the base.[2]

Trading labor is also known as "gaining a worker" (*ganar un peón*), another application of the house schema. The word "gain" is used principally for a movement from outside the doors to inside. Any movement out the doors is a "loss" (*una pérdida*). Unpaid labor that comes in the doors is expended in-house and has to be repaid by a worker going out.

In working for others in a trade, a person gains no rights to the objects on which he works, for these belong to the owner of his labor; but he does gain a claim on the labor of the person for whom he works. When this outside work is repaid, it transforms material things and yields possession of them to his own house. The concept of possession is applied from ownership of objects gained through work within the house to ownership of others' labor, gained through work outside the house; finally, ownership of this outside work, which is brought inside, gives rights of possession to things within the house.

In the people's view, trading labor is a primary way of making savings. When outside help is needed, the choice is between paying others in cash or kind or recruiting them through trading labor. By transacting in labor, a person accumulates his work with others and then regains it, so labor trade is a way of controlling unpaid house effort and a roundabout way of building a base. By trading labor a man effectively is making his own product without the mediation of money or prices. The people explain that since money is scarce, they trade labor; or, as one man said, "What you do without paying day laborers remains for you." The trade of labor is an off-the-market exchange between houses.

The transaction actually is a total house trade, for it is an exchange of both work strength and the food that maintains it. Labor trade draws upon the two main functions of the house and presumes a common set of expectations for them. The intensity and duration of a day's work vary by house, with some starting early and others late, but labor trade has locally shared parameters. When on his own, a person may eat less food "to economize," but in the trade of labor, four or five ample meals, more than in some houses, must be provided. Because there are precise expectations about food to be served and hours worked, a house cycles between the privacy of its own standards and social demands. Trading labor is a transaction between the dual functions of houses, putting these into the public domain and calling for sustained enactment of both; it is a social performance of house processes, representing the domestic economy turned outward, put on display and joined to others.

Labor trade is a total transaction also because it involves both genders in relation to the two flows upon which a house depends. Unlike everyday practices, in which food preparation and field work, female and male, are joined, labor trade splits the performance of gendered tasks. The temporal separation creates a dialectic whose resolution is reached by completion of the exchange.

This aspect of the transaction involves the relation between "use" and "gain" and "from inside the doors" and "from outside the doors." When a man works outside, trading labor, he incurs no expenditures, because he is using up the food of others while gaining a worker. When the work is returned, his house has extra expenditures of food as his own gain of labor, from outside to inside, is repaid. One house has food expenditures and the expenditure of labor as another gains a worker; later, the second has food expenditures and the use of labor as the first pays back its gain of work.

The transaction keeps food and work directly linked. When a man works for another house, it provides him with the force to work; that house's use of labor is also its expenditure of food. In reverse, when that house repays the labor, its workers are fed, because their work is for the recipient house. Work and food are always joined, because the work has come "inside the doors" and is owned. The trade of labor represents an expansion and contraction of domestic boundaries; through the provision of foodstuffs, others are temporarily included within a house's economy.

The male and female contributions operate in reverse. When a male works for other houses, the female "receives" by not having to cook; and when a male receives labor from other houses, the female contributes by cooking for all the workers. A man replicates his labor by working for others over time, storing it with them, and then receiving their labor all at once. A woman saves having to cook for a man over several days but then replicates the labor of others through extra work at a moment in time. And where a woman performs her domestic work alone and in the kitchen, a man performs his material work with others outside the physical house. Material work "moves" the people through the doors, while domestic work does not.

Trading labor thus engages the double functions of a house in opposite ways. Food consumed and work performed, normally joined, are split apart; and the male and female contributions are undertaken in reverse. When a woman is saving domestic work, a man is expending effort in agriculture; and when a man is receiving work, a woman is expending it. Pressure to complete the transaction comes from the need not only to meet external obligations but also to have internal closure of house processes. Labor received and food repaid erase external gains and obligations and rebalance gender-linked tasks within the house.

Labour trade is thus a projection and a transformation of the house model itself. Within a house "working together" is a union of differences in labor between the sexes. By contrast, labor trade between houses is an equivalent exchange that calls upon the separate accumulation of female and male work. This exchange of identities between houses, however, operates by splitting apart normally joint labor within a house and setting it into a dialectical relationship whose resolution also completes the external transaction.

Conversations: reciprocity, exchange, and local traditions

Since the early part of this century, anthropologists have studied exchange and reciprocity in other societies and our own. The collected knowledge, diverse and rich in detail, has stimulated its own increase and textual speculation. But no theory has emerged that seems capable of encompassing all cases, and the anthropological community has never agreed upon a single model. Anthropological views seem to fall within two competing models, one of which comes from economists. This one can be traced to Smith and his portrayal of market trade. For Smith, exchange derives from several inherent features of the human. As animals, humans are endowed with differing natural capacities, although these are not great; humans develop these differing skills through their unique "propensity to truck, barter, and exchange," a disposition that is encouraged by self-interest (Smith 1976[1776]:17). Exchange itself is found in all societies, being an outcome of people behaving in their self-interest, given their differing skills and resources. This market model has been elaborated and amended for two hundred years, and much of neoclassical economics is still based upon its presuppositions. In sociology, echoes of Smith's conversation can be found in the writings of Blau (1955), Homans (1962), and Heath (1976), while in anthropology the principal exponents have been "formalist" economists (LeClair and Schneider 1968; Schneider 1974). Recent work by anthropologists on decision making calls into play related voices (Barlett 1980).

In opposition to this Anglo-American conversation on exchange is the continental one associated with the work of Mauss (1954[1925]), Malinowski (1961[1922]), and Lévi-Strauss (1969) but also elaborated by Polanyi (1968) and Sahlins (1972). According to this model, reciprocity – or the obligation to give, receive, and return – is an irreducible feature of human life. In Lévi-Strauss's argument, which represents a developed form of the model, reciprocity is based upon "certain fundamental structures of the human mind" and is a mode of integrating the inherent opposition between self and other (1969:75, 84). Because reciprocity is the fundamental social act and a mental operation, it is embedded in human institutions, and we should never "confuse the principle of reciprocity, which is always at work and always oriented in the same direction, with the often brittle and almost always incomplete institutional structures used by it to realize the same ends" (Lévi-Strauss 1969:76).

Both these conversations on reciprocity and exchange

suppose the existence of building blocks from which all forms of exchange can be derived. In the Smith model, the irreducible element is the propensity of humans to use the physical and social worlds in self-interested exchange. In the Lévi-Strauss model the building block is the opposition between self and other and its resolution through exchange. The high degree of understanding yet heated difference between the discussants indicates that they share the same mode of reasoning or rhetorical form but differ in their assumptions and ultimate interpretations. The conversation from Colombia offers a different perspective. Certainly, trading labor or helping other houses is an example of reciprocity, and certainly it is a self-interested exchange. But this is not the way the people talk about it. For them, the trade of labor has no rock-bottom feature but draws upon several voices of the house: the base and its uses, the "doors," male and female, force, food, physical work, being thrifty, and help in the divine and domestic spheres. In this perhaps lies a critique of the reductionistic inscriptions that have come to dominate our own conversation.

Chapter 7

REMAINDERS

We never expected the word *"la sobra"* to give us difficulty. According to the dictionary, *"la sobra"* means "surplus" or "excess," and we anticipated that folk usage, from the margin, would provide some insight into the modern uses of "surplus" and "profit" that have long been at the center of theories in economics and anthropology. But as the practices of the rural people unfolded and as we were drawn into conversations, the incorrectness of our initial expectation became clear. *"La sobra"* never fitted the lexical position we had assigned it, its usage remained shifty, and regardless of the conversational ploy we tried, the rural folk could not be induced to talk about it as the house counterpart of corporate profit. Only after some time, and conversations among ourselves, did we come to a better appreciation of the term.

We now gloss *"la sobra"* as the "leftover," "remainder," "remains," or "excess." In rural usage, the word is a shorthand for *la sobra de la casa*, "house leftover." The verb form "exceed" (*sobrar*) is also heard, while *el sobrado* designates the kitchen loft or pantry shelf where the (leftover) crops are stored. *La sobra*, we came to understand, has several applications, although it almost always refers to the flow of crops within the house. Its opposite expression is *el gasto de la casa*, "house expenditure." Together expenditures and remainders make up a processing schema that is applied to agricultural flows: the "expended" and the "unexpended" are paired terms covering a sequence of house uses. The corporate, written schema of accounting has a "bottom line," and this provides the ultimate measure of its success or failure, its competitive position within the market world. The house model has no goal or end; it is a mode of life, a set of practices. The remainder designates not a final state but a momentary leftover within a larger series of house activities.

In the context of the domestic model, the expression "managing well" (*mandar bien*) refers to the interplay of house expenditures and remainders. More pointedly, the frequently voiced reminder to be thrifty or make savings refers to using the schema, for this is the act and the art of turning leftovers to uses, transforming remainders to expenditures, and wasting nothing.

The house remainder is also a category of product distribution. As a harvest is used or expended by a house, the "excess" is always the leftover after a prior expenditure. Needs of the house are sequentially deducted, leaving a series of remainders, so that the excess is the "leavings" of house expenditures just as, in the early Ricardian model, profits are the "leavings of wages" (Dobb 1973:70). But this house schema is also fitted into a larger economic system. Before a harvest reaches a house, it may be partially used to fulfill a rent or crop-sharing obligation. This extrahouse distribution has no effect on the form of the house schema, although it reduces the stock available for use. As the schema is used, the house may also engage in trade. Any volume traded is said to be a "leftover," even if house needs have not been met. The schema thus reveals the way in which house processes are "articulated" with the market. We think that an examination of this connection between the house model of the margin and the corporate model of the center provides a very different perspective on the processes of "underdevelopment" and the ways in which marginality is perpetuated.

The house schema is widely used – in different ecological zones, for different crops, for multicrops, and for cash crops as well. One variation that we have observed may have special implications for theorists of the center. Under extremely poor conditions, the people of the periphery may be reduced to raising one crop only for home consumption; in these instances, the house economy closely approximates a "one-sector" or "one-commodity" economy. Models of the one-commodity economy have been of considerable interest to ancient and modern economists, who have used them to deduce relationships and build more complex models, to generate hypotheses and prove theorems, and to reveal important economic relationships. The advantage of a one-sector model is that it eliminates the need for a separate measure of value by collapsing the distinction between value and physical relationships. As the two are the same, "capital" is not a number but a material, and the reasons for changes in its physical volume – from population increase to technological shifts – can be easily modeled. Blaug has shown how the one-sector model was unwittingly used in the two-Cambridges debate, inspired by Sraffa's (1960) work, about "reswitching capital" and has provided examples of its use in models about investment, capital–output ratios, savings, growth, and the real rate of interest (Blaug 1978:553–4, 264, 539, 566).

But in the positivist tradition of economics, a sharp distinction is drawn between "the model" and "observable phenomena" in the "real world" (Friedman 1953:24–5), and consequently the economists' discussion of the one-commodity economy has been sealed off from the larger conversation, involving practicing humans, of which it is inevitably a part. The one-sector economy is only a textual model. Economists have never discovered or considered the possibility of discovering a one-commodity economy in the "real world." We think, therefore, that our finding of a one-sector model constitutes a true discovery for textual economics. But its occurrence on the margin of the market also inverts many of the standard assumptions, for implicitly (Pasinetti 1977) and sometimes explicitly (Ricardo 1951[1815]) the one-commodity economy has been seen as the logical and historical core or the governing essence of a market system. Should it be considered ironic that we have found the one-commodity economy where it ought not to be – on the periphery not the center, at the margin not the core?

THE HOUSE SCHEMA

House allocation of the agricultural product is based upon repeated application of the division between use and remainder (fig. 7). First, from any harvest, whether in beans, maize, potatoes, or another crop, an initial portion is set aside "for seeding" (*para sembrar*). This amount allows for restitution of the cycle or returning to (*volver a*) planting. The volume sequestered varies by household, year, and plans; for example, a house may decide to start up, to renew, to expand, or to cease planting a crop, its selection being expressed through the amount it sets aside as seed. After the seed has been allocated, a segment of the leftover is earmarked "for eating" (*para comer*). Again, the volume varies, in this case depending on the size of the house and its overall consumption desires and needs. Also, some of the house consumers will be working as they are eating but others will not, so the house may need to plan on feeding outside laborers. This second, consumption use of the crop, like the first, is considered to be a means for returning to planting; it keeps the crop "inside the doors" and within the base→base' circuit.

The third use of the crop is closely linked to the second. In order to purchase "necessities," a portion of the harvest may be earmarked "for selling" (*para vender*). These needs include food and clothes as well as means of production, such as fertilizer, insecticide, and tools. In this use of the crop, said to be a way of replacing (*reponer*) the base, one

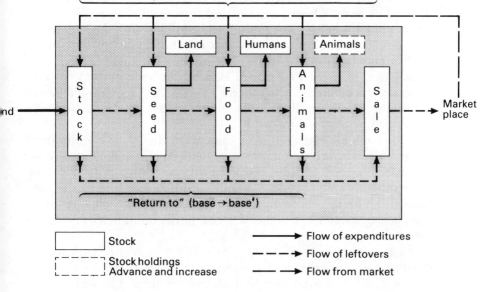

Figure 7 The house schema

part of the harvest is traded through the doors for something different that comes from outside to inside. This, too, is considered to be a house use of leftovers and a way of returning to planting, being an indirect deployment of the crop to meet house needs. It takes the house into the base→money→base' circuit.

Some of the crop may still be left over after these several uses. Occasionally, this remainder is held for a time, but if the crop is suitable as fodder and does not last long before spoiling it may be fed to an animal and "kept" in this form as a "reserve." As the people point out, it is better to feed maize to animals than to trade it for something else, because a market exchange usually does not replace the base. When kept "for the animals" (*para los animales*), the crop remains part of the base, constituting the new portion added to it from the agricultural cycle. This is a base→base' transaction and a house expenditure.

In addition to the several divisions between house uses (for seeding, for eating, for the animals) and remainders, a part of the house figure is used to designate a subpart of the house flow. The longhand expression "kitchen remains" (*la sobra de la cocina*) is used for scraps of cooked or processed foods that are the leftovers on a plate or in the pot. Instead of being allowed to spoil and then thrown away or – in the exact phrase – being "lost to use" (*echado a perder*), they are fed to domestic animals, such as hogs, that are stationed right outside the walls. This is an act of thrift. The kitchen remainder, like a crop remainder, is saved and turned into an advance by feeding it to animals, the difference being that it has traveled an extra step before becoming a leftover. It is cooked versus raw food and has been processed by the force of work.

The people are ingenious at avoiding waste, but not everything from a harvest can be saved, and sometimes leftovers spoil. For example, an abundant harvest of fruit, too expensive to transport for sale and unsuitable as animal fodder, usually spoils before it is totally consumed. This is like throwing it "out the doors." Such items are lost to use, savings cannot be made, and use of the distribution schema comes to an end.

At the other extreme, a crop may not be sufficient to meet the seeding and consumption requirements of a house. This is expressed, as noted, by the spatial metaphor of "not reaching" the next harvest; such shortages are also discussed as a "lack" or "want" of a necessity. These constructs are part of the distribution pattern, too, indicating that the schema of expenditures and remainders cannot be fully used.

Finally, the term "leftover" may be used even when the crop does not restore itself through house use or market trade. Several crops, such as potatoes and beans, do not keep well; maize is one of the few harvests that lasts a year, and that only in the highlands. A harvest volume that cannot be used before it spoils is usually sold. This sold portion is also known as a "remainder," even if the foodstuff has to be bought again later and, furthermore, even if the amount taken to market is not fully "replaced" through the trade. In other words, a harvest may have a leftover even when it does not cover its own needs of reproduction directly or through the market and its lack has to be made up by the expenditure of another crop. The remainder of a crop is figured with respect to its total house uses rather than to the expenditures needed in its next crop cycle. The leftover is the amount of a harvest not set aside for one and then another "use of the house." It is part of a total *domestic* calculation.

The processing schema, then, is based on the opposition of use and remainder, expenditure and leftover. It is a kind of iterative program for distributing the house flow from agriculture. The schema incorporates the major moments of seeding, eating, provisioning the animals, and trading, but it does not specify the amounts for each. Every step is figured in relation to the prior and the proximate, and the schema can feed back upon itself. For example, a house may skip setting aside part of the harvest for seed, allocate something for eating, and then trade the leftover for a different or better variety of seed. A house may also cater to its own tastes by keeping for food a smaller portion of one crop and a larger portion of another. To take account of a change in harvest sizes or to invest more in animals, a house may raise or lower its consumption level. The schema also accommodates varying aspirations or different "subjective utilities" from "Protestant" reinvestment for the future to "Catholic" consumption in fiestas and religious celebrations in the present. It has nothing to do with "motivation" or achievement drive; and this house model – which we believe has wide applicability – is irrelevant for determining whether a society will "take off" into economic growth. By its use of the processing schema, the house is neither a limited nor an ever growing economy.

Conversations: remainders and profit

The people speak little about a "surplus" (*un excedente*), and while they talk about profit this is covered by the word "gain" (*la ganancia*). The remainder is different from both. One distinction is that it is calculated not by matching a harvest with its expenses of production but with reference to future plans. The temporal frame in which a flow of expenditure is set against its flow of revenue is broken apart, and the revenue or stock from one agricultural cycle is set against a planned flow of expenditures in the next, with a remainder emerging after each budgeted deduction. A corporation works up an "after-the-fact" profit statement that makes the two flows of income and costs appear to be simultaneous and brings to a close each independent production cycle, usually conceived of as a year. By contrast, in the domestic economy the returns from one agricultural cycle are forwarded to cover expenditures in the next. The house schema links one cycle and its product directly to the subsequent, bringing a cyclical notion (return to seeding) and a linear construct (the advance) together.

The house schema, in addition, is used only for a flow of goods and is unlike a corporate statement that compares two stocks from different times. A crop leftover is a moment within a larger activity, that of sustaining the house, being relative to what has been done previously and will be done next. By contrast, the corporation calculates both a final yearly outcome, which is profit, and the rate of profit. This involves setting a time period, measuring two flows (income and expenditure), summing up their difference as a stock (the profit), and then calculating the ratio of the incremental stock to the initial one (the rate of profit). The corporate statement brings together a flow of time with moments of time in order to summarize its operations in a final number. A profit or surplus is a fixed amount. When the rural people say that they "do not keep accounts" (*no se lleva la cuenta, no se cuenta*), they are marking one difference between the schema of house flows and the accounting inscriptions of the corporation that fix its profits. This is coordinate with the fact that the house uses mainly circulating holdings, forever being used up and retrieved, while the corporation employs both circulating and fixed wealth, which gives it temporal continuity and "perpetual succession." We surmise that the increase of durable capital itself – whether due to technological change or social reorganization – creates, or at least amplifies, this difference between continuous house making, on the one hand, and the written fictions of the corporation, on the other.

There is a third, important difference between the remainder and profit. No domestic crop is an independent center or costing unit. A crop leftover is figured in relation to its proximate seed costs and to *all* future house expenditures, including feeding the labor for it and feeding the workers in other crops as well as providing for consumption in nonlabor time. The volume of a crop remainder depends on its harvest size and on total house needs as well as the provisions in place from other crops. Within a house, there is cross-commodity feeding; expenditures of one crop support work performed on it and on others, just as the returns from the others sustain work on the initial one. The crops are interlaced as if they were a single commodity, even though the people speak of leftovers in each. One result is that as total house expenditures rise, one or another crop remainder must fall.

The last of the remainders of a crop is what it, in relation to all other production activities, adds to the base.

But because a leftover in one crop may be counterbalanced by high expenditure in another, its appearance does not imply that the base is growing. Furthermore, the leftover itself may be fed to an animal in order to store it as a reserve, and the animal may grow and multiply, which augments the base. The people do say that "a good harvest gives more base," but they also point out that only over time can one tell if the base is increasing. Neither a single agricultural cycle nor an accounting year reveals what is occurring with the holdings of the house, and in this respect also house and corporate models diverge.

POTATOES ON THE *PÁRAMO*: A ONE-SECTOR ECONOMY

The material practices of the campesinos who live on the *páramo* outside Cumbal provide an extreme and clear example of the way the house schema is used. The area can be reached in various ways, and one of the journeys graphically demonstrates the transition from the world of the capital-using, profit making corporation in the center to that of the labor-using house at the periphery. The trip begins in Cali, a major city with direct air links to North America. Nestled against a mountain chain at 800–900 meters, Cali boasts manufacturing and assembly plants and is surrounded by a rich plain, mostly sown in sugarcane. The crop, raised by modern methods, is processed into a variety of products sold in world markets. South of Cali, following the road through Cauca, land use shifts to intensive pastoralism. Then, as the road rises, the land becomes broken and less fertile. Cattle are still raised but more extensively and with less attention to the grasses sown, while interspersed among the pasture lands are small agricultural plots. Finally, at the border between the Departments of Cauca and Nariño, the small farm appears in profusion. Around Pasto, the capital of Nariño, every space is cultivated, the land has a patchwork appearance, and the area is characterized by a plethora of micro-environments. With the exception of the trunk route, which carries on to Ecuador, nearly all the roads are unpaved. Cumbal, some hours south of Pasto, is reached by a dirt road that crosses a plain dedicated to pasture. In the hills around Cumbal, where potatoes, grains, and lima beans are grown on tiny plots, the land is occasionally plowed by a small tractor or oxen. West of Cumbal a dirt track leads upward to the *páramo*. Along the way, pasture quality drops, scrub vegetation increases, and the crops disappear one by one at specific altitudes, except for potatoes. On the *páramo* itself there is no mechanized farming.

Agriculturalists wield steel-tipped tools and sometimes use the ox-drawn plow. In the higher and more distant areas the technology shifts again; slash-and-burn agriculture is practiced, the people relying on nature rather than labor and tools to regenerate the soil, and some of the steel-tipped implements give way to wooden ones. Made in the home, these tools require no command over capital funds for their acquisition. Finally, in the highest reaches of the *páramo*, where the land is rockiest and the weather inclement, even swidden agriculture ceases. At the far end of the *páramo*, a single family lives on a small and infertile plot. This piece of land, which cannot support sustained agricultural activity, marks the limit of human habitation.

By any measure – weather, soil fertility, transportation network, market accessibility – the *páramo* is a marginal area. The people cannot even keep house gardens, for at nearly 4,000 meters the potato is practically the only food crop that grows, and even it is raised with difficulty. If a variety takes six months to grow around Cumbal, it requires seven to eight months at the higher altitude. Yields also drop on the *páramo*, and the people say that the land is "sterile." Frost can wipe out an entire seeding, for which reason the people plant small quantities several times a year and in different areas. Flat bottomland is easier to work but riskier, as the frost falls there rather than on the slopes. Much of the planting, therefore, is done on small hills, and this increases the amount of needed labor. During the day, working conditions in the rain, wind, and cold are harsh, and not even well-built houses provide full shelter from the brisk winds that blow at any hour; in any event, swirling smoke from the kitchen fire makes the warmth of the hearth an ambiguous comfort. In part because of the cold, the earth is difficult to break; if a plow is used, the oxen must make several passes before the land is properly prepared. Sometimes the earth is too hard even for the animals. Once we observed a group of men making furrows with hoes in advance of an ox team; after the oxen had made four passes, the men came back to turn the soil yet again. Here, the "simpler" technology of human-powered, steel-tipped implements had to supplement and replace the more "advanced" technique of the ox-drawn plow. But this tailing off in the use of capital equipment or fixed holdings might be expected at the margin and beyond. In fact, the *páramo* was hardly populated twenty to thirty years ago, and only pressure on better land elsewhere has induced people to live there.

The people of the *páramo* subsist primarily on the potatoes they raise. This has several striking implications. Livelihood on the high plains, in the first place, constitutes an example of the one-sector economy that economists have used in written models. It also illustrates with great clarity the distributional relationships of the domestic economy, for where a single good is being produced and consumed the way the year's product is allocated to different uses – the way the house schema of expenditures and leftovers is applied – is readily observable and talked about by the people. There is no possibility of market mystification here, for distribution is carried out directly after a harvest, first in the field and then at home, as the people sort potatoes. Distribution on the *páramo* does not take place by the allocation of tokens or symbolic counters, such as money, nor does it unfold by disconnected stages through the year. It is enacted at once by sorting and piling potatoes.

On the *páramo* the potato is eaten three to four times a day. A midday meal for field workers may consist of a broth of potatoes followed by a plate filled with seven to ten potatoes, eaten with a hot chili sauce. As one man said, "The potato is the potato; it is a primordial custom to have potatoes. What is more important?" Potato agriculture does not encompass all economic activities on the *páramo*. As we have seen, cattle and other animals are kept, and in the forests high on the mountain trees are felled and split into firewood for sale. But the potato is the focus of the local economy and the principal means for making savings.

We once viewed a potato harvest in which allocation for extradomestic obligations and the process of intrahouse distribution were both revealed. The extradomestic relationships were "encoded" in the physical layout of the potato plot, while the internal distribution became visible in the house patio (fig. 8). A father and son together were sharecroppers with a widowed landowner. They had a single field, on a hill, with potatoes planted in rows running up and down. Father and son shared their work and hired others for the harvest by paying them in cash and in kind. They had divided the field by its rows, with one on the left and the other on the right. They worked across the plot equally and as a team but split their share of the harvest two to one, father to son, as the father had provided the seed and paid most of the money costs. The pair had also planted two varieties of potato, *morazurco* and *sabanera*, which they ended up splitting unequally. Their sharecropping arrangement with the landowner was unusual; normally, the harvest is split evenly or in favor of the landowner, but in this case the ratio was four to one for the croppers. They had borne all the farming expenses, which had been considerable, and the land-owner was principally interested in rejuvenating the field for agriculture, protecting it from squatters, and securing good seed so that her teenage sons could start a cycle of potato agriculture for her house. To

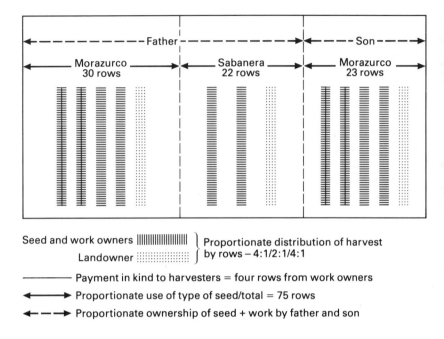

Figure 8 Potato field and harvest

make this distribution with the landowner, the croppers harvested four rows in sequence, leaving every fifth to be seen by the landowner and harvested by her the next day. The croppers explained that this was easier than harvesting all the potatoes at once and then allocating the shares from a central pile. As it happened, the widow's two sons helped the croppers in their harvest, and they assisted later in the harvesting of her share. The sharecropping division, thus, came "off the top." In addition, each of the two harvesters hired for the two days was fed, paid 200 pesos, and allocated a row of potatoes to collect at the end of each day. These four rows were interspersed among the ones earmarked for the croppers. A row, it was thought, would yield approximately one sack of potatoes, which on the market would cost about 350 pesos, though it would sell for considerably less. Both sides did well by this arrangement, and the workers specifically wanted to obtain good eating potatoes. Their total return was rather higher than a cash wage with meals, but they had had to bear travel costs to reach this remote spot. For their part, the croppers saved by avoiding the transport cost to market and receiving only the sale price of the potatoes;

they also made a practice of "cooperating" with others. All these parts of the harvest allocation were displayed in the field itself.

The remainder of the distribution, internal to the house, took place once the potatoes had been dug up and carried home, but a part was begun in the field. Market categories have an impact on the domestic allocation. On the market, potatoes are divided into first-, second-, third-, and fourth-class produce according to size and quality. "Thick" potatoes are the better and larger ones, while "thin" is a residual category. Thick potatoes are first- and second-class potatoes in market terms. In the field, a harvester drags along two baskets, one for each type, and upon digging out the potatoes he sorts them immediately into thick and thin. Only a portion, if any, of the thick potatoes is ever sold, but the people's first selection is influenced by the market classification.

After this initial allocation, the potatoes are usually packed into sacks and carried to the house, where subsequent divisions are made. Here the labor is performed by house members alone, both male and female, whether or not they worked in the field. At the house the potato harvest is sequentially separated into three portions. First, seed for the subsequent year (*para sembrar*) is selected and set aside. As one person said:

> If the seed finishes, everything ends. If I only had a sack or two of potatoes, I would seed them before eating them. And I would never sell the potato completely – how can you end it? You always need some for seed.

A house sometimes finds itself without sufficient or proper seed, in which case it may trade for a different variety, purchase more, or make a different arrangement, as in the case of the widowed landowner. When people speak of going to the market on Sunday, they always mention that they will buy a "a little salt," but as one person then added, "Before salt you need seed. If there is nothing for the salt, worse yet to have to buy seed." The reproduction of seed, because without it one has no chance for making savings, constitutes the first moment of the harvest distribution and the first division of the flow into expenditure and remainder.

The seed is selected from small, equal-sized potatoes – usually thinner ones. Small potatoes, say the people, provide a better and more consistent yield than large ones, but this is also a way of making savings. A sack of small potatoes, because the number of potatoes is greater, yields more seed than a same-sized sack of large ones; to secure the same seed quantity in large potatoes would require twice the number of sacks. On the market, potatoes are purchased by weight, and one sack weighs much the same as another. For eating, too, one sack lasts the same as another, so one makes savings by using small potatoes for seed.

The volume of potatoes put aside for seed varies with the house. On the *páramo* variation in rainfall is hardly noticeable, and potatoes can be seeded in nearly any month rather than just twice a year as in lower areas. The time from seeding to harvest takes longer, but the seeding can be done so frequently that the interval between planting in one field and reaping in another may be short. The tasks of cultivation militate against seeding every day to ensure a daily harvest for the kitchen pot, but some people have as many as four harvests in a year. This temporal separation provides some insurance against bad weather. The frequency of seeding, which sets the interval between harvests, helps determine the size of harvest needed. The harvest, in turn, is linked to seed volume by traditional productivity ratios. The people point out that yields are lower on the *páramo*. In the cold area, seed-to-harvest ratios are one to four or one to six. (In lower areas, the ratio improves to one to eight or as much as one to twenty.) Using these approximations the people convert needed harvest to seed volume and set aside the required quantity. With this in mind, they then prepare sufficient land. It is better, they say, to spend too much time preparing land than to have too much seed. If an abundance of land is readied, one can always seed it later; but if there is an excess of seed, more land must be prepared. One should never lose the seed; even in the case of extreme necessity one should not eat it, for "it is one's lot and obligation to seed."

After the seed has been put into sacks and set aside, a second amount is allocated for eating (*para comer*). This includes the consumption requirements of laborers, from within and outside the house, who will reproduce the potatoes, as well as the needs of the remaining members. This portion also varies according to the proximity of the next harvest, whether two, four, or eight months away. Sometimes the budgeted amount does not "reach" the harvest, and sometimes there are leftovers, but the people generally are adept at earmarking the required supply and never express concern over their ability to project expenditures. This portion is taken from the second-, third-, and first-class potatoes. As this selection is being made, very small and damaged potatoes – fourth-class ones – are set aside to be used as feed for household animals (*para los animales*). This second allocation, then, covers sustenance for the house until the next harvest, including support for needed labor and keeping the domestic animals; along with the first distribution it permits the house to return to planting.

Finally, if any first- or second-class potatoes remain, they are sent to market (*para vender*). The cash received is first used to buy fertilizer for the next crop. Once this production need is met, the money is spent on foodstuffs and clothes. For fertilizer, the house is dependent upon a market transaction; however, its purpose is to replace the base and ensure the agricultural cycle: market sale of potatoes from the margins of the *páramo* signals participation in the base→money→base′ circuit rather than the circuit of money→base→money′. But transport cost from the *páramo* is high, while productivity is low, prices drop at harvest time, frost is unpredictable, and harvests may not yield a first-class product, and consequently the volume of potatoes sent to market is often small. In fact, if the prevailing price does not cover final harvest cost and transport, the people leave a crop remainder in the ground. The *campesinos* certainly cannot withhold potato production, but the supply reaching the market is determined first by harvest size and house need, then by anticipated price.

The distribution pattern, thus, begins with the selection of potatoes for *potential* sale – the thick ones – and then focuses on the potatoes to be used for seed (*para sembrar*), for house use (*para comer, para los animales*), and finally for actual sale (*para vender*). The sequential divisions of the flow are all forms of making savings: producing and saving potatoes for seed offers a costless input for the next harvest and the possibility of costless consumption after it; allocating a portion for house expenditures avoids the purchase of foodstuffs until the next harvest; sale of the leftover provides cash for fertilizer and other foods, which are market goods but purchased from funds ultimately supplied by costless inputs. What the house trades on the market is its remainder after reproducing, as far as possible, its conditions of production.

In the marginal conditions of the *páramo*, potatoes sometimes fail to be self-sustaining and the cycle becomes money-absorbing, maintained only because potatoes are a needed comestible. Several activities support the single-commodity cycle by injecting cash, and for each of these the people make savings by going off-the-market to "produce" something that can be sold. In these cases raising cash is peripheral or subordinated to the project of maintaining the house. At the margin's margin, everything is reversed; money is secured to support making savings, which itself is practiced on the margin of making money. Most of the activities involve using land and labor above.

Wage labor at a potato harvest or on one of the cattle *fincas* helps little, for it is occasional and short-term; to find longer-lasting work the people have to leave the *páramo*. The raising and sale of cattle and sheep provide some cash, and the advent of dairying in the past several years has helped some small farmers, but most lack access to pasture.

Money is sometimes gained through the appropriation and sale of natural resources. High on the mountain above the *páramo* lies a glacier, and a few people journey there, cut blocks of ice, and transport it to lowland towns, where it is crushed, flavored, and sold in paper cups on the street. Sulphur deposits also exist above the *páramo*, and the mineral is occasionally secured and sold in Cumbal for use in local remedies. Securing firewood from the forests for sale in Cumbal is of much greater importance. The usual trip from *páramo* to market takes four to five hours; the wood is carried by horse, each load having a 1986 value of 200–300 pesos depending on its size and dryness. Members of a family usually work together and escort a train of four to five beasts of burden. One family, with a father and two grown sons, depends very heavily on the sale of firewood, as its potato crop often provides only enough for reseeding. Two or more days of work each week felling and splitting wood yields some three to four horseloads, which, when sold on Sunday, return about 1,200 pesos. The return for sale of firewood is roughly equivalent to the going wage (when it can be earned). Charcoal is less frequently brought to market, for it must be made from thick logs, covered, and burned, which requires more labor time. A horseload of charcoal, though lighter than wood, sells for approximately 1,000 pesos.

The volume of wood being taken to Cumbal is difficult to ascertain. Most of it appears on the weekend, having been cut earlier in the week. One Saturday in half an hour five trains passed us; some people who live near the principal track on the *páramo* claim to see thirty to forty horseloads pass each day, a reasonable if not conservative estimate. By all accounts, the wood frontier is retreating, and the people are having to travel longer distances to secure it; in effect, their expenditures at the periphery or "marginal costs" are rising.

Wood, ice, and sulphur are likened to a "savings box." The natural resources are holdings of the earth's strength. The holdings themselves are monetarily costless, and one has only to expend labor "to take out" what nature "gives," while sale of the product "pays" for the work expended. Because they have put in the work, the people also say that they own the wood, the sulphur, or the ice. Through work expended, nature's strength becomes a property of the house to be traded on the market for cash.

This, at least, is the house voice. But the local economy is part of the larger political framework and national economy of Colombia. Forests that lie deep and distant on the *páramo* – at the edge of the market world – are an example in which the legal framework of the state extends beyond the boundaries of profit making, creating a disjuncture that allows the rural folk to bring the private goods of others from "off the margin" for sale in the center. All the resources on the high plains are privately possessed or held by the state, yet the inhabitants treat the forest as a free good. In some instances, the local folk cut trees on land they own or have been given access to, but even they admit that most of the wood being sold, their own load excepted, is "contraband," having been taken from the forests of absentee landowners. For the legal owners, the "transaction cost" – the expense of watching the wood and collecting a rent for its use – exceeds the revenue that might be collected. The forest lies beyond the margin of profit, though within the political and legal framework of society, and within this liminal or remainder zone of the market the local people with their costless labor are able to operate and make savings.

The *páramo*, then, presents an illustration of the domestic economy as it persists on the market's margin. The environment is unfavorable, and the rural folk can move there and use its resources precisely because it lies on and beyond the profit margin. In this peripheral environment, a one-sector economy has emerged, and this living model displays with clarity the house schema of flows, expenditures, and remainders. But this folk practice also provides a critique of the received texts. Drawing upon a part-evolutionary, part-derivational set of assumptions, economists from Ricardo (1951[1815]) to Pasinetti (1977) have assumed that the one-commodity economy comprises the primitive kernel, the essence of market systems. The ethnographic data suggest otherwise. The one-sector model does not lie at the core of economies; it is not historically prior to exchange, nor can the comparative advantages or benefits of trade be derived from it.[1] The single-sector economy does not shift toward greater specialization and display an increasing division of labor over time. It is rather the practices of rural folk who must subsist on the margin, the remainders, of a market economy. The one-commodity economy, in contrast to all assumptions, doubly follows upon the rise of the market, for it emerges in practices only beyond profit's border after the economy of profit is established; and it has emerged in the conversation of theorists who, perhaps unknowingly, have appropriated practices at the periphery for their explanations of the logic of the core.

Conversations: models of the remainder

The house schema is a dynamic and simple model that employs the repeated opposition of expenditure and leftover.[2] The quantities apportioned are relative to one another and do not depend upon the use of a measuring

rod or extradomestic set of values. This easily applied
model serves for different combinations of consumption
crops and for varying combinations of house and market
crops; it is used as houses grow and shrink and as
production volumes change from year to year; it works in
different and changing ecological conditions; and it applies
as the holdings of the house increase, diminish or change in
composition. We think that several dimensions of house
practices can be highlighted and the many variations
summarized in a set of three models drawn from
observation: (1) a single house crop with variations in the
expenditures covered; (2) several house crops with
variations in the conditions of production; and (3) crops
raised for trade as well as for house consumption. For all
these models, we assume that the people work all year or
the same number of days; we assume, too, that house size,
composition, and workforce are constant across the several
contexts.

Model 1: The single crop The one-commodity economy of
the *páramo* is the limiting case. In the first instance, a
sample of the crop has to be obtained for seed. This is
done by sharecropping land or by trade; in the latter case,
the means for acquiring the initial stock have to be secured
by another activity, such as cutting firewood. Once the
agricultural cycle has been started, the house schema is
used. In some instances the harvest covers only the seed
expense, and therefore other activities have to sustain the
house. We term this possibility Model 1A.

If there is a remainder after the seed deduction, this is
for eating; for Model 1B, then, the harvest covers seed and
food. Dividing the remainder after seed deduction by 365
(or the number of days until the next harvest) yields the
daily return that the house has for consumption. In the
lexicon of economists, the daily return might be labeled
"the wage basket" of the house, but we call it the "food
plate." As the rural folk say, they try "to bring back . . .
the potatoes, the beans, the maize" (depending on the
area), meaning food for house consumption. The "food
plate" is a shorthand for "maintaining the house" and for
crops raised "for eating." Consequently, if we assume that
work is performed throughout the year, the daily food

plate is roughly the labor productivity of the crop; not counting the seed, it is the amount produced (and consumed) by a single day of work. In this relatively simple case, the food plate mirrors labor productivity, and the agricultural cycle is precisely self-reproducing.

A conversational qualification should be inserted. The food plate supplies the entire household, but some of the consumers may not be workers. In most houses, the food plate is not automatically translated into labor, a point underlined by Chayanov (1966) in his consumer-to-worker ratio. Houses vary according to their number of "dependents," such as youngsters, old people, and less able workers – all consumers of the food plate who raise the level of house expenditures without turning them into work. As the people well know, a house with teenage working children is in an enviable position. Work intensity also differs from one house to another. These variations raise and lower the size of the food plate itself.

For Model 1C we assume that after deductions for seed and for food there are kitchen scraps that are fed to a hog and chickens. In Model 1D production covers seed, food, kitchen scraps, and a remainder. This leftover may be kept "inside the doors" and fed to a domestic animal in raw form. This base→base' transaction serves to augment the holdings, and by means of it the remainder is turned into an advance.

Conditions of production, however, may shift in space or time. When productivity changes, the volume of the remainders or the food plate must change as well. Inputs readjust to match prior outputs. For Model 1E, we assume that there is a bad year or the land deteriorates. In general, the people first do without the remainders for animals rather than shrinking the amount allocated for the food plate. Then, if conditions worsen, "savings" may be used to replace food not produced. As the rural folk say, when the land does not give, the base shrinks. In more extreme cases, declines in productivity are managed by shrinking the food plate or belt-tightening. In some of the infertile areas of Boyacá, the rural folk speak often of "suffering" in the house, meaning that they are eating as little as possible, not replacing the strength and health that they have used up in work. Conversely, for Model 1F, in abundant years when the land gives, domestic consumption increases, larger excesses are yielded, and savings are put aside.

Model 2: Several crops For Model 2, we assume the people shift across the landscape so that more than one crop can be raised.[3] For example, by descending some 1,000 meters from the *páramo* one can grow lima beans. The possibility of raising a second crop considerably changes the use of the house schema. If "lines of production" – such as potatoes and beans – were "independent," the labor for each could be fed by its per-day return, and for each crop the sum of these per-day returns would be equal to the previous total product less future seed costs; each line would be self-reproducing. But in a house economy the lines of production are not independent; the crops are cooked and served together in the food plate. Through labor's consumption, the production lines are conjoined; the crops are "complementary," as the people say. Because each line feeds the other, the output of each is used to cover its seed costs and *total* house uses, not just its own expenses of reproduction. If, for example, two crops – potatoes and lima beans – are grown and output covers only expenditures for seeding and eating, the yearly food plate for the house will be made up of the two harvests less the two seed deductions, and the daily food plate will be this sum divided by 365. Both potatoes and lima beans will occupy a part of the food plate, their ratio depending upon the volumes raised. If productivity improves over time or in space but equally for potatoes and lima beans – a simple productivity shift that we term Model 2A – each crop will comprise the same proportionate part of the house remainder as it does in the food plate. After seed deduction, the excess proportions and the food plate proportions will be the same.

But this model is relatively simple, and we heard of no instances of equal proportions in the food plate and the remainder. For Model 2B, we assume that the food plate stays the same but labor is distributed differently from the previous year. Over time, work is allocated now to one, now to another crop so that the excess shifts from one line to another. The leftover appears in maize, beans, wheat, or whatever, one crop effectively absorbing and representing the possible remainders of the others. When, for example, labor is shifted to maize, the maize output increases, but house expenditures stay constant (as other crops continue to comprise part of the food plate) and the maize remainder rises. By contrast, the remainders of the other crops fall, for their total outputs fall, while their house uses in the food plate stay the same.

For Model 2C, we assume that the food plate itself is altered from year to year. If the composition of the food plate is changed but not labor's allocation to the crops, then one cultigen has a bigger place in the leftover and a smaller place in the food plate, while the remaining crops are in the reverse position. From the standpoint of the domestic economy, one line is "subsidized" by the others, which are "overreproducing" by supporting labor in the deficit crop. In all these cases represented by Models 2B and 2C, when a remainder appears in one crop it is above all a *house* leftover made through the expenditure of the other crops.

This model of the ever-shifting food plate and remainders bears a family resemblance to a Sraffian system in which several lines of "basic commodities" produce and reproduce themselves by providing for their needed raw materials and the wages of labor. In Sraffa's (1960) model, a set of "basics" – iron, pigs, maize – produces "basics" by feeding into one another. As in the domestic economy, also, one production cycle underwrites the next by providing its foodstuffs and other needed resources. In addition, Sraffa constructs a "surplus" for his system, calculated as the remainder after the strictly material needs of reproduction have been met; because for him these material requirements include only raw materials and tools, his surplus has to cover both wages and profit. Translating to the Colombian countryside, the Sraffian surplus is similar to the leftover directly after the seed deduction has been taken. (On the *páramo*, where only wooden tools are used and baskets are made of fiber, the two models nearly coincide.) The size of the Sraffian surplus depends upon the technological conditions of production – also, much as in the rural model, where the remainder after seed varies with productivity ratios, or how much the land gives. But the similarity we would emphasize is between the Sraffian "standard commodity" and the rural food plate. The standard commodity, made up of basics, is a kind of moving measuring rod for the system. It is carefully designed by Sraffa to mirror its own means of production; its own proportional composition of basics mirrors the proportion of basics that it takes to produce it. Everything else is in surplus, and when the conditions of production change, the standard commodity alters, as does the surplus. In a rather similar way, the daily or yearly food plate conjoins and reflects what the house economy produces for its own reproduction. The standard commodity and the rural food plate are made up of the necessary commodities produced – the one of basics, the other of foodstuffs. There are differences, however. The rural food plate feeds labor, while the standard commodity does not. (Again, in Sraffa's system, the wage basket comes from the surplus.) Sraffa's system also presumes trade; the output of each production line is exchanged against the others at a rate sufficient to secure from them its required means of production. In contrast, within the domestic economy agricultural products are not exchanged against one another "inside the doors" but conjoined in the food plate. In addition, in the Sraffian system the standard commodity readjusts immediately as the conditions of production change; since its composition is in the same proportion as the means by which it is produced, it shifts as these need to be combined in different ratios. Certainly, the rural food plate also changes through time and over space, but it does not immediately mirror all the shifting conditions and forms of production. Only under specific conditions does it actually reproduce the proportion of inputs that have produced it. Still, there is a sense in which the Sraffian economy is the house economy writ large and the standard commodity is like the food plate. Sraffa himself pointed to the connection between his work and that of Ricardo, Smith, and the Physiocrats (Sraffa 1960:v, 93–4); and in fact, Ricardo's early "corn model" had a special influence upon Sraffa. But the corn economy itself is a one-sector model (Sraffa 1951), and we have suggested that it is modeled after the domestic economy, although ethnographically we find the house model, and especially the one-commodity form of it, located on the margin of the market and not at its "basic" core.

We have assumed for Models 1 and 2 that the house provides for its own reproduction and keeps remainders "inside the doors"; the crops are for house expenditures, and savings are made. The house workforce is fed by a composite plate of food that is a product of that work. One of the crops may yield a remainder for saving, but the leftover appearing in that crop is underwritten by the others, which will have a smaller remainder themselves or subsidize it through the food plate.

The domestic economy, however, is embedded in the market, for the people may wish or need to consume a good they do not produce. Salt and *panela* are apposite examples, but depending on the area there may be a desire for coffee, potatoes, rice, maize, or some other foodstuff or for clothing or some other domestic item. We must consider, therefore, how trade is woven into the house schema.

Model 3: Trade For Model 3, we assume that the house procures from others; it does not maintain itself from its own crops. Purchased items are like deficit or underreproduced products in the domestic system. To secure them, some portion of the crops must be set aside for sale and traded "outside the doors" in a base→money→base' transaction. The remainder may be traded for foodstuffs, but often it is used to obtain seed, tools, fertilizer, or insecticide – things for seeding – or for animal supplies or an animal, which augments the base and transforms the remainder into an advance. All uses of the product for seeding and for eating in the direct (base→base') or indirect (base→money→base') sense are considered house expenditures. In contrast, use of the product to buy new animals is a way of increasing the base.

The crop that is traded for cash may be maize or potatoes, also eaten in the house, or it may be sugarcane or tobacco (whose seed may even need to be purchased). In either case, the house schema is used to constitute trade: the volume for sale is termed a "remainder" and is taken after the amounts for seeding and for eating have been set aside. The cash crop or sold portion of a domestic crop thus represents a leftover of the domestic economy, and it is "fed" by all the others, draining their potential remainders into its production. In addition, the traded leftover is not a preset surplus but varies directly with and has an effect upon the size of the deductions previously made. The amount traded in the base→money→base' circuit can be very large, if a house's expenditure of its own products is depressed.

The trade of leftovers itself is neither beneficial nor detrimental. The consequences of trade depend on its terms: everything rests on the exchange rate between the house and market dealers, for depending on what comes back, the food plate, seed volumes, or, more generally, the base will increase or diminish. Thus, an understanding of how the house constructs its trade relation to the market provides only a partial view of a total process and ultimately raises three new questions: How do the people model market trade itself? How does their model fit the corporate one? And what happens to the house when it enters the market?

Chapter 8
THE HOUSE AND THE MARKET

The house economy exists within a political and legal framework that defines how access to property is gained, and it is located within a market system characterized by the unequal control of wealth. This structural placement has an important impact on its functioning, for the rural areas of Colombia are penumbral to the use and concentration of capital, and the house must survive in the spaces left empty by profit-seeking organizations. There is a dramatic asymmetry between the power of the corporation and that of the house. Corporations move within the market, extending it and using it in their project of turning a profit. The house cannot. As the people say, it is "a struggle, a fight," to maintain the house, which is always "in the making." Even haciendas perpetually struggled to maintain and enlarge themselves only to dissolve under the impact of the market.

The way that the house economy fits into the larger market world is variantly voiced, for the house conversation lacks unity (although it echoes one that goes back to Aristotle), while the corporate discussion, inscribed in texts, models exchange yet differently. But these several conversations illuminate processes at the periphery and even hint at ways to alleviate certain modern struggles. An examination of the coexistent models and of their conjuncture through trade reveals what is happening in markets at the periphery: the picture gained is very different from current theory.

RURAL MARKETS

The market extends everywhere in the countryside; land, labor, tools, equipment, goods, and houses all "have their price." Even in the most remote areas, where the domestic economy thrives, all productive factors are privately held and exchanged at prices that are market-determined. Whether or not there is much hiring, there is always a wage rate. Land has everywhere a cost, though we encountered only one instance of a rental paid in money and but a few instances of land pawning. One of the puzzling features of the countryside is precisely that the house economy exists within a market context yet survives by avoiding purchases. The house and the corporation are connected within the same world but are unlike.

The most visible interchange of the house with the larger economy is through the weekly markets. The rural folk buy at small stores, sell their crops to intermediaries and traders, visit banks and government agencies, and have experience with the larger *fincas* and older haciendas in their area, but they participate in and depend most on markets. Every town has a weekly market, and "to go to market every week" (*ir a mercar cada ocho días*) is a household habit. This is also the time when the campesino goes to church for baptisms or marriage, to the government office, or to the larger grain dealer. In every town, too, the government agrarian bank is open on market day.

Local markets are organized confusion. Market preparations start between two and three in the morning, when the out-of-town sellers arrive. Buying begins in earnest by six or six-thirty, with activity reaching a peak in midmorning, and by early afternoon the entire area may be deserted. The early-arriving sellers set up stalls of wooden frames with canvas or plastic coverings, but some towns have permanent structures for the entire market or for the butchers and fruit sellers. There is no single market layout, with one type of seller to the east, another to the west, but sellers of the same goods are grouped together, heightening competition while providing the opportunity for sellers to gather timely information about price shifts. And everyone knows about prices. A campesino on the way home can detail the cost of his every purchase and the current prices on other provisions. The sellers have a keen notion of buying power, for they will talk about the state of local crops and whether the people have much money to spend. For example, they say that the market is good when the harvest is abundant locally but has failed in adjacent areas, for then the buyers – who have brought produce to the market – have plenty of money.

The weekly market is the domestic economy put on display. Markets do vary in the goods offered – more fruits and "hot-country" produce in the low areas, warm clothes, potatoes, and grains in the higher zones. But certain goods are seen again and again, and the markets offer everything that will be found in a rural home. The main market commodities include foods, tools, clothes, household items, and sundries, with foodstuffs occupying the largest portion of the market. There are fruits, wheat, barley, and oats, along with packages of noodles, maize and potatoes and lesser amounts of yucca and beets, beans of many varieties, cattle, sheep, goat and hog meat, and usually some live chicks and pigs. Salt, coffee, and sugar along with *panela* are popular. There are inexpensive clothes, ruanas, and rubber boots for working in the fields, pots, baskets, soap, mirrors, combs, playing cards, matches, batteries, and wallets. Finally, one or two vendors offer "irons," the steel tips for tools; wooden shafts for them are locally fashioned.

The town market is a campesino market in another sense, too. Items are sold in very small quantities – one or two oranges, a small sack of salt or coffee –partly because the local folk lack purchasing power and partly because intermediaries make money by buying in bulk and breaking to small lots. But this is also part of the corporate world's adaptation to the countryside; smaller-sized packages are made for sale in regions of lesser purchasing power. Only in small rural stores is coffee found in 1/8-kilo packets. In addition, the commodities themselves are of a less expensive variety. One rarely encounters first-class potatoes or fruits in town markets, and some goods, such as the iron tips for tools, fashioned from car springs, as well as sandals made from used rubber tires, are exclusive to these markets.

Many of the products, such as crops, meat, and handicrafts, are locally produced. Processed foods, however, are nationally distributed; some clothes and fruits come from Ecuador and Venezuela, while small household items often are imports from the Far East. The people talk, validly or not, about point of origin for some of the goods. In the higher altitudes, buyers explain that fruits and *panela* come from the lower regions, while in these latter areas they say that potatoes have to be brought from the higher zones. In this respect, the people see the market as an arena for the redistribution of goods from different regions. They also say that goods from Ecuador and sometimes Venezuela are less expensive, but they do not explain why, except for noting that exchange rates often shift. They talk little, however, about the influence of the Far East or the United States on what they purchase. For them, the weekly market is the focus of a local region and the nation, not the end point of a world system.

These are markets of the margin also in the sense that many of the goods offered are produced and sold by other householders. Transporters and intermediaries gather up produce from houses in small trickles, then store, transport, and resell it to small vendors, who themselves are a diverse lot, including older men, younger women, and families. Some make a living at this, selling at two or three markets per week, traveling by bus and toting small wares. Others journey to a town and are supplied by a transporter there, while still others keep an inventory of durables where they sell. But some of the vendors are local, and many link their market activity to making savings and what they do in the house. An older man we once encountered sold *panela* each Sunday as much for the activity as for the profit. His house, which he rented to lodgers, was two blocks from the plaza, and he brought the *panela* to the market in a wheelbarrow. Having located a site, he would remain there for several hours, selling once or twice an hour and conversing with acquaintances. The unsold inventory went home with him, for it was relatively durable. By contrast, another man had a small store (*una tienda*) in the same town, and what he did not sell of his perishable fruits and vegetables on Sunday he sold in his store during the week. Families also sell small quantities of foods, purchased from the transporters, to finance their weekly needs, returning home with the unsold portions for consumption there. They try to break even on the purchases and sales with domestic use of the remainder as the gain. Others have a single item or two to hawk, such as cheese or a pig, and the transporters themselves sell directly from their trucks what remains after supplying the market vendors. Sellers thus have many ways of participating in the market: some buy to sell on that day only, others link the occasion to another market activity or to domestic use. Likewise, the wares in each market stall are put together differently by each seller. One woman sold hinges, rings, and hasps made by an uncle in a neighboring town, but she also bought metal locks from manufacturers' outlets.

Rural buyers in the market explain their purchases in terms of necessities. They speak of the need for salt, then mention *panela* or sugar, maize, potatoes, wheat, and rice, beans, coffee, and meat, and this is not to speak of clothes and tools. In this, they see the domestic economy as being embedded within an exchange system, although they wish it were otherwise:

> You could have everything if you had the land. You meet the needs by raising for the house, if you can. But you cannot produce everything or store it for the climate. For this, you need the city. For example, you can't store lard, but we could produce it and soap from hogs. Salt is about the only thing you cannot produce here. The center serves for trading.

This same view, repeated by others, specifies two functions that the market performs. Some goods do not keep, so the market has a *storage* function that cannot be performed by the house. The people say that merchants have warehouses or deposits (*depósitos*) from which they sell and for which they buy. The market also has a *trade* function, being a site where a house can exchange what it has for what it cannot produce (salt usually being given as an example).

The rural folk use the word *"cambiar"* for market transactions. At the outset we translated this as "exchange," but the context of use and our own conversation led to a different gloss, "trade." The people themselves explained, "I sell potatoes and with the money buy the rest of what I lack. Thus, I 'trade' [*cambiar*] one thing for another." Or, as one person said:

> I take maize and sell it for money and use the money to buy beans or whatever. There is no gain in this; it is a "trade." We are selling to replace.

The purpose of trade is to shift the composition of the base. The rural folk "sell to buy" (base→money→base') rather than "buy to sell" (money→base→money').

The people likewise hold a "trading view" of money. Money serves in the countryside as a common measure and as a medium for trading. The rural folk do not sell goods to obtain money as an end, nor is cash held as a store of wealth, although the people keep small amounts within the home. One afternoon an older gentleman in Cundinamarca explained:

> Money is a movement, for circulation, to trade one thing for another, for whatever else. Money is not a useful thing [*una utilidad*] itself but serves to buy a cow or hog as a savings for tomorrow. All useful things are products of the earth; although it sometimes does not give them, the market never gives them. Money serves only to make trades.

The people sometimes do without money as a medium of exchange, for they occasionally engage in barter (*trueque*). Because the rural barter rate is determined by prevailing market prices, however, money provides the standard for determining the amounts traded. Rural barter is an "off-the-market" exchange, a way of gaining access to market functions without having to control a money fund.

This house model of the market is quite different from Adam Smith's. For Smith, there exists a human propensity to "truck, barter, and exchange" regardless of immediate need (Smith 1976[1776]:17–19), and the market and the division of labor are its products. The rural folk start from the needs and capacities of the house, using the market not to make a living but to purchase what they cannot produce and store what they cannot hold. For Smith production is a type of market practice, while in the rural conversation production occurs in the house, the circulatory processes of the market serving to redistribute products between houses.

In the people's assessment, market trades seldom replace the base; as they say, "One is losing the base little by little to the market." They have, in fact, a critical commentary about what actually happens in the market and some thoughts about what it should involve. But this domestic conversation is unfinished, having no point of verbal agreement, as if the problem itself could not be resolved. The rural folk talk about seeking a "fair trade" in the market and receiving a "just price" for their products, but there are many voices about what constitutes a just price. For some, a fair trade would be like an identical exchange of money; it would be based on the money value of the products so that, without loss, a purchase could be changed back to what was initially sold. Implicitly, these people are saying that the seller of an object, in buying another object, does not receive the full value of the object sold; something is lost when money is used as a medium of exchange. By a second view, goods should trade "bundle for bundle," meaning that equal volumes should be exchanged – a sack of maize, for example, for a sack of beans. When we probed this proposal, it often led to a third – that goods should trade according to the amount of work they contain; two different bundles produced by the same amount of work should trade equally. This was linked to a fourth view – that a fair trade is based on the equivalency of expenditures in the products exchanged. According to this "cost-of-production" view, "both know what they expended. You make an account of the food used to set the trade." Lastly, there is the idea that a fair trade replaces the base. Susceptible of various interpretations, "replacing the base" could mean trying to reach equivalency of costs, of labor, or of volume in a trade. But the view also implies that because the base is used to meet the necessities of the house, a just price or a fair trade allows a house to meet its needs: "It depends on how much need they have." The trade reestablishes a house's ability to sustain itself. This final notion of the just price is linked to an ethical view of the market, for it is also said that a trade should be based on "one's conscience." A person of "good conscience" helps others when they have problems, when a harvest is lost, or when they cannot pay back a loan. Such a person also attends to the needs of others and does not take advantage of them; for a person of good conscience the price paid is just when it allows the recipient to meet house necessities. The just price, in this case, varies with buyer and seller.

These voices about market trade are connected to lending practices. As we have seen, no interest is charged on loans between rural houses. Seed, tools, food, labor, and even money are borrowed and returned at no cost. In effect, they are delayed trades of equivalents; when the loan is repaid, the base is replaced. Of course, most base items themselves – as circulating wealth – are not productive. Only when they are used to support work do they help provide for house continuance and increase. Thus, a loan from unused reserves has no price, while collecting interest on money lent between houses is "usury" (money→money′):

> It is a sin to collect more than you are owed. You take away the bread of another. With interest, one takes back more than one gave. A trade, such as work for work or food for food, this is just. These are equal trades, but taking interest is not. It depends on God if he wants there to be more ... from the land.

A conversation: the just price

These rural voices about trade, the just price, and usury are part of a very long conversation that started with Aristotle, reached a crescendo in medieval Scholasticism and, though partly silenced by Smith, continues to this day, at least in the market peripheries of Latin America. From today's vantage point, the traditional concerns about usury and the just price seem to reflect abstract ethical thinking that drew variously upon Greek philosophy, Roman law, and Christian morality. But this understanding of the historical voices severs them from institutional practices, and if concerns about establishing what the just price was and varying understandings of its nature persisted right up to Smith it was not because ethical thinkers were in the vanguard of social practices but because the social context to which they were responding was continuing to shift. In our view, the ruminations on usury and the just price are linked to a modeling problem of the domestic economy. If this long conversation has shifted but never reached closure after two thousand years, it is because the house world does not encompass or control the world of exchange for gain. Only when the practices of the core shift do the textual voices about the just price become stilled; on the margin, the folk continue to articulate the hope for fair exchanges.

In *The Politics* Aristotle set forth a model of the domestic economy. The broader context was that of political association, and he examined the family-based household as it fitted into the village and the *polis*. According to Aristotle, the aim of the house was to achieve sufficiency, and he identified five forms of household "acquisition" in service of this goal: farming, pastoralism, freebooting, fishing, and hunting. The products from these activities, said he, are "given by nature to all living beings" (1946:20). He further suggested, much as the rural Colombians do, that "it is the business of nature to furnish subsistence for each being brought into the world . . . Plants exist to give subsistence to animals, and animals to give it to men" (pp. 28, 21). The household lives from and manages these returns. Aristotle argued that early transactions between houses were immediate or direct and took the form of barter. The barter rate or terms of transaction between houses, he said, should satisfy "the natural requirements of sufficiency" (p. 24). This formulation – that the purpose of trade is to meet the needs of survival – corresponds to one of the rural voices. Aristotle's notion of trade for sufficiency also contains the "ethical" view that – in Colombian terms – one house in good conscience should help another; although this might make the real terms of trade between them unequal – a bundle of maize for a bundle of beans depending on "reciprocal" needs – it would allow each to persist.

In Aristotle's account of history, after barter developed, money came into use, "retail" trade arose, and then profits began to be made through trade. But in this latter form of acquisition, "there is no limit to the end it seeks" (p. 26). Aristotle insisted upon the difference between limited acquisition for household use and acquisition for retail gain. As Polanyi (1968) once observed, he had "discovered" the difference between the house economy and business.

Having located a contradiction between household and "retail" organisation, Aristotle turned to other subjects, but in the *Nicomachean Ethics* he again considered price and exchange, although within the context of "corrective justice." The discussion is not entirely lucid nor amenable to a single interpretation, but the ideas are resplendent because they lead in many directions: the just price is linked to the social status, the value, and the labor of the transacting parties and to establishing a "reciprocal proportion" between them (1926:283–5). For example, there is the hint that rates of exchange might be set in accord with relative statuses or positions, which is a social and political construction of market transactions. There is the suggestion that the value of an object made and the personal worth of its maker are intertwined, and this can lead to a labor–value theory of price. Aristotle's long explanation of reciprocal proportions also seems to be an attempt at "mathematical modeling," though the meaning is opaque (Gordon 1975:62–5). In his commentary on these variant voices, however, Schumpeter simplifies and claims that Aristotle was "groping for some labor-cost theory of price" (1954:61), while in Polanyi's view (1968:108) Aristotle wanted to establish a theory of prices that would "restore self-sufficiency." For a house economy Schumpeter's and Polanyi's readings coincide; restoring self-sufficiency or meeting the needed expenditures of the house (Polanyi) is almost equivalent to paying for the cost of production (Schumpeter) when all house members are workers. In a reproductive system, sustained by liquid holdings, production cost and the needs of self-sufficiency are the same, especially if tools last less than a year. Aristotle, in other words, was examining price formation from the perspective of the house economy. He was projecting the house model on market transactions – as do the rural Colombians.

Aristotle's views on usury were part of this larger way of modeling exchange. In his words (1946:28–9), the "natural" form

of acquisition is always, and in all cases, acquisition from fruits and animals. That art, as we have said, has two forms: one which is connected with retail trade, and another which is connected with the management of the household. Of these two forms, the latter is necessary and laudable; the former is a method of exchange which is justly censured, because the gain in which it results is not naturally made, but is made at the expense of other men. The trade of the petty usurer is hated most, and with most reason: it makes a profit from currency itself . . . Currency came into existence merely as a means of exchange; usury tries to make it increase. This is the reason why usury is called by the word we commonly use [for breeding]; for as the offspring resembles its parent, so the interest bred by money is like the principal which breeds it, and it may be called "currency the son of currency." Hence we can understand why, of all modes of acquisition, usury is the most unnatural.

For Aristotle, usury was the most extreme way of unjustly securing a gain, its unusual feature being that the gain is made through buying and selling money alone rather than buying goods with money in order to sell them, however unjust that set of transactions also may be.

Aristotle is a source of voices on labor value, usury, price, mathematics, trade, and related topics because he was responding to and helping to formulate social practices concerning household exchange, and if his textual voices remained important for the Schoolmen and others it was because the domestic economy continued after his time, from the Roman villa to the hacienda. Clearly, the house economy changed in function, size and proliferation through medieval times, and the market sphere grew considerably in importance and respectability. But throughout this long stretch of time, marked by political shifts, technological change, and "capital" accumulation, there was a remarkable persistence of the house world or, as it was once called, the "natural economy." Even in the thirteenth century, St. Thomas Aquinas was, in the *Summa Theologica* (1265–73), concerned with many of the Aristotelean problems. Aristotle's ideas on "utility," satisfying needs, and the social standing of the trading partners are reflected in the *Summa*, although Aquinas more firmly offered a "cost-of-production" view of prices. In these changed times, Aquinas also approved of both merchants and retail trade (Gordon 1975:172–6), and while he was concerned with the just price, a shift had occurred in the expression's use. The just price was defined in terms of the market itself, being the commonly held or generally charged price, unaffected by individual control, fraud, or monopoly (Baldwin 1959; Roll 1973; Schumpeter 1954).

We are tempted to suggest that the rural Colombians are thoroughgoing Aristoteleans (influenced by medieval Scholasticism), but the larger issue is that from the viewpoint of the house economy, which "acquires" fruits and animals (Aristotle) or gathers up nature's force (Colombia), gain made in exchange – by trading money for goods or money for money – poses a problem of modeling. In the domestic model all increase comes from nature, and human activities are a using up of this gain. Trade is secondary to production and has the purpose of redistributing goods among houses; it adds nothing to the flow. By contrast, in the corporate model gain is made only through exchange. The business organization assumes that persisting commercial trade surrounds it and that there is a living intake and output of goods that yields growth. Today, as in ancient Greece, the domestic and the business organization coexist, but their practices do not mesh. The construct of a just price and the condemnation of usury are the voice of the house as it enters the market. This voice is first heard in Aristotle and remains remarkably strong for nearly two thousand years; in fact, the textual concern with just prices and usury persisted until Smith offered a different model of the market. Among the folk, however, the voice and the angst have lasted well beyond this.

CIRCULATION AND THE PROFITS OF TRADE

To engage in fair exchanges and encounter just prices may be the people's hope. The reality is different, and about this the rural folk have much to say. Part of their discussion focuses on the relation between the *campo* (countryside) and the *centro* (the center) and on what happens to goods in circulation between them. The people sometimes have to make allocations from their annual product for the church and government, but their main concern is with the commercial "center." We have listened to voices in different places, and though repetitious they provide a glimpse of the way the rural folk are modeling their contemporary situation. They say:

> The land is giving to the *campo* and *centro* both. The land produces – for those in the market; from this they live.
>
> The gains of the trader come from the *campo* itself, not from the city; only the land gives.
>
> The campesino is the only one who produces – in Bogotá what do they produce? The city consumes, the campesino produces.
>
> The *centro* needs the *campo*, it depends on the *campo*; if everyone stopped in the *campo*, the *centro* would stop. If there is no movement in the *campo*, there is none is the *centro*.
>
> The *centro* doesn't produce anything; it lives from the *campo*, from the work of the *campo*.
>
> In the *campo*, people live from work; if no one were in the *campo*, the *centro* would die of hunger.
>
> What does the *centro* give in return? The *centro* gives almost nothing – it only produces study and teaching. We need the *centro* only for schools.

The *centro* is finishing off one's account; where would the *centro*'s money come from if the *campo* stopped sending it?

One takes a thousand times more from inside to outside than from outside to inside.

The *centro* takes advantage of the warmth (i.e., sweat) of the agriculturalist.

We see trucks going to the city. Where did their money come from? – from business and work. They buy to consume, so they have to live on what the *campo* produces. This can be just, because they have worked for it.

This varying commentary provides a house critique of the encompassing economy. The touchstone is the idea that because only the earth is productive "the campesino sustains the nation." City dwellers do work, which justifies a return to them, but trade with the "center" is unjust because traders take more than they give, whether through the pricing of goods or through interest on loans.

This constellation of critical voices, however, poses the further problem of explaining how one party in an exchange takes advantage of another. If the countryside maintains the city, how does it happen that trade is unjust? Again, the people have views:

Merchants make money because they buy at a price that they put on – they don't pay all to the campesino.

If you take something to the market and sell it, you sell at a lower price than what you buy the same thing for. You have to carry five times more of the crop for the money than what you can buy with the money.

You get little for what you sell, but it certainly values what you buy.

The merchant gets his gain from this difference of the buying and selling price. Sometimes it is the same person who buys and then sells it back.

Merchants live on unjust prices. They make money because they don't trade equally. The center is a con game.

They know the prices better; they do have gains and losses, but they know the prices better than the campesino. They know if something will be scarce tomorrow so it will be worth more.

Traders' money comes from cleverness and luck. The merchant has competition, so luck also enters their practices.

People with money can buy and sell better.

Markets go up and down – the rich bear it, the poor cannot.

The rich have more base – the deposit of the merchant is like a base; they come out better.

The merchant buys in times of abundance and keeps it in deposits and sells later for much more, double. We cannot keep it here.

You cannot buy in large lots. You may sell in quantity, but you have to buy in smaller volume.

You may go to the market with a goat; you have to take what the people offer, you have needs. You could come back with the goat, but if you come back with the animal, what will the children say? They ask, "What did you bring?"

According to these voices, commercial gains come through control over circulation. Merchants' profits are founded on their ability to store and redistribute local goods. The rural commentary also suggests that the city makes gains through control of knowledge. The people claim that merchants and traders have information about supplies and possible future price changes that allows them to take advantage of market conditions. This was exemplified one afternoon in Boyacá as we followed a road upward through the mountains until it ended amidst boulders. Toward the end of the track a new solar-powered telephone station had been built as part of the expanding national communication network. Along the way we asked people what they thought about the telephone. One man spoke at length about the difficulty of selling cattle in town at a just price and added that the telephone might be a great help; rather than taking an animal to market and having to sell at that day's offering, he could call and wait until prices were favorable. In theory at least, the telephone could help erase a market "imperfection" by improving the knowledge infrastructure and lowering the transaction cost to the campesinos.

Traders' control of information, the people's little withholding power, and the market's function as a storehouse are linked to the merchants' financial power. The rural folk, drawing upon their house model, say that merchants have deposits or stores of goods that are a base. Market traders control money, which allows them to postpone buying or selling and to take advantage of price differentials. They enter the market only to make a gain, using their oligopoly command over money to do so; and because they are "farther ahead" with their deposits, they can bear up longer in adverse times. Personal need for a commodity never forces traders to enter the market. In contrast, say the rural people, they themselves lack withholding power and have to make transactions based on necessity, which lowers their bargaining power. They are of the opinion that the differential control of deposits or the base accounts for the gains that traders reap. Curiously, the other rural voice calling for a just price in circulation does not apply to this difference in the initial allocation of the holdings. The just-price voice is not a critique of the class structure or the asymmetrical pattern of property control, of which the people are also cognizant.

The rural folk do have some ways of avoiding the trader's gain. For example, by feeding accumulated maize to a domestic animal as opposed to selling it, they internalize the exchange function of the market. Some people argue that the government should have store-houses for buying and selling local goods at just prices and stores that guarantee quality and set fair prices for basic items not produced in the countryside. A salient feature of this solution is that it would shift control over the circulation of goods to the polity. Another solution, proposed in some of the rural areas by one of the revolutionary groups – the M19 – is to use armed force to block roads and halt transport of all local goods to the market. One campesino explained that the M19 wanted to cut off the "center," raise prices on agricultural goods, and make the city people aware of their dependence on the countryside. This proposed action, directed at the market itself, is particularly interesting because it is based on the critical commentary of the rural folk yet fits a Marxist and dependency theory of the economy.

Conversations: terms of trade, the margin of capital, surplus and remainder
The pricing problem in the weekly markets is one instance of a larger issue facing the people: disadvantageous terms of trade in all markets – labor, tools, goods, and money. Throughout the countryside, the daily wage is seldom high enough to purchase the foodstuffs necessary to sustain a worker and his family for a day. Similarly, most of the cash crops, such as sugarcane and tobacco, are unprofitable; even the tobacco companies and intermediaries admit that if the people had to hire labor instead of providing it themselves, many of the cash crops could not be raised. But to say that the center gathers up gains by controlling exchange makes it appear as if the problem resided in the markets themselves as if regulating the activities of traders, intermediaries, moneylenders, banks, market consortia, suppliers, transporters, and small vendors to create a "perfect" market would solve it. A close examination of the house and corporate models yields a different perspective.

According to one voice, the market model, stemming from Smith and Ricardo, the transaction between house and corporation is like international trade. In fact, according to one interpretation, Aristotle's analysis of household trade is much like "that of the two-country, two-commodity case in international trade" (Gordon

1975:67). In this case, according to Ricardian theory, a unit trades to achieve comparative advantage; each sells what it can produce more efficiently and buys what it produces less efficiently. The result is specialization by country and a larger overall return for each. But the theory of comparative advantage does not attend to differences in absolute advantage – that is, where one partner can produce both products more efficiently than the other, which certainly is the case in trades between domestic units and corporations. Furthermore, while house–corporate exchange may be like "international" trade in its crossing of economic frontiers, it occurs within a single polity and legal system, which in turn has facilitated the expansion of the capital market into the resource space of the house and perpetuated the absolute disadvantage. And there is another factor. According to the market model, specialization is a result of trade, competition, and the seeking of comparative advantage. But this is the textual theory of the corporation, and the rural house does not become specialized through trade as the model predicts. The domestic economy, located beyond the margin of profit, cannot specialize by purchasing inputs and covering costs through the sale of a product, and when it is encouraged or forced to attempt this its living standard usually declines.

Dependency theory, which attends to absolute advantage in trade, emphasizes the impact of a spreading capitalist system upon its surrounding environment (Cardoso and Faletto 1979; Frank 1967; Furtado 1976). It looks at international and national processes and is historical in scope. The dependency model suggestively underlines the importance of capital control and how this structures the relation of metropoles and satellites, or centers and peripheries, but it says little about processes at the periphery. For example, it is not clear from the dependency model how a supposed "surplus" is extracted from peripheral areas or how "development" depends upon the "development of underdevelopment." The model is also silent about the independent historical trajectories or self-modeling processes that characterize peripheries.

Marxist contributions to this same general topic are diverse and without agreement among themselves. Most

are based on the "law of value," which usually means that
only the efforts of labor create value, that (labor) values
are transformed to (money) prices in the market, that
average rather than marginal prices prevail, and that
surplus value is extracted in the process of production. For
example, according to some Marxist models, an
agriculturalist puts a large quantity of labor into a product;
his efforts are above the "social average," and in exchange
for his product he receives goods containing less labor
value. This difference – between the labor in the products
that he sells and the labor in the products that he receives
– can be very large, and it constitutes the surplus that is
taken over by market traders. The model, in its way,
attends to differences in absolute advantage and to gaps in
dependency theory, but it does so only by applying
concepts developed for capitalism. For instance, Bartra
(1982) has attempted to apply a Marxist perspective to
campesino life in order to reveal how exploitation of rural
areas occurs. He agrees that the house does not buy to
make a profit or sell to realize one (p. 73); nevertheless, he
uses the Marxist armature of capitalism for the rural
sector, distinguishing among "cost of production," "price
of production," "surplus," and "profit" within the house
itself. Ultimately, he holds that "the true measure of the
expropriated value from the campesino does not reduce
itself to production price less cost but is elevated to a
larger magnitude: the difference between cost and value"
(p. 80). In other words, for Bartra surplus in the house
economy is comprised of the difference between labor
performed (or labor value) and *its* cost of production (or
value of support), which is much the same as Marx's
definition of surplus for a corporate economy. Bartra's
model assimilates the house to the corporation, converting
heterogeneous use values and work in the house to
homogeneous labor as in the corporation. In his view, the
sole difference between the two contexts lies in the fact
that surplus is appropriated from the campesino through
market exchange, while corporate appropriation takes
place in production. Not surprisingly, his model leads right
back to the medieval concern with establishing a just price
in the market. In effect, Bartra wants to show what a fair
exchange for the house would be, and so he deploys a

labor theory of value to show that a just price is not established. Not without reason did Tawney once remark: "The descendant of the doctrines of Aquinas [on the just price] is the labor theory of value. The last of the Schoolmen was Karl Marx" (1926:36).

Our Colombian conversations make us hesitate to embrace these several and discordant texts. In our view, the peripheral context needs to be seen differently – by examining the house and corporate models separately, considering their articulation, and seeing how the corporation's power to take over areas of profit defines the trading processes for the domestic economy.

From the perspective of the dominant economy, the house is located "off the margin." It occupies, and sometimes has to fight for, spaces left empty by the larger system. As soon as these rural spaces become profitable, however, the capital-backed organizations enter, buying land and controlling resources, and the local people are pushed again beyond the frontier of profit. Throughout the Andes and elsewhere, the central, fertile land is held in large tracts by cattle owners and agrobusinesses, while surrounding hill land is held in small plots by campesinos. For the last 150 years and more, campesinos have been expanding the spatial frontiers of the Colombian economy only to find that after they have cut down the forest, planted it in domestic crops, and built homesteads, the land is taken over by large owners by political and economic means.

The house economy, thus, remains in a state of perpetual marginality relative to the corporate system. The production–possibility frontier, which defines the boundary of profit making, excludes the house. When this frontier does expand or move outward spatially, so does profit-seeking capital (and vice versa). As the market moves outward, the local inhabitants are incorporated within it as itinerants, shantytown dwellers, the homeless, laborers, and even profit makers, or are squeezed into the ever more marginal spaces. Capital creates its own margin, with escalating entry costs, and, at least for some of the people, it perpetuates the house economy.

Situated in this off-the-margin context, the domestic economy almost never commands a competitive position in

the market. Most of the products yielded by the rural
dwellers are "high-cost"; because of lack of resources,
infrastructure, or productive methods, the domestic
economy is at an absolute disadvantage in production. One
response of the domestic economy is to keep its base
"within the doors," but household autarky is impossible
given the demand created by the larger economy; and, as
the people point out, the house needs to trade for things it
cannot produce. One person, who raised maize for the
home and tomatoes and onions for sale, said, "We only do
this to have money in order to buy what the land doesn't
give here."

This marginal position of the house in relation to the
dominant economy can be seen more clearly in terms of
land productivity and the gathering of rent. In a profit-
making system, better holdings of land are able to claim a
positive, differential rent; the rent of a plot corresponds to
its larger yield. For example, where two equal-sized pieces,
side by side, are farmed with the same amount of capital
and labor, the more fertile one yields a greater volume of
product. The amount received for this greater volume is
paid to the owner of that piece and comprises the
differential rent. Now, if land fertility diminishes from the
center to the periphery, with the result that each land plot
contributes less and less differential rent, eventually there
will be some land so infertile or distant from the market
that it cannot return any rent above the costs of
production and may not, given the current level of
demand, even be able to meet the cost of investment or of
capital. At least for the profit making entity, this marks the
limit of production. In the Colombian countryside,
however, production continues beyond the frontier of
profit. This submarginal zone is the home of the domestic
economy, and its conditions of existence are quite different
from those of the corporation. We suggest that just as
inside profit's border a positive rent is garnered in accord
with the land's fertility, so outside it a negative rent has to
be paid in accordance with the land's infertility – if a
product is to compete on the market. Given the land it
occupies or the resources it can use, the house can trade its
products only by providing a subsidy on everything it sells.

It must incur a negative profit or negative rent to trade in the profit making arena.

We further propose that the house pays its negative rent through persistently adverse terms of trade. The "unjust prices" about which the people complain reflect the uncompetitive position of the house economy. For example, if tools, fertilizer, insecticides, seeds, food, and clothes are all purchased, the money return for a market crop will be lower than the price of the materials used in its production. To phrase it differently, the labor of household members yields a low return because the people are selling labor-expensive goods. In this situation, a business would either make a profit but lose its labor force because of low wages or it would pay the competitive wage but go broke for lack of profit. In either case, it would suspend operations, because it would be unable to cover the cost of its inputs with the sales of its output. In contrast, the house trades "at a loss" or unequally yet never "goes out of business."

To understand how it persists, one must consider first what the house must do. It has no money reserves to subsidize deficits, nor does it receive transfer payments from the government to cover cash losses. It can bring a crop to market only if it can make its total cash costs fall below the selling price; and to accomplish this it must "off-load" or "part-cost" what would otherwise be the full money expenses of production.

This magic is effected through the domestic model. Part-costing and off-loading are accomplished by trading remainders and practicing thrift. When a house makes savings, it converts money costs (*costos*) to material expenditures (*gastos*). To compete in the market a house replaces market-purchased items with home produced materials, or substitutes *gastos* for *costos*. The more *gastos*, the lower is the monetary cost of production. This process of parsimony ends in the selling of the uncosted remainder in a base→money→base' trade.

In some cases, for example, one crop, such as onions, is raised for sale and another crop, maize, for home consumption. If the onion crop were fully costed (if its inputs were entirely purchased), the house would incur a loss. But by the practice of thrift, the house substitutes for some of the onions' potential monetary costs by expenditure of the maize. The domestic remainder of the maize is reduced, but the onions reach the market from conditions – beyond the profit margin – that would otherwise be prohibitive. One afternoon in the mountains to the east of Bogotá, a woman observed that her house raised maize for eating and onions for sale. The maize, she said, had more house uses (*más gastos de la casa*) than the onions, for maize was used to maintain the people of the house, the workers in the fields, and animals. Onions had fewer house uses but more money costs (*menos gastos pero más costos*), and money could be made on them only by feeding the workers maize and selling some of the maize to obtain fertilizer for the onions. This use of the maize reduced the monetary cost of the onions (making savings). The "low-expenditure" (i.e., nonmonetary and productive) maize supported the "high-cost" onions. As our discussant summarized, "If you can't make savings using maize, you can't make money with onions. If one had to keep monetary accounts [*poner la cuenta*] or buy everything for the onions, there would be no gain." This process is in fact analogous to producing and selling uncosted firewood on the *páramo* in Nariño.

In effect, then, a market crop is raised by using some or all of the potential remainders of other crops, draining their uncosted leftovers into its production; this saves money. Furthermore, since house leftovers are figured in relation to future house expenditures, and since these can be lowered, it becomes quite clear how a cash crop not only lives off house ones but can depress the house project of maintaining itself or perpetuate economic stasis by choking off a domestic increase.

Even with these practices set before us every day, it took some time to sort out or "hear" the people's conversation about money cost and material expenditure. If we inquired about the production of domestic crops, they would tell us about seed ratios, land areas used, and the amount of labor required; but if we talked about "profit," they would say, "We don't keep accounts of that." In contrast, when we asked about market crops, the rural folk could and would tell us about money costs and revenues, adding that a profit was seldom made. But if we then asked about the domestic labor or foodstuffs that went into the cash crops, they answered, again, "We don't keep accounts of that, we don't count that, they are a house expenditure." This last voice did not betray an inability to calculate – for everyone knew what *volumes* of labor, food, and land went into the crops – but rather expressed the way the house and corporate calculations were being used together, through the substitution of "nonaccountable" expenditures for "accountable" costs. Accounting for profit and loss, and being accountable for them – as Weber (1947[1922], 1958[1920], 1961[1923]), Sombart (1915[1913]), and many others (Swetz 1987) have emphasized – is a phenomenon of the corporation and the market.

In their material practices and conversations the rural folk distinguish between homogeneous money costs and heterogeneous material expenditures. One is linked to profit making, the other to having remainders of incommensurate goods. Textual conversations, however, equate the two and subsume the latter within the former in order to model and to measure it. If we listen to the rural voice, a remainder (*una sobra*) is not a profit (*una ganancia*), and what the house loses to the market is never a measurable "surplus" produced during a prior production period. Trade from the margin is modeled in terms of the house schema of future material uses and leftovers rather than past monetary costs and profits. And what the house pays for entry into the market can have differing effects on it, for when the house trades, its leftovers may come from the part for seeding, for eating, for the animals, from the yearly savings, or from reserves in crops and animals. The house schema, with its continuously changing expenditures and remainders, its variable food plate, and its iterative application, determines the placement and effect of the transaction loss. One or another component of the heterogeneous holdings – crops, animals, tools, land – plays a part. Still, regardless of its immediate origin, this expenditure translates into a diminution of the base. Sometimes the base is replaced through trade, but usually it is not, so over time the house is ever evaporated by the market and must struggle to survive.

Chapter 9
MAKING SAVINGS

On the first day of our fieldwork, a discussant spoke at length about "making savings" (*hacer economías*) and "economizing" (*economizar*). The need to make savings and ways of doing so entered our discussions many times after, but the construct proved difficult to place. "Making savings" applies to a diverse and changing list of practices whose connection is not immediately apparent. It also belongs to two worlds, the house and the market. Since that initial talk, we have come to realize that "making savings" has a double, overlapping sense – being thrifty and hoarding – and that our contemporary usage is not coincident with the rural Colombians'. In the attempt to sort out these varying usages, we followed several textual trails, but when we realized that the distinction between being parsimonious and making hoards had been used to advantage by John Maynard Keynes (1964[1936]) the historical discussion became much clearer. The long conversation about "making savings" is complex, as is the local ethnography, but an examination of it has much to suggest about the relations between practice and text, margin and center.

We often use "making savings" to translate *hacer economías*, but terms such as being "thrifty," "parsimonious," "frugal," "abstinent," or "economical" can also be employed. Economizing is common to both house and corporation. In the rural economy, being thrifty means controlling expenditures to have leftovers; these increase savings or the base. In the market economy, economizing controls disbursements to have retained earnings or controls consumption to have unspent income; these also increase savings. Leftovers in the domestic economy and the unspent income of the market participant are both savings, but they are used differently. House remainders are held "inside the doors" as a precaution; they are kept as part of the base, and when they are traded the purpose is to replace the base or keep the advance. Leftovers are a savings that draw no interest. In the market economy, savings are exchanged (or lent) to secure more inputs (or achieve a return) with the purpose of increasing capital. In the corporate economy, savings become investments that draw a return.

But keeping and exchanging savings are actually practiced in both house and market economies, though in different ways and ratios. This can be seen by looking at the way income is allocated. In effect, following Keynes, two decisions about income are taken. The first concerns the making of savings through frugality. In the house economy, all returns are divided between expenditures and remainders; in the market economy, income is divided into immediate consumption or costs and deferred consumption or savings. In both contexts, savings are the residual of expenditure, and in both cases the admonition to be frugal is voiced. This can be summarized as follows:

In the house economy, returns = expenditures + remainders (savings)
In the corporate economy, income = consumption + savings

Once savings have been amassed, a second decision is taken concerning their use. The house makes savings "to keep" (*guardar*) them as a hoard. In contrast, market participants usually part with accumulations to secure a return, although they may keep a portion as a precautionary measure against the future. (In fact, the house also "invests" but by increasing its expenditures or consumption before remainders are secured.) This second decision can be summarized as follows:

In the house economy, remainders = hoards
In the corporate economy, savings = new investment + hoards

The contrast, then, lies in this: in the house economy, hoarding predominates over investing, while in the corporate economy investing predominates over hoarding. Still, in the latter there exists a tendency to hold wealth, and this is what Keynes termed "liquidity preference." But until he wrote about this propensity to hoard and explained its impact on the functioning of the market system, the long-dominant house practice of keeping the savings was passed over in the central market texts, even though the making of savings was not. Keynes's recognition of the desire to keep or to hold, it might be argued, allowed him to construct a new macro-economics or total model of the market that included practices of the house in addition to those of the corporation.

A consideration of the Colombian practice of making savings, we think, helps to elucidate the local model as well as two moments in economics texts and history. One textual discussion, between Weber and Sombart, concerned the origin of capitalism. We think that their argument, never fully resolved, would have been much clearer had it not confounded consuming versus saving, on the one hand, with hoarding versus investing, on the other. A different discussion took place in economics texts themselves, from Turgot through Mill. Most classical economists projected the house practice of making savings upon the corporate economy in order to explain the rise of capital, to develop a rationale for the taking of profit, and to build a model of a smoothly working economy. But, ironically, in so doing they appropriated the house practice of being thrifty to mark the distinction between modern society and its predecessors, while leaving aside any consideration of the reason for this practice. For a long time, economics texts had everything back to front: the major difference between house and corporate economies lies in their differing propensities to hoard, not in their differing propensities to be thrifty. There were countervoices in this discussion, such as T.R. Malthus, but until Keynes these remained subordinate. All of this material illustrates, then, the way in which practice and text, voices "on the ground" and "in the air," and dominant and subordinate texts are appropriated and transformed, become intertwined, and play themselves out in long and ever-thicker conversations.

WAYS OF BEING THRIFTY

In the house economy, the practice of making savings is part of the larger task of managing a house well (*mandar bien*). Managing well means ensuring the smooth working of all the house's relationships. The man and woman must assist one another, the children must be trained to respect authority and to work. When there is shared labor and shared ownership, the house is "well run." In the context of material life, managing well means making savings. A house gathers up agricultural produce from the land in a venture that it does not fully control. But once gathered, the harvest constitutes a stock for living that the house does control. The practice of being thrifty presumes that the resources of a house are already given, and it applies to the way a flow is used. Economizing is the human management and judgment that must be exercised whenever goods are expended in the house. Specifically, it is the process of allocating and expending goods so that there are leftovers and of turning these leftovers to other uses so that nothing is wasted or lost. Through the practice of making savings a remainder is gained and a reserve built for the future. A house's continuity, through the making of leftovers and savings and the growth of the base, depends upon its being "well run." Making savings stands in opposition to waste, prodigality, and luxury. Being thrifty runs through all the practices of the house from housekeeping to householding, preserving, conserving, and storing.

Care in the use of money is one aspect of being thrifty. Just as making leftovers and making something of them are ways of being frugal, so avoiding the expenditure of cash by substituting material uses for money costs is a way of being thrifty: "One uses up the base but in order to avoid buying. Don't sell anything; keep it for eating, and less will need to be bought." If the base is sufficient and carefully used, if something is replaced inside the house, money does not have to be secured and expended: "When it does not go out the doors, that is making savings." The rural folk also explain that to make savings one must have the materials in the house, by which they mean producing the means for living and for working to avoid the need to buy and the trader's gain.

When the rural folk do purchase, they try to spend as little as possible in stores, for then "money remains." Men especially should avoid wasting money in a bar; and buying less, for example, owning fewer clothes, and buying inexpensive goods are ways to be thrifty. As we have seen, this has an impact on the way small stores stock and sell their inventory. Market goods come in specially packaged sizes as the people ration their money in purchasing. For their part, stores "make money" in much the same way. The inventory of small lots is itself small, and the goal is to have rapid turnover so that less financial investment is needed. For both houses and stores, these practices save money though they require the expenditure of more labor. For those with some financial wealth, buying in bulk is thrifty because it is less expensive per item. But this is difficult to do, given the present marketing structure in the countryside, the small packages produced for most consumers, and the way merchants make money through small-lot sales or taking over the bulking and breaking function.

Parsimony in the use of house materials is of a piece with the way cash is expended. Economizing in the home is a shifting set of experiments. In production there are many ways of making savings. The harvest of a domestic crop provides food for the house, which means it does not have to be bought: this is thrift. The people try to provide their own seed, obviating the need for its purchase; and in the selection of the seeds there are ways to make savings. Some crops serve several purposes, such as providing food for humans and fodder for animals, and this is a way of making savings because there is less loss of the harvest. Certain crops, such as maize, require less labor or materials to raise, and this makes savings by releasing money or work time for other household activities ("The worker uses less food, so more remains to sell"). Then, too, the thriftiest way to raise crops is by using house labor, although trading labor with others is also economical. If laborers must be hired, paying them in kind rather than in cash saves money, and remunerating them partly with meals is a way to be thrifty. For those with ample land, using sharecroppers who receive part of the harvest instead of money is a form of frugality; and sharecroppers bear some of the costs of the crop, a further saving to the landowner. Finally with ample land, more can be raised in quantity and variety, and less needs to be bought; in the smallest house, too, a garden with herbs and tomato plants or a patio with a few fruit trees aids in making savings: "Everything serves."

The domestic production of commodities is also done parsimoniously. A potter tries to secure clay from land he owns or to which he has free access. If stubble from the fields can be used instead of wood or charcoal to fuel the kiln, more economies are made. All the working of the clay is done at the house, which supplies the processing shelter.

Comparable strategies are employed in consumption. The people are careful not to cook up too much food, for it may be wasted and the need to buy will arrive sooner. There are limits to belt-tightening, however; the laborer must have enough food to work, and the fire in the kiln must be hot enough to bake the pottery, so if scrub from the field is not sufficient to provide the heat, wood must be purchased. To expend beyond what can be replaced is not thrifty, but to go below what the house needs means that the base will not be restored.

Another way of making savings is to prolong the useful life of an object. For example, being careful not to lose possessions is a form of parsimony. (Also, to pay a loan back slowly rather than quickly is thrifty – unless one has to pay interest.) But the stretching out of a material service is particularly characteristic of tool use. Machetes are domestically repaired; plows are locally made. All the tools have a patchwork and patched-up quality. Most of the small iron sugarcane mills originally came from the United States and were made in the early part of this century. Over time gears, casings, and pistons all break; if the grinding equipment had been held by a profit making unit, it would long ago have been discarded. But the rural people are adept at "making do," and therefore mills and other instruments last well beyond their anticipated lives – a lengthening of their service time bought at the expenditure of local labor. This is true house*holding*.

"Making do" itself is an important way of being thrifty, and getting along with what one has or doing something with what remains is practiced with invention in the countryside. Materials are not only fully used and then reused but are put to new uses – a process applied especially to the leftovers and the waste of the larger society. Plastic containers made originally to hold petroleum products for market sale are used to carry and store liquids or to catch rainwater, and with their tops sliced off they serve as measuring containers for seed. Old tires are remade into sandals, small oil tins become kerosene lamps. The usages and the examples change over time, but the practice of using the no-cost "remainders" of the market is surely old. Objects already held in the countryside also are given many tasks. One afternoon we joined a family baking bread, pastry, and cookies for a holiday. As the food emerged from the outdoor oven, they used metal pot lids and roofing materials for trays, and the dough was rolled on a bed.

But making do is possible only because the people have many and broad skills and readily learn new ones. Some structures are made without the use of a nail, and if constructing this type of building is the skill of only a few, most can make a bed of cane and wood in place of buying one. For sending tomatoes to the market, the people make crates from wood scraps and used nails. Women, aside from their domestic duties, tend animals and harvest cash crops, although to use a woman's skills most fully the people sometimes spend money – to buy a sewing machine. The very act of forming a household is considered an act of parsimony; the woman prepares a brew for field laborers and the man provides the materials for it, with neither paying for the work of the other.

Making savings means engaging in ceaseless activity, for this also is a careful use of materials. Working long hours, continuously and without vacations, means that one is not wasting time, which implies the house is not wasting food. The people's definition of being rich, to repeat, is having sufficient base that work is unnecessary. Luxury – as in the pure waste of owning and feeding pigeons – means that savings are not being made.

In addition, owning land is a way to be thrifty. By raising a variety of crops, trading use of the land for labor via sharecropping, combining agriculture with pastoralism, and relying on the latter – all of which are ways of "internalizing exchange" – the market can be avoided and money saved.

Finally, keeping animals helps make savings. Holding the agricultural leftover in animals keeps the base for future use. Cattle and sheep also provide manure, which reduces the need to purchase fertilizer. Cows and goats yield milk, a no-cost foodstuff, while hens provide eggs and sheep wool. Most of the animals require little expenditure of labor, and their maintenance costs are low, which helps make them a thrifty holding. Animals, of course, have the further advantage that they grow, can be sold for cash, and may augment the base, although this is not itself thrift.

A long conversation: thrift
The project of the corporation in the market is to make money; the project of the house is to save on the use of money. The house saves and hoards, the market participant saves and expends. Market actors do use thrift to manage their flows and build reserves, but money saved may be used for further investment by returning it to the sphere of exchange and subsidizing profit making activities. In fact, too much hoarding by market participants leads to underconsumption, oversupply, and lassitude in the general economy. By contrast, rural saving preserves the base and may help augment it later; these savings are kept off-the-market, for the house that overspends destroys itself, although not spending anything is impossible given that land access must be gained and some inputs must be purchased. Thus, practicing thrift is common to both house and corporation, yet it has a different position in each. What is the connection? Is the practice of material thrift in the house evidence of the market's influence, or is economizing with cash a domestic carryover?

In our view, the practice of being thrifty began in the domestic economy and was then transformed by market actors. But the relation between practice and text also enters here, and the textual history of thrift alone is complex. Briefly, the inscribed model of the domestic economy, as we have seen, begins in Greek times or earlier. The main Greek texts emphasize the importance of managing a house well; the subsequent Roman ones give attention to agricultural techniques and practices but hint at the importance of care in the expenditure of money. As the market sphere grew, the house had more and more to handle money, and by the fourteenth century running a household well had much to do with cash and exchange. Leon Battista Alberti's (1971[1433–41]) *Della famiglia* is a benchmark here, with its contrasting voices concerning the house and its handling of money. After Alberti, the route of inscription takes several paths, two of which we shall follow. According to Max Weber, being thrifty is a central component of the Protestant ethic, culturally and ideologically crucial for modern capitalism. Sombart (1915[1913]), Braudel (1986), and others partly disagree, holding that capitalist relationships began far earlier, but concur that the practice of making savings is important in their development. Part of this older argument, then, hinges on the origin of parsimony, and we think that this argument may be incorrectly focused. The second path leads into modern economics itself, for starting with the Mercantilists and early French writers and continuing through Smith and Mill, the concepts of thrift and abstinence are linchpins in the textual understanding of the way capital funds are created, augmented, and used. This line of argument ends in a contradiction with Mill's claim that abstinence from current consumption creates capital yet does not influence spending patterns in the market. There are countervoices, for early on Malthus disagreed; but his voice – to stretch the argument in time – remained "unheard" until the work of Keynes. To recount every step in this long history is not our project and is well beyond our capacities. We do want to suggest, however, some of the ways the house practice developed, was appropriated and transformed, and eventually gave rise to contradictions in models of the center, all the while remaining a practice of the house and the periphery.

The practice of thrift does not appear in Aristotle's seminal text. He focuses upon the management of the household and especially upon its internal relationships, such as the relation of master to slave, husband to wife, and parents to children: "the business of household management is concerned more with human beings than it is with inanimate property" (1946:33). Household management, Aristotle maintains, is not directly concerned with "production" or acquisition. House provisioning is limited to securing necessities, while household life is not a means to an end but an action (praxis) complete in itself. Aristotle is keenly aware that monetary gains can be made, and he recounts some of the ways in which fortunes have been amassed through monopoly control of resources (1946:30–1). But household possessions are for use; they are not instruments for the accomplishment of something else, nor is the house directed to ceaseless acquisition, which falls within the unnatural realm of exchange.

Because the use of currency pertains mostly to "retail trade," not a proper household function, the house management of money is not Aristotle's concern.

Like Aristotle's *Politics*, Xenophon's fourth-century B.C. text on household management (1923) had a formative impact on those to follow. It was translated from the Greek by Cicero and became known among the Roman writers on agriculture, who through their own texts also influenced the practical and verbal conversation of the succeeding centuries. Because Xenophon's work is cast as a Socratic dialogue on good estate management, themes emerge through the articulation of many voices and countervoices; and the themes are many. To be certain, Xenophon does speak of increasing "the estate by showing a balance" (p. 363), but the voice of gain is subsidiary to that of running the estate through careful management (p. 517). A central assumption of Xenophon (p. 401) is that only the earth yields food and all the things on which people live; this stated, he moves swiftly to household administration. The text is surely one of the earliest written on management practices, and Xenophon is a delight to read both for his enthusiasm and for his use of the dialogic form to experiment with different house models. Some parts may offend the modern ear, for in long passages Xenophon speaks of taking a young wife, training her, and teaching her to obey male authority. A wife is to remain indoors and learn domestic practices so that she can properly superintend servants; she should be orderly and diligent in her own work and keep household utensils and other belongings in good condition. But the husband must also work diligently to keep the house going and to serve as a model for the servants and other workers. In Xenophon's estimation, it is not the knowledge of farming itself or the intelligence of the farmer that makes for success but the care, hard work, and trouble of the manager (p. 521). In fact, precepts of farming occupy a small place in the text, while dialogue and conversation themselves (pp. 461, 473) are held to be formative of behavior.

Throughout the work, Xenophon uses metaphors to explain and construct the roles of female and male in the household. The tropes are taken from the world of animals, such as the beehive with workers and a queen,

from the military with armies and commanders, from ships
with captains and crews, from the polity, and from music.
In this respect, Xenophon's house is modeled after other
domains. But the successful house also has its own
characteristic: ceaseless work. Slack and slothfulness are to
be avoided especially (p. 517), as these

> are the evils that crush estates far more than sheer lack of knowledge. For *the*
> *outgoing expenses of the estate are not a penny less* [emphasis added]; but the
> work done is insufficient to show a profit on the expenditure . . . to a careful
> man, who works strenuously at agriculture, no business gives quicker
> returns than farming. My father taught me that and proved it by his own
> practice.

In Xenophon, as in Aristotle, the focus is upon good
management, but he emphasizes more the importance of
working assiduously and having care in spending money.
The admonition to use materials and money carefully –
which is also the calling to ceaseless work – is hardly the
monopoly of capitalist ideology and the Reformation.

The principal Latin texts on the household, estate, or
villa are by Cato, Columella, Varro, and Palladius
(Amerlinck 1987). The emphasis in these times shifts from
social relationships within the house to farming practices.
Greater recognition is also given to the villa as a user of
money. For example, Cato recognizes the estate as a locus
of currency circulation, but he emphasizes the importance
of care in expenditure so that there may be remainders
(Cato 1933:5–8). "Remember that a farm is like a man –
however great the income, if there is extravagance but little
is left" (Cato 1934:5). His discussion mingles money
accounts with product calculations; he talks about villa
processes, not corporate functions. He recommends
(1934:9), for example, that after reviewing the tasks
accomplished the owner

> give orders for the completion of what work remains; run over the cash
> accounts, grain accounts, and purchases of fodder; run over the wine
> accounts, the oil accounts – what has been sold, what collected, balance due,
> and what is left that is saleable . . . let the supplies on hand be checked over.
> Give orders that whatever may be lacking for the current year be supplied;
> that what is superfluous be sold . . . Sell worn-out oxen, blemished cattle,
> blemished sheep, wool, hides, an old wagon, old tools, an old slave, a sickly
> slave, and whatever else is superfluous. *The master should have the selling*
> *habit, not the buying habit* [emphasis added].

Cato continues with admonitions and practical advice. His text is not about profit making in the sphere of exchange but about running a house through careful administration by setting aside sufficient amounts from returns to cover subsequent expenditures, by keeping superfluities intact within the villa, and by reproducing the estate by replacing its holdings.

Precepts on farming and on stock raising have a prominent place in the texts of Varro (1934), Palladius (1976), and Columella (1941). For example, the latter says (p. 333),

It is of the greatest importance that a cutting which is set in the ground should heal over and quickly form a callus at the point where it is cut from the mother vine. For, if this does not happen, excessive moisture is drawn up through the open pith of the vine, as though through a tube, and makes the stock hollow; and the result is that hiding-places are provided for ants and other creatures that cause the lower part of the vine-stalk to rot.

This concern with the maxims and techniques of estate functioning is a new voice, but it fits the domestic model; attention is being given to controlling house expenditure, while little emphasis is paid to market activity itself or to profit making. The notion of being thrifty with money is voiced but as part of the practice of good housekeeping.

The Roman and Greek texts on the domestic economy proved to be influential models right through the Middle Ages, and they were intensively reworked in the Scholastic thought of Aquinas and others (Roll 1973). But it is most interesting to reengage this long conversation on the domestic economy at a later period, when the market economy was more fully developed. In his masterful study of the development of the market economy, Fernand Braudel, with some reluctance, turns to the question of when capitalism truly began. Max Weber had argued that the crucial moment was the sixteenth century, when the Protestant ethic called for a new form of wordly action, but Werner Sombart thought that capitalism had arisen earlier, and Braudel agrees. "Fourteenth-century Florence," he says (1986:578), "was a capitalist city." Regardless of who stands in the right, some of the textual evidence cited is of capital interest. Sombart drew ammunition for his argument from Alberti's *Della famiglia* (1971[1433–41]), in which he claimed to find a new set of themes: forethought, the considered use of money and of time, and "thrift exercised willingly" (Sombart 1915[1913]:106). Braudel calls these "good bourgeois principles" (p. 579); although he admits that Alberti's work is one of a long line of "housekeeping manuals" filled with homely advice and of little "relevance to the world of trade" (p. 580), he argues that it bespeaks the existence of a capitalist spirit in the Florence of the time.

Thrift, along with hard work, has often been identified as "the bourgeois virtue" (Fox-Genovese and Genovese 1983). Parsimony is said to be the practice of the rising and prosperous middle class, being a willingness to forgo present pleasures and amusements in the service of the future. As linked to rational action, it implies controlling and disciplining current wants in the service of greater ends. Sombart called this *The Quintessence of Capitalism* (1915[1913]), and on this point he and Weber agreed. Weber (1958[1920]) had proposed that parsimony, as opposed to prodigality, was a key feature of the Protestant ethic. Faith was to be proved by objective results, achieved consistently over a lifetime. In certain forms of Protestantism there was not only a "this-world" turning but a "calling" to ceaseless work in order to show signs of being one of the elect through worldly success. The pure pursuit of money and gain were condemned, for these were not to be enjoyed, nor was individual industry to cease with success. Ostentation and self-indulgence were detestable to the asceticism that was inherent in this religious form. On Weber's account, religiously impelled asceticism, directed to the material realm, led to thrift and the accumulation of capital. The religious model of Luther and Calvin produced both industry and frugality and ultimately riches.

We enter a demurrer; we have found thrift to be pervasively and intensely practiced in rural Colombia, among Roman Catholics and within a cosmological framework in which labor is an effort and creation of God, and all success (*abundancia*) is a result of His power expressed through nature. Weber might have countered that this discovery does not belie his argument because the particulate features of the Protestant ethic are not unique to it and, once articulated or modeled, the ethic shifts in a secular direction; this response admitted, the historical roots of Colombian rural culture, it must be said, do predate the presumed rise and spread of the Protestant ethic. Thrift, savings, ceaseless work, and avoiding the unnecessary use of resources are found precisely where – on Weber's argument – they ought not to be.

This would seem to align us with Sombart (and Braudel) as opposed to Weber, for if being thrifty predates the rise of ascetic Protestantism and is separate from it, Weber must be wrong. On our view, however, monetary thrift is initially the voice of the domestic economy as it encounters the growing sphere of market exchange. It is the domestic making of monetary and exchange relationships. One must disagree with Sombart not only for fixing on economizing or making savings as the original capitalist essence but for locating this activity within the market as opposed to the house. Yet this was exactly Weber's (1958[1920]:194–8) critique of Sombart in a learned footnote that placed the work of Alberti in the stream of Greek and Roman texts on the house economy. The point at issue involves not only the practice of making savings but the way the resulting accumulations are used.

How, then, shall we read Alberti's *Della famiglia*? The scholarly argument has centered on only part of the work which consists of four parts or books, all with a domestic focus. The first concerns relations between the generations, the second love and marriage, and the fourth friendship, while attention has been drawn to the third, which concerns "good management." This third section is about the well-run house, not the profit making individual, and the conversation, cast in a form recalling Xenophon's dialogue, ranges widely over many domestic themes of the period. But the discussion of material practices would be especially well understood in contemporary Colombia (Alberti 1971[1433–41]:169–71):

Those who use no more than is sufficient for whatever is needed and save the rest . . . I call good managers . . .

For every expenditure, see to it that it is not greater than necessity requires nor smaller than decorum demands . . .

Men labor to earn money so that they will have it in case of need. While in good health, they provide for illness, just as an ant in the summer provides for the winter ahead. Possessions, therefore, are to be used to satisfy needs;

when there is no necessity, they are to be saved. Thus you may conclude that good management consists not so much in saving things as in using them when needed.

This is a house text about frugality and hoarding, written within the context of the long conversation that began in Greek and Roman times even though it gives more attention to money use. Sombart, however, gives it a "capitalist hearing," and he particularly draws attention to one phrase: *sancta cosa la masserizia*. Sombart first terms this the principle of "Holy Economy," then says that what Alberti meant by *masserizia* is not clear, and finally treats the Italian *masserizia* as meaning "economy" in the modern sense (1915[1913]:105). Our English text, however, reads: "Thrift is a sacred thing; how many evil desires and dishonest appetites it curbs!" (1971[1433–41]:168). Weber (1958[1920]:195), too, was worried by Sombart's understanding of "sacred thrift," and he interpreted it as "a principle of maintenance . . . not of acquisition." Sombart dissimulates here, for *masserizia* has several usages that make quite good sense in the context of Alberti's discussion, are instances of the domestic voice, and can be seen as applications of the house model as it encounters the market. According to one authoritative dictionary (*Sansoni Dictionary of the Italian and English Languages*, 1972), *masserizia* can be used for

1 Furniture and fittings or household goods
2 Fittings and stock, such as equipment, tools, and implements
3 Stewardship
4 Saving and economy

The meaning could not be clearer: *masserizia* is the good management (or stewardship) of the domestic holdings, and this includes, but is not limited to, frugality with money. In addition, *far masserizia* means "to economize or save," "to do or make," and this is comparable to the Spanish *hacer economías*. Sombart, in the service of his argument, revoices Alberti's domestic use of "economy" as if he intended it to apply only to exchange and to the market. But Alberti was expressing not so much a "bourgeois mentality" as the domestic economy's response to exchange. Sombart's argument, while ostensibly calling on "history," lacks historicity, for it displaces Alberti's voice from its position within a long and changing conversation to make it a reflection of his own. Alberti's voice is particularly interesting because it is one of the first written expressions of the way the house was managing itself in the market – by trying to save on the expenditure of money and to keep it. In short, we claim that the practice of being thrifty with money developed out of good housekeeping. The latter has always meant care in the use of materials, but as the market grew and domestic units became greater participants within it, careful house management came also to be applied to the use of currency. The aim was to create reserves. Eventually, the house practice was appropriated for conversations about market transactions themselves, but this takes us ahead to the texts of economists.

Several stages may be distinguished in the written, market conversation. In the view of Tribe (1978), the period from 1600 to 1800 saw the final development and then the demise of the "agricultural treatise." During the early years of this period, writers were still listening to, and sometimes plagiarizing, Xenophon and the Latin authors; emphasis was placed upon the relation of the house to land and on its internal "good ordering" (Tribe 1978:55). The husbandman was visualized as a solitary figure, not even linked to the local economy. In most of the texts the larger system itself was seen as a form of householding. The Mercantilists, for example, were broadly united in the view that goods were produced as the nation provided for its needs just as a house did; any remainder could be sold internationally, with the balance received in goods, imperishables, and currency, thus increasing national wealth over time. Certainly, Mercantilism displayed a special interest in trade, but this was linked to ensuring national self-sufficiency, and it echoed the house problem of achieving a just price and fair exchange. As one Mercantilist said, there is "a great similitude between the affairs of a private person, and of a nation, the former being but a little family, and the latter a great family" (quoted in Haney [1949:143]).

By the 1750s, however, a new model was emerging according to which the house farm is enmeshed in a system of exchange and its produce is circulated within the larger

society. Calculation, landlord–tenant relations, and record
keeping all became subjects for textual conversation, and
the house was no longer seen as "the economy" itself
(Tribe 1978:78). This period, however, did not mark the
complete disappearance of the house model, for it was now
projected upon the more inclusive state. "Political
economy" was seen as the wise regulation of a royal
household, in which the monarch helps to guide the
circulation of the national product. This use of the house
model for the nation culminated in James Steuart's *An
Inquiry into the Principles of Political Oeconomy*
(1966[1767]), which began with a consideration of thrift
(pp. 15–17):

> Oeconomy, in general, is the art of providing for all the wants of a family,
> with prudence and frugality. If any thing necessary or useful be found
> wanting . . . we immediately perceive a want of oeconomy. The object of it, in
> a private family, is therefore to provide for the nourishment, the other wants,
> and the employment of every individual . . .
> The whole oeconomy must be directed by the head, who is both lord and
> steward of the family . . .
> What oeconomy is in a family, political oeconomy is in a state: with these
> essential differences, however, that in a state there are no servants, all
> are children: that a family may be formed when and how a man pleases,
> and he may there establish what plan of oeconomy he thinks fit; but states
> are found formed, and the oeconomy of these depends upon a thousand
> circumstances . . .
> The principal object of this science is to secure a certain fund of subsis-
> tence for all the inhabitants . . . to make their several interests lead them to
> supply one another with their reciprocal wants . . .
> It is the business of a statesman to judge of the expediency of different
> schemes of oeconomy, and by degrees to model the minds of his subjects.

Steuart's text, like a statesman's function, was an act of
modeling or persuading. He projected the known house
model upon the political ordering of the larger economy.
But, notably, while he assumed frugality to be an
important part of household and state management, he did
not apply it to market practices. Soon after, this was done
by Adam Smith.

We have argued that Turgot's *Reflections* (1898[1770]),
which followed upon Steuart, was both a Physiocratic text
and a precursor of later conversations. As the work
unfolded it evinced a shift from the house to the corporate

model – and it mixed the two by using thrift as the
continuous practice. For example, Turgot claimed that the
land provided all wealth and consequently capital was
accumulated only by economizing on what the earth had
already yielded (p. 97). This was the house model. But he
also stated that capital existed as money, that it was used
in the entire economy, and that money itself was the
"subject of saving" (p. 98). This was the emerging
corporate model, and it implied that capital was not
accumulated solely by making savings from the land. The
French term used here is *l'épargne*, which has the
ambiguous triple meaning of "thrift," "economy," and
"saving." Turgot's work in some respects captured the
very process of a conversational shift or appropriation in
which the domestic lexicon was used and then taken apart
and reprojected on exchange as if the two applications –
for materials in the house and for money in market
transactions – were the same.

But it was Smith who made greatest use of the construct
of thrift, and he did so in the context of the market. His
Wealth of Nations was published only nine years after
Steuart's *Principles*. The latter may have brought to a close
the period in which the domestic model was maximally
projected outside its "home domain," and Smith may have
established a new model for the market, but his text
retained parts of the earlier conversation. He argued
(1976[1776]:358–9) that savings from current consumption
were made through frugality and that these constituted
capital:

Capitals are increased by parsimony, and diminished by prodigality and
misconduct. Whatever a person saves from his revenue he adds to his capital
. . . Parsimony, and not industry, is the immediate cause of the increase of
capital. Industry, indeed, provides the subject which parsimony accumulates. But whatever industry might acquire, if parsimony did not save and
store up, the capital would never be the greater.

This was different from Turgot's text, with its special
emphasis on the land as the first source of wealth, and
more fully projected the practice of thrift upon the market
actor. But because the market enterprise itself was not
completely established in the text, most of Smith's
examples had an individualistic and house resonance; in

effect, this helped bridge the two domains of house and business.

Smith saw frugality as involving the interplay of expenditures and leftovers, of controlling one to have the other; but this house practice was now elevated to the status of a human "principle" (pp. 362–3):

> The principle which prompts to expence, is the passion for present enjoyment; which, though sometimes violent and very difficult to be restrained, is in general only momentary and occasional. But the principle which prompts to save, is the desire of bettering our condition, a desire which, though generally calm . . . never leaves us . . . the principle of frugality seems not only to predominate, but to predominate very greatly.

Smith placed great trust in self-interest, but he did not attend – from within the economic realm – to the determinants of parsimony and prodigality; they were rather counterpoised "passions" whose balance was perhaps determined, as Weber was later to argue, by something like the Protestant ethic. Still, along with his contemporary David Hume,[1] Smith produced a ringing defense of frugality: "Every prodigal appears to be a public enemy, and every frugal man a public benefactor" (p. 362). This textual appropriation of the house practice for the market, however, ultimately led Smith along a new path. He argued not only that parsimony increased capital but that the latter was used by its holder to produce more: being thrifty and spending the savings were welded together, while being thrifty and holding the savings were teased apart (p. 359).

> What is annually saved is as regularly consumed as what is annually spent, and nearly in the same time too; but it is consumed by a different set of people. That portion of his revenue which a rich man annually spends, is in most cases consumed by idle guests, and menial servants, who leave nothing behind them in return for their consumption. That portion which he annually saves, as for the sake of the profit it is immediately employed as a capital, is consumed in the same manner, and nearly in the same time too, but by a different set of people, by laborers, manufacturers, and artificers, who reproduce with a profit the value of their annual consumption.

Smith's main theme was that all money accumulated by thrift, or restraint from consumption, is ultimately spent rather than hoarded. He linked this to the idea that some spending goes on food and services in the home, while

other spending is used on the manufacture of goods; one is
unproductive expenditure, the other productive. Thus, all
money saved is spent, and cash has no store-of-value
function: "The sole use of money is to circulate
consumable goods" (p. 361). This was an appropriation yet
a crucial reevaluation of the house practice of thrift, and it
gave making savings a new rationale. We might summarize
the developing model by saying that thrift yields savings,
savings make capital, and capital is spent on goods and
labor, which are employed productively to provide more
goods. There are no pauses, there is no keeping of wealth.
For Smith, the crucial distinction was between spending in
manufacture and purchasing domestic services; one creates
growth, the other does not. The house rationale for being
thrifty and accumulating savings – to have a reserve for
future use – was thus deleted from the conversation.

In France, Jean-Baptiste Say interpreted and elaborated
upon the work of Smith. In his *Treatise on Political
Economy* (1964[1803]) he argued that productive capital is
augmented only by saving and that savings are made from
current consumption by the exercise of frugality. He agreed
with Turgot and Smith that the practice of frugality had
increased in modern times but considered this due to "the
advances of industry," more efficient processes of
production having tempted the owners of capital to use it
for making profit. For Say, capital could be endlessly
accumulated through industry and frugality, and these
heightened practices of his time quite undermined the older
one of hoarding wealth (pp. 116–18).

Say's rereading of frugality as prompted by profit
seeking was of a piece with his larger model of the
economy. A savings, he contended, was always expended
or consumed; and he attacked the countervoices of
Sismondi and Malthus, stating that "the accumulations of
the miser are now either vested in reproduction . . . or . . .
production" (p. 111). All this fits "Say's Law," which in
many ways was the logical conclusion of the
thrift→savings→capital argument (p. 135):

When the producer has put the finishing hand to his product, he is most
anxious to sell it immediately, lest its value should diminish in his hand. Nor
is he less anxious to dispose of the money he may get for it; for the value of
money is also perishable. But the only way of getting rid of money is in the

purchase of some product or other. Thus the mere circumstance of the creation of one product immediately opens a vent for other products.

In different terms, or according to "Say's Law," there is no overproduction of goods or shortfall of demand, for the sale of a product yields – through the return it gives on land, labor, and capital – the purchasing power to secure it on the market; and this power is exercised. For the economy as a whole, returns from production make up exactly sufficient demand to purchase what has been produced. The act of "saving" only influences the distribution of spending between present consumption and investment for the future. Monetary savings are always offset by their expenditure.

The classical model of the economy that emerged was finally and fully articulated by Mill. In keeping with prior arguments, he held that all capital is the result of saving, even when there are increases in productivity: "To consume less than is produced, is saving; and that is the process by which capital is increased" (Mill 1929[1848]:70). Mill, who like Smith was an observer of the world, admired peasant smallholders, and to some degree he used them to model middle-class savers. Both, he said, are frugal; they economize and exercise self-control. In contrast, day laborers are "usually improvident" and "spend carelessly" (pp. 286–7). Savings are the result of abstinence from consumption, and saving enriches while spending impoverishes; consequently the prodigality of some, such as day laborers, forces others to economize (pp. 163, 72–3). Thus, Mill saw thrift as being common to both the house and corporate actors but not the laborer.

Mill went on to reason, as we have seen, that profit is the return for abstinence (p. 462). To persuade a holder of capital to forgo current consumption a return has to be paid, and because the person who supplies the means of production must have abstained from their use, profit is his reward (p. 36). Mill also argued that cultures differ in their propensity to accumulate and that this motive itself varies with the profit or income it can be expected to realize (pp. 164–5, 173, 728–9). He clinched the profit-as-reward-for-abstinence argument by drawing an analogy between the house and business (pp. 416–17):

The cause of profit is, that labour produces more than is required for its support. The reason why agricultural capital yields a profit is because human beings can grow more food than is necessary to feed them while it is being grown . . . from which it is a consequence, that if a capitalist undertakes to feed the labourers on condition of receiving the produce, he has some of it remaining for himself after replacing his advances.

Mill's claim "from which it is a consequence" was intended to persuade the reader of an identity between house returns and expenditures in agriculture, and corporate income and costs in manufacturing – that making savings has the same function in both, to create capital. But Mill, an ethnographer of his time, did know that savings were not always accumulated for investment and that he had not taken full enough account of the link between being thrifty and building reserves in the house (pp. 286–7):

The tendency of peasant proprietors . . . is to take even too much thought for the morrow . . . They deny themselves reasonable indulgences, and live wretchedly in order to economize. In Switzerland almost everybody saves . . . among the French . . . the spirit of thrift is diffused through the rural population . . . there are numbers who have hoards in leathern bags, consisting of sums in five-franc pieces.

This recognition of contrary practices at the European periphery posed a paradox for the new model of the center. Specifically, Mill argued that profit arose from the investment of savings accumulated by thrift; profit was the reward for this abstinence, and it motivated different degrees of thriftiness. Yet he knew that peasants practiced thrift simply to have savings and never received a reward for their abstinence. If both had capitalist practices, how could the difference of the two economies be explained? Mill "rid" himself of the problem by the textual device of redefinition – or perhaps omission. Pure savings, he said, are not capital. "If merely laid by for future use, it is said to be hoarded; and while hoarded, is not consumed at all. But if employed as capital, it is all consumed" (p. 70). To preserve the profit-as-reward-for-abstinence argument, Mill – with Say – had to omit the possibility of hoarding in the market economy. But with this, the textual conversation had come full circle: capital was made by abstinence or hoarding, yet capital was not a hoard! Mill had drawn a similarity between capitalists and peasant householders on the basis of their common practice of economizing, giving thought to the morrow, and having the spirit of thrift. This provided a model of the way capital was built and was used to justify the taking of profit. But among householders thrift is practiced to have a reserve, so to keep the profit argument intact Mill deleted this implication of the older, appropriated model.

After Mill, discussion of hoarding fell aside until Keynes (1964[1936]) reinstituted it, neatly turning everything about by claiming that interest paid on money is the reward for not hoarding. He thus distinguished making savings from keeping them. In Keynes's model, interest is not a reward for abstinence, for thrift or for waiting but a return for giving up the security of keeping a liquid hoard. Keynes did not write about the domestic economy, but his transformed model allowed him to draw an implicit distinction between the house and the corporation: "In the absence of an organized market, liquidity-preference due to the precautionary-motive would be greatly increased; whereas the existence of an organized market gives an opportunity for wide fluctuations in liquidity-preference due to the speculative-motive" (pp. 170–1).[2] With this, hoarding and temporal hitches reentered the market model, and the phenomena of business cycles and of political action in the economy again became textual concerns. By his implicit recognition of domestic practices, Keynes was able to construct a new macroeconomics, but in a sense he was only restating the Colombian folk voice that being thrifty or making economies is not the same as seeking a profit or making money.

Thus, what had begun as the house modeling of exchange – and still persists in Colombian practice – was appropriated and slowly reevaluated in the texts of economists in order to model the accumulation of capital. In this intellectual appropriation and transformation of a practice, the act of perpetual thrift or hoarding – with all that it potentially implied about liquidity preference, money used as a store of value, the occurrence of gluts, and underconsumption – was for a long while effaced, perhaps to distance the new model from those from whom it had been taken. Thrift and saving had been shifted from one conversation to another and reapplied. Only after some time was the original voice and practice "rediscovered."

Keynes himself once justified his profession in a grand set of phrases (1964[1936]:383):

The ideas of economists and political philosophers, both when they are right and when they are wrong, are more powerful than is commonly understood. Indeed the world is ruled by little else. Practical men, who believe themselves to be quite exempt from any intellectual influences, are usually the slaves of some defunct economist. Madmen in authority, who hear voices in the air, are distilling their frenzy from some academic scribbler of a few years back.

But the anthropologist wonders whether the economist has it back to front, for to judge by the Colombian ethnography it would appear that many of those "voices in the air" come first from the practices and articulations of living folk and are then frantically distilled and transformed by academic economists into textual forms that – as the writings of Aristotle, Xenophon, Cato, Aquinas, Smith, Mill and Keynes all suggest – have their persuasive force on one another and on the long conversation in which we all participate.

Chapter 10

FROM HOUSE TO CORPS

The conversation from Colombia is unfinished; much remains to be said by the rural folk and by us. But our purpose – to present the Colombian model of the house economy – has been mostly accomplished. We call this model a finding or discovery. Clearly, the idea of the domestic economy is not new, but a portrayal of the way it is practiced and voiced has, we think, some claim to originality; and we suggest that this is not without moment given the model's continuing presence in most rural areas of Latin America, its historical importance there and its genesis and original florescence in Europe.

The house is an institution of long standing, a kind of "infrastructure" that runs "underneath" and has been used within many economic forms: colonialism, imperialism, slavery, feudalism, seigneurial society, early capitalism, and others. To place the house economy in context today, we have used the triangular set of market, corporation, and house. The market now is home to the corporation; as markets have spread, so have corporations; and as markets become more specialized and marketing covers more spheres, so corporations multiply in number, deepen their capital, and grow ever larger. But markets also have seams and crevasses, boundaries and frontiers, and these marginal or liminal regions are today's home of the house economy and its many variants.

We think that this interplay between, or dialectical relation of, house and corporation has much to suggest for rethinking past and present economies. For example, there were house economies in colonial and postcolonial North America in addition to markets and businesses; in the southern portion of the hemisphere, the plantation and mining venture were forms of the corporate economy, while the hacienda and the peasant house were their domestic counterparts. Today, the small business and even the large family one – whether in Mexico, the United States, Africa, or elsewhere – often has an interstitial character, conjoining features of both house and corporation. By fate's irony, this division, which might have recommended itself to anthropologists and been found congenial to their social and institutional perspective, never found its way into anthropological theory. For a long while anthropologists, especially those who focused on lineages in Africa, were influenced by the model of the corporation as developed by Sir Henry Maine and others. Like the corporation, they claimed, the lineage "never dies," has an "estate" and "offices," and acts as a single "body" in feuds or the collection and distribution of bridewealth payments. When ethnographic material from Asia and New Guinea was collected and closely studied, corporate lineage theory seemed to have been dealt a mortal blow. But all the while it was only a model, and the onlooker can only wonder how the history of descent theory might have appeared had theorists of the 1940s, instead of exporting their own market experience, used a model of the home and the hearth, as Evans-Pritchard's own foundational work suggested (1940:192, 195, 204, 222, 247; 1951:6, 7, 21, 127, 141), or the local imagery for kin groupings. We might never have established such trust in the existence of the corporate descent group or even, for that matter, the lineage (Kuper 1982).

A conversation: house and corporation contrasted
The contrast between house and corporation is always in flux, but we have examined a number of features in the Colombian situation that may bear weight elsewhere and are worth summarizing:

1 The house is at the margin of profit making, the corporation at the center: the opposition is not absolute, for clearly many corporations are themselves marginal or fail, while houses can and do enjoy the fruits of profit taking; and, as we have indicated, there are many transitional forms, especially in situations often labeled "development." But there is a clear difference in locus between the two.

2 The house project is to maintain itself, to meet its necessities, and to increase its holdings by keeping its remainders as a reserve. The corporation aims to make a profit and to increase this profit over time by reinvesting its retained earnings. The house primarily hoards; the corporation primarily invests.

3 The corporation is embedded in exchange; it buys to sell and sells to buy, with the purpose of realizing a profit and engaging in the venture without cease. Its moments of keeping are transitional. The house economy is not

built around the need to exchange, and though it is
never autarkic, it might be if it could. When the house
trades with other units, it tries to replace what it began
with, and the trade is its own finality; each trade is
unique and for different purposes. The corporation,
thus, produces for others and becomes itself through this
act, while the house produces for itself and is a making
through itself.

4 The corporation sometimes keeps wealth as a precaution
against the future, but it is highly susceptible to that
practice in others. The house generally holds its wealth
as a precaution, but the size of this holding is susceptible
to the rates of trade that the house encounters in the
market and to changes in the physical environment upon
which the house depends.

5 The house generates, uses, and holds mostly circulating
forms of wealth; the corporation has at its command
both circulating and fixed capital. This difference is
closely connected to technological change and to the
differing capacities of the two to develop, buy, and
control its benefits.

This difference in the type of wealth controlled yields
what seems to be paradoxical consequences. We are of
the opinion, for example, that low velocity of exchange
in an economy is connected to a high ratio of
circulating-to-fixed wealth within it; conversely, a lower
ratio of circulating-to-fixed wealth is linked to a higher
velocity of exchange. Circulating holdings lend
themselves to hoarding and to conversion into keepings
or even monuments of wealth to be put on display. This
at the same time slows down circulation and is practiced
because exchange is slower.

6 The need for good management is common to both
house and corporation but has different specifications in
each. In the house, the practice of being thrifty pervades
most material acts. The house uses up what it has
gathered from nature in agriculture, pastoralism, or
mining. It controls expenditures from this stock by
economizing on current consumption and by turning
leftovers to new uses or putting them into storage.
Allocation of its stock occurs through a sequence of
budgeting or earmarking divisions directed to

maintaining the group or meeting its necessities and governed by the injunction to be frugal. The corporation also practices thrift, but it allocates its resources, or so some say, on the basis of rational calculations directed to achieving the most efficient relation possible between inputs and outputs. And while the house attempts to make economical use of objects so that it does not have to buy, the corporation makes economical use of money so that it can sell at a profit. The house practices thrift on a heterogeneous flow of material objects; the corporation practices its rationality on a homogeneous stock created by the common standard of money.

7 Both house and corporation change in size but differently. The house augments itself by increasing its holdings and the work group that is supported by these holdings. Many houses are built around a kin group, and as this grows or diminishes so does the economic unit. In contrast, the corporation hires and dismisses its members in accordance with its material assets and profitable activities.

As its holdings grow, the house may also rent out land, take on sharecroppers, or utilize some other form of labor management such as taking on tenants; in these modes of growth, the house preserves its form as a house and accommodates another, wholly or in part. The house form itself is not changed. But the domestic economy, as house and "large house" (hacienda or manor), experiences organizational limits. These do not so much "block" growth as compel it by its expansion to become something other than what it is: a corporation. In contrast, the corporate mode of grouping has no organizational boundaries. It persists without cease and enlarges itself by accumulating capital, people, and techniques, by altering its form through changing the functions it undertakes or dividing them into new specialties, and by purchasing other corporations and incorporating them as subsidiaries.

8 The corporation and the house both require that their members work continuously – perhaps the latter more so than the former – and are characterized by task specialization. But the work is arranged differently between the two. Corporations specialize among

themselves, and an individual corporation features changing and increasing specialization within it. As the corporation differentiates its functions, specific tasks are assigned to individuals with the aim of achieving efficiency in the totality and control over the workforce. In contrast, members of a house all have specific tasks, but each member undertakes many and changing ones and therefore skills have to be at once finely honed and diverse.

9 Innovation, invention, imitation, and improvisation – which overlap one another – have differing emphases in the house and the corporation. The house worker improvises with materials at hand rather than buying them. As the available materials change and the tasks shift, the householder pours creative energies into "making do" – making something do something. Improvisation also has a place in corporate beginnings and in their mythologies, but because it is unplanned and practiced on a small scale its role in the corporate world is small. Corporations rather assign the tasks of imitation, invention, and innovation to their research-and-development departments or to marketing groups; the work of the engineer, the technocrat, replaces that of the handyman and handywoman.

CONVERSATIONS AND COMMUNITIES

We have viewed conversations as practices and voices that are themselves a form of practice. Because conversations are unbounded in topic, in history, and between communities, our focus on the practices of the Colombian rural folk has led us to consider, however briefly, many voices from the past and from texts. Conversations are a process, a use, and as they are in history and make it, a model – such as the widespread domestic one – is connected to others through the historical and contemporary conversations by which it is made.

But the fact that conversations spread, are transformed, and are rejected draws attention again to their many links with power. Certainly, a conversation may be "persuasive," and it may be "about" power as well. Clearly, too, the exercise of force by a military unit can be an effective way, at least in part, of building a shared conversation. But we have been more concerned with the way economic power, through appropriation and control of wealth, can build or at least perpetuate divisions between communities of people who are themselves modelers. As long as there is a margin of an economy, and as long as there is a community of the marginalized, we may confidently expect models of the margin to be made and perpetuated. But this is not what economics texts reveal to us; the authoritative texts suppress the economic models of others though also drawing upon them. This, then, is another connection between power and conversation: "textual power" – the social "authority" of the writer, the capacity to freeze a conversation in an inscription, the command of written arts and persuasive skills, the faculty for disseminating a particular conversation – and the way in which we ourselves have used it yet struggled to reject its claim to superior knowledge has been a concern of ours since the first days of fieldwork. The problem draws us back to the relation between practice and text and to expressed epistemologies in economics.

Most histories of economics, and there are some very good ones, present the development of economic theory as a linear, self-contained sequence. The narrative is marked by revolutions and disruptions, but it is written as a form of "intellectual history" in which ideas are compared and contrasted according to their positions on a time scale. The implicit theme is the postutilitarian one that "truth will out"; the tone is progressive and often rather self-satisfied. The relationship between economic knowledge and society is not considered an issue for puzzlement; most writers – Schumpeter (1954) and Blaug (1978) are apposite examples – treat ideas or models as a separate, autonomous historical sequence.

The explicit theories of knowledge proposed in economics are at one with the way the history of economics is written. At one end of the continuum, for example, there is the well-articulated view of Friedman (1953), who has proposed that economics adopt a Popperian methodology. In Friedman's view, economics is an "objective" science that tries to locate the "essential features of complex reality" (pp. 4, 7). The economist proposes theories or hypotheses and tests them in appropriate ways in order to disconfirm or provisionally accept them. The more a hypothesis withstands chances or tests of rejection, the more we may have confidence in it. A recent version of this positivist view, incorporating Lakatos's arguments, has been offered by Blaug (1978, 1980). In this, the falsificationist method of Popper is converted from a normative prescription to a description of economists' behavior in the handling of theory. The revised claim is that in the long run economists actually do invent hypotheses and then seek to falsify them as Popper said they ought to do. The "ought" of Popper becomes the "is" of

Blaug, or at least Blaug would have us consider the history of economic theory itself as an arena for falsifying a theory about the falsification behavior of economists! But it seems to us that the relation between text and practice becomes especially complex here, for a sceptic might argue that if economists are "falsificationists," they are so because they themselves have been persuaded by the canons of the central texts. Whether one follows Friedman–Popper or Blaug–Lakatos, a line is always drawn about an inner, progressive sequence of ideas and everything else, which is relegated to footnotes, the "context of discovery," personal motivations, and the like.

At the other end of the continuum, McCloskey (1985) has recently directed our attention to and persuaded us to look at the "conversations" and inscriptions that economists make. He offers a kind of literary criticism, a postmodern deconstruction, a close look at the tropes of the text, and this is not only enlightening but amusing.

But none of this breaks with the idea of a dominant text. Ultimately, the intellectual historians, contextualists, verificationists, falsificationists, and literary critics in economics (and anthropology as well) focus upon inscriptions. But the text is only part of the story, because it leaves out practices. By "practice" we do not mean something by which to "verify" or "falsify" theory, for this serves only to subjugate practices to the hegemony of the theorist and writer; instead, practice refers to the actions and voices of people in history that are sometimes inscribed in texts and of which the inscription is itself an example. We find it useful to talk about all this – the practice, the inscribing, the text, and its readings – as a long conversation in which folk, inscribers, readers, and listeners are all engaged.

One part of our argument, then, is that the folk have economic models, too. Their behavior and talk, patterned and changing, is an act of modeling. Often, they are very articulate about what they make, and some of their historical voices have been incorporated into textual theories. But the shift from practice to text is hardly one-way, for just as Aristotle may have been influenced by early Greek practices or Mill by his observations of European peasants or Smith by what he observed in France and Scotland, so their texts have had a profound influence on the way life was conducted and texts were written in the centuries thereafter. We have further suggested that connected to these shifts between practice and text was the developing opposition between house and corporation and that elements of the former were appropriated and transformed in the modeling of the latter.

This leads us, then, to argue for a new look at the communities within which models are made. Most accounts of economic theory make it appear as if hypotheses, paradigms, or ideas were the inspiration of a single theorist who had hit upon contradictions in earlier writings and imaginatively invented a new model (Friedman 1953:13). We think rather that there are communities of modelers and that the boundaries or compositions of these are problematic. There are many voices in conversations that are thick with history and laden with memory. But if science is not just done by scientists, or economics by economists, the idea of a discipline, with a scientific method, a canon, a discourse, an "objective" and "essential" grasp on reality, dissolves. This part of our argument is at the opposite pole from Friedman's, which seeks to separate the "amateur" from the "professional" and the "crackpot" from the "scientist" (p. 25). The proper discourse or method is – from an anthropological standpoint – only what the central practitioners do or say they do.

But just as there are "voices in the air" (by which Keynes meant texts), so there are "voices on the ground." Contemporary conversationalists situated at the periphery of economies have models of livelihood, too. Should we call their study "ethno-economics" (Mayer 1987)? Certainly, when we turn to problems and puzzles of "economic development," we might think first about expanding and democratizing the community of modelers. Rather than using the various forms of power – from monetary control of capital to the writing of texts – that subjugate and exclude these other voices, rather than offering prescriptions for "deepening capital" or raising agricultural productivity through doses of technological improvement (as in the Green Revolution), we might try to develop an "appropriate economics" that would expand the community of conversationalists by drawing upon the work of both the marginalized modelers and the inscribers. In a curious, almost paradoxical way, this would return us to the tradition of Smith, Mill, Marx, and others, whose work was embedded in their experience of contemporary practices.

But what might we expect from such a venture? We have seen how the house model – with the practice of making savings and the schema of sorting flows into expenditures and remainders – helps us to understand what is occurring in trade between the rural house and the marketplace agent. Starting with this model we might view trade relations themselves as simply one dimension of the larger, two-way, "flotsam-and-jetsam" or remainder relation between house and corporate economies. Leftovers from corporate units are turned to new uses in the countryside. Old rubber tires are recycled into sandals, discarded plastic sheeting becomes a windbreaker and raincoat; distant forests are used for firewood, leftover grass by the roadside becomes pasture for animals. This is a perpetual, ever-changing relationship corresponding to the house practice of putting remainders to use. In the model of the larger economy, however, it is viewed differently: there, the tires, the plastic sheeting, and the old tins are "garbage" because they cannot be used for profit. By expanding our community of modelers, our community of material makers, we come to a better understanding of this total relationship and to the proposal that we search for ways in which one group's leftovers can be used by the other. Viewed from the other side, the expenditure/remainder relationship in the house may be beneficially connected to market sale. In southern Nariño, as we have mentioned, a small dairy began operations a few years ago. Its transportation network has slowly expanded, and now some of the rural folk are able to sell milk on a daily basis. Most of these people already had cattle, and they were consuming some milk in the home. The opportunity offered by dairying has allowed them to expand and transform what was a partly unused remainder into an item for sale. The signal feature of this change is that money has been gained exactly by practicing thrift, since cattle are raised at little monetary cost where pasture is available, cattle husbandry requires little expenditure of human work, and an item previously lost to use has been transformed into a usable and salable good.

The larger issue, however, concerns communities of conversationalists. We argue these are never bounded, except for social reasons, and that one purpose of anthropology is to bring to the bar of discussion different conversations in space and history. This principled starting place is just the reverse of that of other disciplines. Much of modern economics, for example, starts from a Cartesian ego or from a reified model of the individual from which behavior in any aggregate is deduced; much has been lost by effacing the vocal presence of the other, and if we are once again to take cognizance of human experience, daily lives, and the shifting problems of survival – whether in the rural areas of Colombia or the peripheries of the market in modern cities – we must expand our conversation to include other communities of people, their practices and their voices, which, to judge by Colombia, are sometimes not so different from our own.

NOTES

I CONVERSATIONS

1 The literature on these subjects is large. As examples, see Popkin (1979), Scott (1976), Barlett (1980), Taussig (1980), Meillassoux (1981), and Wolf (1969).

2 A considerable body of research exists on the rural areas of Colombia. Some of the useful ethnographic studies include Fals Borda (1955), Ortiz (1973), Reichel-Dolmatoff (1961), and Salazar (1982). For studies on neighboring areas, see Gudeman (1978), Roseberry (1983), and Johnson (1971).

3 See, for example, Clifford (1983, 1988), Clifford and Marcus (1986), and Marcus and Fischer (1986). In economics, McCloskey (1985) has adopted a rather similar approach, but he is a practicing economist and directs his analysis toward achieving greater clarity in the work of his colleagues.

4 In recent years especially, studies of Colombia's socioeconomic history have grown in volume and sophistication. We have found useful the work of Colmenares (1979, 1983), Fals Borda (1976, 1982, 1979), Twinam (1982), and Villamarín (1975b).

2 THE STRENGTH OF THE EARTH

1 Some of the useful studies include Colmenares (1983), Fajardo M. (1983), Fals Borda (1979, 1982), Gaitán (1984), Kalmanovitz (1982), LeGrand (1986), McGreevey (1971), Perry (1983), and Zamosc (1986).

2 The pattern goes right back to colonial times. Villamarín (1975a:13) states that on the Bogotá plain in the late 1500s, 94 percent of the population – who were Indians – held less than one-twentieth of the land. At the beginning of the nineteenth century, 2 percent of the population still held over 60 percent of the land (p. 15).

3 In Consacá 87 percent of the holdings occupy 31 percent of the land, in Samaniego 91 percent of the holdings cover 51 percent of the land. Samaniego has a number of small sugar-mill (*trapiche*) owners who raise sugarcane for grinding and therefore contains more small holdings than Cumbal; its large holdings also occupy a smaller land area. Consacá shows much the same pattern, but it has seen a large hacienda sold and parceled out within the past generation and therefore contains an even greater number of small holdings.

4 This is a common pattern; for example, according to studies of potato production in Bolivia, the use of chemical fertilizer is accompanied by the destruction of microorganisms and brings increasing dependence on market purchases (Dandler and Sage 1985).

5 The principal Physiocratic texts are Quesnay (1972[1758–9]) and Turgot (1898[1770]); useful selections of other writings are found in Meek (1963, 1973). Summaries and commentaries on Physiocracy have been offered by Fox-Genovese (1976), Gudeman (1986), Marx (1963[1905–10]), Meek (1968), and Weulersse (1910, 1931), among others.

3 THE HOUSE

1 Figueroa (1984) provides a formal model, using input–output relations, of a peasant economy in Peru. His "intersectoral relations" (p. 5) can be sorted into base→base' and base→money→base' circuits.

4 THE BASE

1 Salazar (1982:85) claims that the term *sacarruinero* is used for sharecroppers who are occasionally employed for cash by other sharecroppers, but she also notes (p. 109) that the practice is a form of subsharecropping, and this more closely fits our understanding.

5 THE ADVANCE AND THE INCREASE

1 For descriptions and discussions of some of the historical relations between Indians and campesinos on the one hand, and haciendas and large landholders on the other, see Deas (1977), Fajardo (1983), Fals Borda (1955, 1975, 1979), and Taussig (1977). On advances see Fals Borda (1976:39; 1982:49, 113, 131).

2 Dobb (1973:131–2) has summarized the wages-fund doctrine as:

> the view that total wages were limited by the existing fund of capital, moreover by that part of capital that was earmarked (in some fashion unexplained) for paying wages. Given this total, wages per head were arrived at by a simple process of dividing the total by the labouring population that competed for employment. This view that wages are "paid out of capital" regarded as advances of wages, and hence "limited by capital" . . . was first cousin . . . to the doctrine which many have seen as implicit in classical political economy that industry . . . is limited by capital.

6 WORK FOR THE HOUSE

1 The national census reports similar figures. For example, in the Federal District of Bogotá, the wage with food rose from 133 to 621 pesos per day from 1980 to 1986; without food the wage went from 183 to 1,028 pesos. In Boyacá, wages rose from 70 to 360 pesos without food and from 139 to 658 pesos with food during the same interval (DANE 1987:158–9).

2 In the city, the "comparable" expression would be *ayudar unos a otros*, which appears similar but has a different sense. The city form signifies that some help others, and this help is repaid; but the relationship is not one of mutual need and comparable aims, and the act of offering help places one of the parties in a superior, paternalistic position.

7   REMAINDERS

1 The argument that the one-commodity economy has "heuristic value" for modeling the entire economy assumes a single metric or that heterogeneous things are already comparable, as capital. In this case, it presumes what it is often supposed to show.

2 Physiocracy might be "reread" in terms of the house schema. Quesnay's *tableau* is a system of flows with repeated expenditures and remainders. Some of Quesnay's own wording (1963c:233) and Mirabeau's (1973[1760]:121) explanation of the *Tableau économique* suggest that the house model had a pervasive influence on their vision of the larger economy. See also Turgot (1898[1770]).

3 In the one-commodity economy, different varieties of the same crop may be grown. In the case from the *páramo*, two varieties of potatoes are raised, but because these are roughly equivalent in productivity this has no impact upon the size of the remainders. A difference in productivity, however, does exist between the *páramo* and lower land, which means that the same volume of work in potatoes on the high plain produces a smaller harvest than below. If the people descended meter by meter from the *páramo* and continued to raise potatoes, the leftovers after the seed deduction, the food deduction, and the animal deduction would successively grow. If, however, they continued to grow potatoes on the *páramo* as well as on lower land, this would be a multicrop case as described in Model 2. The shift downward from the *páramo* is a way of describing the move from marginal to inframarginal or better land.

9   MAKING SAVINGS

1 For Hume the need for thrift was almost an obsession, as he felt luxury might become "vicious":

> Prodigality is not to be confounded with a refinement in the arts. It even appears, that that vice is much less frequent in the cultivated ages. Industry and gain beget this frugality . . . idleness is the great source of prodigality at all times. (Hume 1955[1752]:31)

2 Keynes may sometimes have overdrawn the case, but he was insightful:

> The weakness of the inducement to invest has been at all times the key to the economic problem . . . The desire of the individual to augment his personal wealth by abstaining from consumption has usually been stronger than the inducement to the entrepreneur. (Keynes 1964[1936]:347–8)

REFERENCES

Alberti, Leon Battista. 1971[1433–41]. *Della famiglia*, trans. Guido A. Guarino. Lewisburg: Bucknell University Press.

Amerlinck de Bontempo, Marijose. 1987. "'Praedium', 'fundum', 'villa' y hacienda: La perspectiva de los agrónomos latinos," *La heterodoxia recuperada*, ed. Susana Glantz, pp. 375–95. México: Fondo de Cultura Económica.

Aristotle. 1926. *The Nicomachean Ethics*, trans. H. Rackham. London: Heinemann.

1946. *The Politics*, trans. Ernest Barker. London: Oxford University Press.

Baldwin, John W. 1959. "The Medieval Theories of the Just Price," *Transactions of the American Philosophical Society*, vol. 49.

Barlett, Peggy F. (ed.) 1980. *Agricultural Decision Making*. New York: Academic Press.

Bartra, Armando. 1982. *El comportamiento económico de la prodúccion campesina*. Mexico: Universidad Autónoma Chapingo.

Beardsley, Monroe C. 1981. "The Metaphorical Twist," *Philosophical Perspectives on Metaphor*, ed. Mark Johnson, pp. 105–22. Minneapolis: University of Minnesota Press.

Blau, Peter M. 1955. *The Dynamics of Bureaucracy*. Chicago: University of Chicago Press.

Blaug, Mark. 1978. *Economic Theory in Retrospect*. Cambridge: Cambridge University Press.

Bloch, Mark. 1966. *French Rural History*. Berkeley: University of California Press.

Braudel, Fernand. 1986. *The Wheels of Commerce*, trans. Siân Reynolds. New York: Harper and Row.

Brush, Stephen B. 1977. "The Myth of the Idle Peasant: Employment in a Subsistence Economy," *Peasant Livelihood*, ed. Rhoda Halperin and James Dow, pp. 60–78. New York: St. Martin's Press.

Cardoso, Fernando Henrique, and Enzo Faletto. 1979. *Dependency and Development in Latin America*. Berkeley: University of California Press.

Cato. 1933. *On Farming*, trans. Ernest Brehaut. New York: Columbia University Press.

1934. *On Farming*, trans. William Davis Hooper. London: Heinemann.

Chayanov, A.V. 1966. *The Theory of Peasant Economy*, eds. D. Thorner, B. Kerblay, and R.E.F. Smith. Homewood, Ill.: Irwin.

Clark, Christopher. 1979. "Household Economy, Market Exchange, and the Rise of

Capitalism in the Connecticut Valley, 1800–1860," *Journal of Social History*, vol.13, pp. 169–89.

Clifford, James. 1983. "On Ethnographic Authority," *Representations*, vol. 1, pp. 118–46.

1988. *The Predicament of Culture*. Cambridge, Mass.: Harvard University Press.

Clifford, James, and George E. Marcus. (eds.) 1986. *Writing Culture*. Berkeley: University of California Press.

Colmenares, Germán. 1979. *Historia económica y social de Colombia*, vol. II, *Popayán: Una sociedad esclavista, 1680–1800*. Bogotá: La Carreta.

1983. *Historia económica y social de Colombia, 1573–1719*, 3rd edn. Bogotá: Tercer Mundo.

Columella. 1941. *On Agriculture*, trans. Harrison Boyd. London: Heinemann.

Dandler, Jorge, and Colin Sage. 1985. "What is Happening to Andean Potatoes?" *Development Dialogue*, vol.1, pp. 125–38.

DANE. 1987. *Colombia estadística*, vol. II. Bogotá: Departamento Administrativo Nacional de Estadística.

Deas, Malcolm. 1977. "A Colombian Coffee Estate: Santa Bárbara, Cundinamarca, 1870–1912," *Land and Labour in Latin America*, ed. Kenneth Duncan and Ian Rutledge, pp. 269–98. Cambridge: Cambridge University Press.

Dobb, Maurice. 1973. *Theories of Value and Distribution Since Adam Smith*. Cambridge: Cambridge University Press.

Duby, Georges. 1968. *Rural Economy and Country Life in the Medieval West*, trans. Cynthia Postan. Columbia: University of South Carolina Press.

1974. *The Early Growth of the European Economy*, trans. Howard B. Clarke. Ithaca, N.Y.: Cornell University Press.

Evans-Pritchard, E.E. 1940. *The Nuer*. Oxford: Clarendon Press.

1951. *Kinship and Marriage Among the Nuer*. Oxford: Clarendon Press.

Fajardo M., Darío. 1983. *Haciendas, campesinos y políticas agrarias en Colombia, 1920–1980*. Bogotá: La Oveja Negra.

Fals Borda, Orlando. 1955. *Peasant Society in the Colombian Andes: A Sociological Study of Saucío*. Gainesville, Fla.: University of Florida Press.

1976. *Capitalismo, hacienda y poblamiento*. Bogotá: Punta de Lanza.

1979. *El hombre y la tierra en Boyacá*, 3rd edn. Bogotá: Tercer Mundo.

1982. *Historia de la cuestión agraria en Colombia*. Bogotá: Carlos Valencia.

Faragher, John Mack. 1986. *Sugar Creek: Life on the Illinois Prairie*. New Haven: Yale University Press.

Figueroa, Adolfo. 1984. *Capitalist Development and the Peasant Economy in Peru*. Cambridge: Cambridge University Press.

Fox-Genovese, Elizabeth. 1976. *The Origins of Physiocracy*. Ithaca, N.Y.: Cornell University Press.

Fox-Genovese, Elizabeth, and Eugene D. Genovese. 1983. *Fruits of Merchant Capital*. New York: Oxford University Press.

Frank, Andre Gunder. 1967. *Capitalism and Underdevelopment in Latin America*. New York: Monthly Review Press.

Friedman, Milton. 1953. *Essays in Positive Economics*. Chicago: University of Chicago Press.

Furtado, Celso. 1976. *Economic Development of Latin America*, 2nd edn. Cambridge: Cambridge University Press.

Gaitán, Gloria. 1984. *La lucha por la tierra en la década del treinta*, 2nd edn. Bogotá: El Áncora.

Georgescu-Roegen, Nicholas. 1971. *The Entropy Law and the Economic Process*. Cambridge, Mass.: Harvard University Press.

Gordon, Barry. 1975. *Economic Analysis Before Adam Smith*. New York: Harper and Row.

Gudeman, Stephen. 1972. "The *Compadrazgo* as a Reflection of the Natural and Spiritual Person," *Proceedings of the Royal Anthropological Institute for 1971*, pp. 45–71.

1978. *The Demise of a Rural Economy*. London: Routledge and Kegan Paul.

1986. *Economics as Culture: Models and Metaphors of Livelihood*. London: Routledge and Kegan Paul.

Hahn, Steven, and Jonathan Prude. (eds.) 1985. *The Countryside in the Age of Capitalist Transformation*. Chapel Hill, N.C.: University of North Carolina Press.

Haney, Lewis H. 1949. *History of Economic Thought*, 4th edn. New York: Macmillan.

Hart, Keith. 1973. "Informal income opportunities and urban employment in Ghana," *Journal of Modern African Studies*, vol. 11, pp. 61–89.

1988. "The Idea of Economy: Six Modern Dissenters," *Beyond the Marketplace*, ed. M. Friedlander and A.F. Robertson. Chicago: Aldine. Forthcoming.

Hayes, E. Nelson, and Tanya Hayes. 1970. *Claude Lévi-Strauss: The Anthropologist as Hero*. Cambridge, Mass.: Massachussetts Institute of Technology Press.

Heath, Anthony F. 1976. *Rational Choice and Social Exchange*. Cambridge: Cambridge University Press.

Henle, Paul. 1981. "Metaphor," *Philosophical Perspectives on Metaphor*, ed. Mark Johnson, pp. 83–104. Minneapolis: University of Minnesota Press.

Holland, Dorothy, and Naomi Quinn. (ed.) 1987. *Cultural Models in Language and Thought*. Cambridge: Cambridge University Press.

Homans, George C. 1962. "Social Behavior as Exchange," *Sentiments and Activities*, pp. 278–93. New York: The Free Press.

Hume, David. 1955 (1752). *Writings on Economics*, ed. Eugene Rotwein. Edinburgh: Thomas Nelson.

Hutchins, Edwin. 1980. *Culture and Inference: A Trobriand Case Study*. Cambridge, Mass.: Harvard University Press.

Johnson, Allen W. 1971. *Sharecroppers of the Sertão*. Stanford, Calif.: Stanford University Press.

Johnson-Laird, P.N. 1983. *Mental Models*. Cambridge, Mass.: Harvard University Press.

Kalmanovitz, Salomón. 1982. *El desarrollo de la agricultura en Colombia*. Bogotá: Carlos Valencia.

Keynes, John Maynard. 1964 (1936). *The General Theory of Employment, Interest, and Money*. New York: Harcourt, Brace and World.

Kuper, Adam. 1982. "Lineage Theory: A Critical Retrospect," *Annual Review of Anthropology*, vol. 11, pp. 71–95. Palo Alto, Calif.: Annual Reviews.

1988. *The Invention of Primitive Society: Transformations of an Illusion*. London: Routledge and Kegan Paul.

Leach, Edmund. 1954. *Political Systems of Highland Burma*. London: G. Bell.

LeClair, Edward, and Harold Schneider. 1968. *Economic Anthropology*. New York: Holt, Rinehart and Winston.

LeGrand, Catherine. 1986. *Frontier Expansion and Peasant Protest in Colombia, 1850–1936*. Albuquerque, N. Mex.: University of New Mexico Press.

Lenia, V.I. 1956 (1899). *The Development of Capitalism in Russia*. Moscow: Foreign Languages Publishing House.

Lévi-Strauss, Claude. 1969. *The Elementary Structures of Kinship*. London: Eyre and Spottiswoode.

McCloskey, Donald N. 1985. *The Rhetoric of Economics*. Madison, Wis.: University of Wisconsin Press.

McGreevey, William P. 1971. *An Economic History of Colombia, 1845–1930*. Cambridge: Cambridge University Press.

Malinowski, Bronislaw. 1961 (1922). *Argonauts of the Western Pacific*. New York: Dutton.

Marcus, George E., and Michael M.J. Fischer. 1986. *Anthropology as Cultural Critique*. Chicago: University of Chicago Press.

Marx, Karl. 1963 (1905–10). *Theories of Surplus Value*, vol.I. Moscow: Progress Publishers.

1967 (1867). *Capital*, vol.I, trans. S. Moore and E. Aveling. New York: International Publishers.

Mauss, Marcel. 1954 (1925). *The Gift*, trans. Ian Cunnison. London: Cohen and West.

Mayer, Enrique. 1987. "Macro-Ethno-Economics," *Reviews in Anthropology*, vol. 14, pp. 250–6.

Meek, Ronald L. 1963. *The Economics of Physiocracy: Essays and Translations*. Cambridge, Mass.: Harvard University Press.

1968. "Ideas, Events and Environment: The Case of the French Physiocrats," in *Events, Ideology and Economic Theory*, ed. R.V. Eagly, pp. 44–64. Detroit: Wayne State University Press.

ed. 1973. *Precursors of Adam Smith*. London: Dent.

Meillassoux, Claude. 1981. *Maidens, Meal and Money*. Cambridge: Cambridge University Press.

Merrill, Michael. 1977. "Cash is Good to Eat: Self-Sufficiency and Exchange in the Rural Economy of the United States," *Radical History Review*, vol. 4, pp. 42–71.

Mill, John Stuart. 1929 (1848). *Principles of Political Economy*, ed. W.J. Ashley. London: Longmans, Green.

Mirabeau, Marquis de. 1973 (1760). "The *Tableau économique* and Its Explanation," *Precursors of Adam Smith*, ed. Ronald Meek, pp. 115–46. London: Dent.

Ortiz, Sutti Reissig. 1973. *Uncertainties in Peasant Farming*. London: The Athlone Press.

Palladius. 1976. *Traité d'agriculture*, trans. René Martin. Paris: Société D'Edition "Les Belles Lettres."

Pasinetti, Luigi. 1977. *Lectures on the Theory of Production*. New York: Columbia University Press.

Perry, Santiago. 1983. *La crisis agraria en Colombia, 1950–1980*. Bogotá: El Áncora.

Polanyi, Karl. 1968. *Primitive, Archaic, and Modern Economies*, ed. George Dalton. Garden City, N.J.: Anchor Books.

Popkin, Samuel L. 1979. *The Rational Peasant*. Berkeley: University of California Press.

Postan, M.M. 1972. *The Medieval Economy and Society*. Harmondsworth: Penguin Books.

Pruitt, Bettye Hobbs. 1984. "Self-Sufficiency and the Agricultural Economy of Eighteenth-Century Massachusetts," *The William and Mary Quarterly*, vol. 41, pp. 333–64.

Quesnay, François. 1963a (1766). "Analysis," *The Economics of Physiocracy*, ed. Ronald L. Meek, pp. 150–67. Cambridge, Mass.: Harvard University Press.

1963b (1766). "Dialogue on the Work of Artisans," *The Economics of Physiocracy*, ed. Ronald L. Meek, pp. 203–30. Cambridge, Mass.: Harvard University Press.

1963c (1766). "General Maxims for the Economic Government of an Agricultural Kingdom," *The Economics of Physiocracy*, ed. Ronald L. Meek, pp. 231–62. Cambridge, Mass.: Harvard University Press.

1972 (1758–9). *Tableau économique*, trans. and ed. M. Kucynski and R.L. Meek. London: Macmillan.

Reichel-Dolmatoff, Gerardo, and Alicia Reichel-Dolmatoff. 1961. *The People of Aritama*. London: Routledge and Kegan Paul.

Ricardo, David. 1951 (1815). *The Works and Correspondence of David Ricardo*, vol. IV, ed. P. Sraffa. Cambridge: Cambridge University Press.

1951 (1817). *On the Principles of Political Economy and Taxation*, ed. P. Sraffa. Cambridge: Cambridge University Press.

Ricoeur, Paul. 1977. *The Rule of Metaphor*, trans. R. Czerny. Toronto: University of Toronto Press.

Robinson, Joan. 1962. *Economic Philosophy*. New York: Doubleday.

Roll, Eric. 1973. *A History of Economic Thought*, 4th edn. London: Faber and Faber.

Roseberry, William. 1983. *Coffee and Capitalism in the Venezuelan Andes*. Austin, Tex.: University of Texas Press.

Sahlins, Marshall. 1972. *Stone Age Economics*. Chicago: Aldine-Atherton.

Salazar, María Cristina. 1982. *Aparceros en Boyacá: Los condenados del tabaco*. Bogotá: Tercer Mundo.

Say, Jean-Baptiste. 1964 (1803). *A Treatise on Political Economy*. New York: Sentry Press.

Schank, R., and R. Abelson. 1977. *Scripts, Plans, Goals, and Understanding: An Inquiry into Human Knowledge Structures*. Hillsdale, N.J.: Lawrence Erlbaum Associates.

Schneider, Harold. 1974. *Economic Man*. New York: The Free Press.

Schumpeter, Joseph A. 1954. *History of Economic Analysis*. New York: Oxford University Press.

Scott, James C. 1976. *The Moral Economy of the Peasant*. New Haven: Yale University Press.

Senior, Nassau W. 1938 (1836). *An Outline of the Science of Political Economy*. London: Allen and Unwin.

Smith, Adam. 1976 (1776). *An Inquiry into the Nature and Causes of The Wealth of Nations*, ed. Edwin Cannan. Chicago: University of Chicago Press.

Smith, T. Lynn. 1967. *Colombia: Social Structure and the Process of Development*. Gainesville, Fla.: University of Florida Press.

Sombart, Werner. 1915 (1913). *The Quintessence of Capitalism*. New York: Dutton.

Soto, Hernando de. 1989. *The Other Path*. New York: Harper and Row.

Sraffa, Piero. 1951. "Introduction," *The Works and Correspondence of David Ricardo*, vol.I, pp. xii–lxii. Cambridge: Cambridge University Press.

1960. *Production of Commodities By Means of Commodities*. Cambridge: Cambridge University Press.

Steuart, James. 1966 (1767). *An Inquiry into the Principles of Political Oeconomy*, ed. Andrew S. Skinner. Chicago: University of Chicago Press.

Swetz, Frank J. 1987. *Capitalism and Arithmetic*. Peru, Ill.: Open Court Publishing.

Taussig, Michael. 1977. "The Evolution of Rural Wage Labour in the Cauca Valley of Colombia, 1700–1970," *Land and Labour in Latin America*, ed. Kenneth Duncan and Ian Rutledge, pp. 397–434. Cambridge: Cambridge University Press.

1980. *The Devil and Commodity Fetishism in South America*. Chapel Hill, N.C.: University of North Carolina Press.

Tawney, R.H. 1926. *Religion and the Rise of Capitalism*. New York: Harcourt, Brace.

Thünen, Johann Heinrich von. 1966 (1826). *Von Thünen's Isolated State*, trans. Carla M. Wartenberg. Oxford: Pergamon Press.

Tribe, Keith. 1978. *Land, Labour and Economic Discourse*. London: Routledge and Kegan Paul.

Turgot, Anne Robert Jacques. 1898 (1770). *Reflections on the Formation and the Distribution of Riches*. New York: Macmillan.

Twinam, Ann. 1982. *Miners, Merchants, and Farmers in Colonial Colombia*. Austin, Tex.: University of Texas Press.

Varro. 1934. *On Agriculture*, trans. William Davis Hooper. London: Heinemann.

Villamarín, Juan A. 1975a. *Factores que afectaron la producción agropecuaria en la sabana de Bogotá en la época colonial*. Bogotá: Pato Marino.

1975b. "Haciendas en la sabana de Bogotá, Colombia, en la época colonial: 1539–1810," *Haciendas, latifundios y plantaciones en América Latina*, ed. E. Florescano, pp. 327–45. Mexico: Siglo Veintiuno.

Weber, Max. 1947 (1922). *The Theory of Social and Economic Organization*, trans. A.M. Henderson and Talcott Parsons. Glencoe: The Free Press.

1958 (1920). *The Protestant Ethic and the Spirit of Capitalism*, trans. Talcott Parsons. New York: Scribner.

1961 (1923). *General Economic History*, trans. Frank H. Knight. New York: Collier Books.

Weulersse, Georges. 1910. *Le Mouvement Physiocratique de 1756 à 1770*, 2 vols. Paris: Félix Alcan.

1931. *Les Physiocrates*. Paris: G. Doin.

Wolf, Eric R. 1969. *Peasant Wars of the Twentieth Century*. New York: Harper and Row.

Xenophon. 1923. *Oeconomicus*, vol. IV, trans. E.C. Marchant. Cambridge, Mass.: Harvard University Press.

Zamosc, Leon. 1986. *The Agrarian Question and the Peasant Movement in Colombia.* Cambridge: Cambridge University Press.

INDEX